Brahms 2

biographical, documentary and analytical studies

EDITED BY
MICHAEL MUSGRAVE

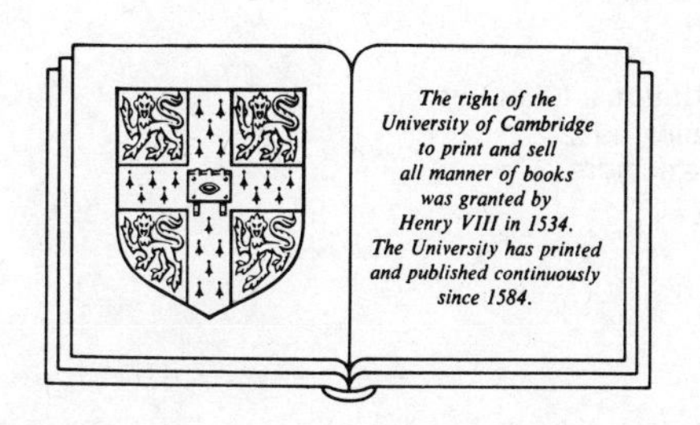

CAMBRIDGE UNIVERSITY PRESS
CAMBRIDGE
LONDON NEW YORK NEW ROCHELLE
MELBOURNE SYDNEY

Published by the Press Syndicate of the University of Cambridge
The Pitt Building, Trumpington Street, Cambridge CB2 1RP
32 East 57th Street, New York, NY 10022, USA
10 Stamford Road, Oakleigh, Melbourne 3166, Australia

First published 1987

Printed in Great Britain at
the University Press, Cambridge

British Library cataloguing in publication data

Brahms 2: biographical, documentary and analytical studies.
1. Brahms, Johannes
I. Musgrave, Michael, 1942–
780′.92′4 ML410.B8

Library of Congress cataloguing in publication data

Brahms 2: biographical, documentary and analytical studies.
Companion to Brahms: biographical, documentary and analytical
studies/edited by Robert Pascall.
Bibliography.
Includes index.
1. Brahms, Johannes, 1833–97. 2. Brahms, Johannes,
1833–97. Works. I. Musgrave, Michael, 1942–
ML410.B8B64 1986 780′.92′4 86-11718

ISBN 0 521 32606 0

Contents

Illustrations

Preface

That the measure of Brahms's artistic stature was inadequately reflected in scholarly activity after the 1933 centenary of his birth, not least in England, has long been acknowledged: Brahms may have been twenty years Wagner's junior, yet the nature of his achievement can now be seen to have offered far fewer and less direct lines of access than those of his many-sided contemporary. The scope of the work which has attended the sesquicentenary celebrations (coincident, as it just so happens, with the centenary of Wagner's death) shows Brahms to be a figure of immense fascination, however: one still insufficiently known, both in the range of his output and in the adventure of his techniques, and one offering fields for further exploration as rich in their way as those of Wagner.

No apology is therefore needed for a collection of essays which accommodate themselves easily to the outlines established in Robert Pascall's signal volume of 1983, to which the present volume now becomes the companion, though the origins lay in a specific event: the London Brahms Conference, held in the University of London, at Goldsmiths' College, from 8 to 11 July 1983 in celebration both of Brahms and of his links with England. The latter emphasis informs the opening chapter, as it does the concluding exhibition handlist, introducing biographical and documentary themes which are taken up in the German context by Siegfried Kross and pursued in different ways by Imogen Fellinger, Otto Biba and George Bozarth. The complementary, analytical focus of the Conference is present in varied approaches to the first, Op. 51 String Quartets, by Arnold Whittall and Allen Forte, raising issues further reflected in Christopher Wintle's view of Brahms's harmony. Links of a different nature appear where broader aspects interrelate, as in the approaches to Brahms's creative relationship to the past by Virginia Hancock and Robert Pascall and the exploration of analytical implications of manuscript clues by Louise Litterick.

Many acknowledgements are due for the event which

prompted it as for this volume itself: first to my contributors, who travelled distances small and very large to devote a memorable weekend to Brahms; to Robert Pascall, for first mooting the idea and helping it along; to Nigel Simeone, for bringing the English connection to life with his Exhibition; to Vanya Milanova and Jonathan Dunsby for memorable performances of the violin and piano works; to Goldsmiths' College for its facilities and to the staff and students of the Music Department for practical help, as to its Head, Stanley Glasser, for his support; to the British Academy and to the Institute of Advanced Musical Studies at King's College, London, for financial support and to the King Edward Professor of Music at King's, Brian Trowell, for his constant interest; to Rosemary Dooley for setting this publication on its way and to Penny Souster and Victoria L. Cooper for their patience and expertise in seeing it through.

In conclusion, grateful acknowledgement is made to the following institutions for permission to reproduce materials in their possession: the Royal College of Music, London (plate 1); the Gesellschaft der Musikfreunde in Vienna (plates 2 and 3); the Allgemeine Musikgesellschaft, Zürich and the Zentralbibliothek, Zürich (plate 4).

Michael Musgrave
University of London,
Goldsmiths' College

MICHAEL MUSGRAVE

Brahms and England[1]

Of the many facets of investigation prompted by a great composer's work, the nature of its reception is one of the most broadly revealing, not least of the ever-shifting patterns of response and evaluation. The story of Brahms's music in England is no exception: it attracted interested reaction from relatively early in his career and he was soon installed as a leading representative of 'the modern movement in Germany'.[2] Whilst fear of the inevitable lionization discouraged Brahms from accepting repeated invitations to visit England – 'I know', he said to Ethel Smyth, 'how you went on with Mendelssohn',[3] he clearly knew much of the English scene and of the performers and performances of his works, not least through his tireless ambassadors Clara Schumann and Joseph Joachim. They seem to have been almost as frequently in England as on the Continent and, with other great German performers of the day, notably Julius Stockhausen, Hans von Bülow and, later, Hans Richter – together with expatriates like Hallé and Henschel – founded a powerful tradition of Brahms performance in England. In their turn, prominent English musicians and their students, familiar by tradition with Germany and its musical culture, sought the composer out and provide us with some first-hand material, a notable example existing in the study by the pianist Florence May, for a time Brahms's pupil.[4] The fol-

[1] This paper was first given in conjunction with the exhibition 'Brahms and England' organized by Nigel Simeone in Goldsmiths' College during the London Brahms Conference, 8–11 July 1983, the handlist of which is reproduced as the Appendix on pages 237–45. Where it adds supportive information, it is cited in the present text in brackets (hereafter List).

[2] General acceptance was slower elsewhere, especially in France. The title of Françoise Sagan's novel *Aimez-vous Brahms. . .*(Paris, 1959; English trans. P. Wiles, Harmondsworth, 1960) – 'a vague social enquiry that requires no answer' – reflects the new interest in the late 1950s.

[3] Ethel Smyth, 'Brahms as I remember him', *Radio Times*, 39 (5 May 1933) 266.

[4] Florence May, *The Life of Johannes Brahms*, 2nd edn., rev. and enl. (n.d.; repr. Neptune City, N.J.: Paganiniana Publications, 1981) 2 vols. (hereafter May).

lowing letter from an older acquaintance, Sir George Grove, reflects the contact which existed within the right circles.

Dear and honoured master,
I hope that you will forgive me for thus writing to you; but I heard your new Symphony for the first time on Saturday finely played by Mr Manns's band and I cannot help sending you my deep and heartfelt thanks for the pleasure and delight you have afforded me by that noble and beautiful work. There is much in it that I could not appreciate at first and which will come to me after hearings; but I heard enough to make me thankful for your existence and grateful for the opportunity of profiting by your deep and lofty genius. . . .[5]

This letter is in a sense symbolic of the world into which Brahms's music came. The Concerts of the Crystal Palace, conducted by the pioneering August Manns (1825–1907), signalled a new era of cultural opportunities, heralded by the Great Exhibition of 1851. First located in Hyde Park, the Crystal Palace subsequently was rebuilt in Sydenham, then outside the metropolis, where it became the focal point for the display of all that was new and exciting in science and art, not least its own spectacle. Thus, Clara wrote to Brahms in 1859 that she was 'once more overwhelmed by the magnificence of man's handiwork'.[6] Shortly after, in 1858, the less spectacular St James's Hall was opened between Piccadilly and Regent Street, its Monday and Saturday Popular Concerts rivalling those of the Palace. Outside London, the work of Hallé made Manchester an especially important centre attracting important Germans, most notably Richter. It was largely through these new venues – with the newly emerging music societies of the universities of Oxford and Cambridge – as well as through the continuing role of such established locations as the Hanover Square Rooms in London, that Brahms's music was first absorbed.

Brahms's music becomes a subject for serious discussion in the middle 1860s. A key moment identifies itself with the publication of a letter to the editor of the *Musical World* on 7 May 1864 in response to a recent article on Brahms's music in the *Niederrheinische Musik-Zeitung*. The apparent purpose is to remind readers that this is the composer of whom Schumann had made such ambitious prophesies, to which end the writer, one Groker

[5] George Grove, unpublished letter to Brahms of 20 October 1884, reproduced by kind permission of the Gesellschaft der Musikfreunde in Vienna.
[6] *Clara Schumann–Johannes Brahms Briefe aus den Jahren 1853–1896*, ed. Berthold Litzmann (Leipzig, 1927) (hereafter *Schumann-Brahms Briefe*) I. 509.

Roores, reproduces the essay 'New Paths'. But, in subsequently chiding the German critics for so undiscerningly accepting Schumann's claims, he reveals a strong reserve towards Brahms's music, specifically the two Piano Quartets. Thus: 'It struck me that the composer's talent was so wrapped up in, and smothered by, the fearful confusion of tone from all the four instruments played together without calm, without cessation, and without any light spots of melody, that it is nearly impossible for anyone to think of comprehending the works as a whole, far less of having any pleasing or elevating effect produced on his mind or imagination.' However, this view was not without implicit challenge – indeed it may even have encouraged response by the younger generation; for, on 6 July of the following year, Agnes Zimmermann, an outstanding pianist and well-regarded composer who had just left the Royal Academy of Music, gave the Piano Quartet in A major with a distinguished group associated with the Academy – Ludwig Straus, Alfredo Piatti and Septimus Webbe – at the Hanover Square Rooms. Perhaps because it was intended for the subscribers to the library of the publishers Ewer and Co., and therefore presumably private, it attracted no critical attention and only comes to notice through May's informal listing (May II, 451).

Chamber music was to remain the chief vehicle through which Brahms's music was introduced and can be traced, though it was not until 1867 that another chamber performance was given, this time by the more prestigious Joachim at the Monday Popular Concert of St James's Hall on 25 February, with Louis Ries, Henry Blagrove, Henri Zerbini, Alfredo Piatti and Guillaume Paque. The work was the String Sextet in B flat Op. 18 (List, 15). Clara wrote directly to Brahms:

> your Sextet was produced with great success at the Popular Concert yesterday. Joachim had, of course, practised it well and played magnificently. The reception was most enthusiastic, particularly after the first three movements. The Scherzo was encored, but Joachim wanted to keep the audience fresh for the last movement and did not respond to the call. I enjoyed it thoroughly and would have loved to have been the first violin. I really wanted to play the A major Quartet but Joachim insisted on the Sextet which he considered more appropriate for the first performance of one of your works in England. I gave way, but most unwillingly. . .I really played with them in spirit. (*Schumann-Brahms Briefe* I, 503)

However, her report seems to show more loyalty to Brahms than to the facts, for Florence May states that it made 'no impression' and that as a result Brahms was not heard at the Popular Concerts for another five years (May, 387). Reaction was strongly echoed by the critic of the new *Monthly Musical Record* (1871–1960) who noted divided opinions on Brahms, finding 'harshness, want of mastery of form, and immaturity' in the work of one clearly regarded as a progressive. Reviewing several works from score he observes with special reference to the Sextet in B flat major:

The first thing that strikes us. . .is that Herr Brahms is a very unequal writer. By far the best of the compositions before us is the sextet for stringed instruments. The ideas are original throughout, and often very striking, and the work is to a great extent free from that over-elaboration and diffuseness which seem to be Brahms' great fault. The opening movement is charming, from beginning to end; the variations in d minor. . . are very interesting. More generally, he is evidently a man who thinks for himself; his subjects are always unborrowed; but there is a want of clearness of form, and a tendency to over-development, which seems more or less to characterize all the modern German school of composition, and which greatly impairs the effect of the whole. We do not forget that the same criticisms were made with reference to Beethoven's music at the time of its appearance; and it is possible that the time may come when Brahms's works may be accepted as a model; but until thought and idea comes to occupy only a secondary position, and elaboration is considered the one thing needful, we do not see how this can take place. (April 1871)

When the work's companion, the Sextet in G major Op. 36, was first given publicly (having been heard previously at Holmes's private concerts) on 27 November 1872 at St George's Hall in London, the critic of the *Monthly Musical Record* found it 'certainly in advance of the earlier work', whilst having 'equal attractions for the general listener', concluding that 'it is satisfactory to feel that this clever composer's works are surely though slowly, making their way in England'. But the critic of the *Musical World*, though accepting the cleverness and 'powers of no common order' was less keen. 'The Quartet is thoroughly representative of the modern German school, wherein its composer is a "shining light". We may be excused for not as yet pretending the meaning which Herr Brahms wishes to convey. That he has a meaning courtesy must assume.'

By May 1873, when the *Requiem* was reviewed, the critic of the *Monthly Musical Record* could state that performances of the two Piano Quartets in G minor and A major, the two Sextets, the Serenade for Orchestra in D and several piano works including a concerto 'have been heard respectively at Mr Coenen's concerts of "Modern Music", at Mr Henry Holmes's Musical

Evenings, at the Crystal Palace, at the Philharmonic Society's Concerts and at the Monday Popular Concerts'. Of these, by far the earliest was that of the Serenade, given even before the Sextet in B flat, by Manns at the Crystal Palace on 25 April 1863, though not noted critically.[7] The performance of the Concerto (the Piano Concerto in D minor) offers another example of Manns's initiative. The soloist in what was soon to be regarded as the most daunting of modern concertos was not a famous name, but a pupil of Holmes's, one Miss Baglehole, who apparently made a good attempt at it on 9 March 1872. The growing interest in Brahms's piano music was, of course, based on published works, though England had heard its first Brahms in the form of two piano pieces destined to wait until after his death for publication, a Sarabande and Gavotte which Clara included in a recital of 17 June 1856 at the Hanover Square Rooms, together with a 'Clavierstück in A major' by Scarlatti, as well as Schumann's Variations Op. 9, *Carnaval*, Beethoven's Variations in E flat and two pieces by Sterndale Bennett. However, if the Scarlatti was acceptable, Schumann's young prophet was certainly not: 'The *Sarabande* of the "new man", Johannes Brahms, is extremely difficult, extremely uncouth and not at all "in the style of Bach"' wrote the critic of the *Musical World* on 21 June 1856, though it was the Gavotte which she encored at the end of the concert (May I, 208); this critic's attribution of the encore to Scarlatti detracts from the value of his observations on the 'style of Bach', however. Clara retained her interest in Brahms's historical inclinations as a composer for keyboard. In March 1872 she gave his new transcription of the Gavotte from Gluck's *Alceste* in a St James's Hall concert which was well received, and destined to become a popular recital piece thereafter. Yet she did not attempt to repeat her great success in Germany with that most powerful pianistic expression of earlier idioms – the Variations and Fugue on a Theme of Handel Op. 24. Florence May names herself as having given the first performance on 12 November 1873 at the Crystal Palace, though contemporary reports indicate that it was played by Clara, as also by von Bülow after his first London performance in the same year. An important year in the dissemination of the piano music was 1876, in which Augener published a popular edition of all the works hitherto available

[7] See: H. Saxe-Wyndham, *August Manns and the Saturday Concerts: A Memoir and a Retrospect* (London, 1909) 62–3. The author quotes from Manns's programme note that the work 'exhibits perhaps less individuality than his later works, which are more independent of preceding composers'.

only in German editions which, as the *Monthly Musical Record* noted, were of greater expense. In setting the emergence of Brahms's music in a broader perspective, it is worth noting that the chamber works had been known in America since 1855, thanks to the efforts of Liszt's pupil William Mason, who gave the first performance of the B major Trio Op. 8 with Theodor Thomas and Carl Bergmann on 27 November of that year in New York.

The 'sure and slow' progress noted earlier was sharply interrupted by the growing reputation of *Ein deutsches Requiem*, which, as in Germany, made Brahms's name. It was first performed in England on 10 July 1871, the score having appeared in 1868, a private performance taking place at the house of Lady Thompson – the former Kate Loder – a prominent pianist of the day and teacher at the Royal Academy before her marriage (List, 3). The performance was of the piano duet version in which she was accompanied by Cipriani Potter and 'a large number of ladies and gentlemen' conducted by Stockhausen. It obviously stimulated immense interest. Stanford recalls that the Royal College wanted to get the first full performance, but that it went to the Royal Academy, predictably so with the contacts from the first private performance, and was first given at the Hanover Square Rooms under the choral conductor John Hullah. In fact, this performance was actually a 'public rehearsal' which featured 'sections from a *Requiem in F* by Brahms', namely 'Blessed are they', 'Behold all Flesh' and 'Ye who now have travail', with a Jessie Jones and Mr Popp as soloists. It escaped press attention, which was directed to the performance of the Second Philharmonic Society concert of the 1873 season on 2 April under W.G. Cusins at the St James's Hall noted as 'first time of performance in this country' (List, 7). The soloists here were Sophie Ferrari and Charles Santley, the rest of the programme including the Adagio and Rondo from the Violin Concerto by Vieuxtemps and 'The First Walpurgisnacht' by Mendelssohn. Critical reaction to Brahms's work can be seen to sharpen up with the appearance of the *Requiem*. The unqualified supporter was George Macfarren, friend of Stanford and Professor of Music at Cambridge, and one of Brahms's staunchest supporters. His important 'analytical and historical' programme note states: 'It is impossible in the space of these comments even to hint at all the extraordinary merit, technical and aesthetical, of the composition under our notice. . .When the *German Requiem* becomes known, lovers of music in England will feel, indeed, that their art has a living representative, that the greatest masters have a successor, and that the line of Purcell, Handel, Bach, Haydn, Mozart, Beethoven, and those great men who have yet shone since through the blazing of his transcendent light, is not extinct.'

But the *Musical Times* detected some weariness in the audience, though not seeking to criticize from a single hearing: 'The Philharmonic concert room is not the place for a funeral service' and the work should not be surrounded by compositions 'in such violent contrast'. The *Monthly Musical Record* was also qualified, noting diffuseness, though also stressing the abundance of ideas and 'harmonic and contrapuntal treatment of amazing skill'. This favourable criticism is in accord with the reaction two years earlier to the work in score in May 1871, in which the critic of the *Record* considered it definitely superior to anything previously noted, citing particularly originality of form throughout and an admirable relationship of music and words, though also preoccupied with its 'over-elaboration' of ideas and counselling 'judicious curtailment'. In commending the 'artistic earnestness' in giving a difficult modern work, the critic noted, interestingly, 'a small but efficient chorus'.

The Piano Concerto in D minor, intimately associated with the *Requiem*'s origin, encouraged less general support at its second performance on 23 June 1873 at the Philharmonic concert, now with the established virtuoso Alfred Jaell, the critic of the *Record* still finding the first movement laboured, though powerful, and acknowledging the 'real beauty' of the slow movement and animation of the finale (List, 37). Response to the purely orchestral works was more encouraging. The Serenade in A, first given on 29 June 1874, at St James's Hall by the Philharmonic under Cusins, was preferred to the Serenade in D by the critic of the *Monthly Musical Record* (16 August 1874) because it was shorter, though not quite as short as implied by comparison with the observation of the critic of the *Musical Times* (August 1872) of the D major work: 'A Serenade in eight movements is too much for an English audience, however it may be endured in Germany.' As in Germany, the orchestral breakthrough came with the *St Antoni Variations*, first given in March 1874 and clearly indicating the greater rapidity with which Brahms's music now travelled to England. The critic of the *Record* picked up all the contrapuntal ingenuities, though stressing that they were not in conflict with the work's beauty and emphasizing the quality of the instrumentation, a point interesting in relation to the observation of the 'brilliance' of the instrumentation of the *Requiem* in the *Musical Times* review noted.

With the completion and successful first performances of the

Requiem and *St Antoni Variations*, it had become inevitable that Brahms's First Symphony, when it appeared, would attract intense interest and demand for performance; and so it was. The contact with England was through Joachim and Stanford. The University had determined to honour Brahms and Joachim, so Stanford conceived the idea of inviting Brahms to come and conduct his new work, and Stanford one of his. Stanford describes the event fully.[8]

On my return to Cambridge in January 1877, I found the organization of the Joachim-Brahms concert well advanced and everything promised success for the responsible undertaking. We were however to experience a severe disappointment. The rumour of Brahms' approaching visit got around with disastrous speed, and the Crystal Palace authorities publicly announced that they hoped for a special concert of his works conducted by himself. This ill-timed advertisement reached his ears and effectively stopped his coming. It had been a hard task to induce him to consider the journey at all, and it had necessitated all the pressure of Joachim and the humouring of Madame Schumann to get him within range of an acceptance, so greatly did he dread the inevitable lionizing which he would have had to face. He intended to visit Cambridge only, and to leave London severely alone. Curiously enough he told Mr John Farmer that his chief interest in London would be to explore the East End and the Docks. As soon as he saw what the Crystal Palace meant to do, he retired into his shell, and the opportunity was lost for good. The concert was fixed for March 8th, and the programme was as follows:

Part I

Overture, "The Wood Nymphs", op. 20	Sterndale Bennett
Violin Concerto, op. 61 (Joachim)	Beethoven
"A Song of Destiny", op. 54	Brahms
Violin Solos, Andante and Allegro in C major	J.S. Bach
Elegiac Overture (in memory of Kleist), MS	Joachim

Part II

Symphony in C minor, MS	Brahms

There was an orchestra of fifty-one, led by Alfred Burnett, and a chorus of about 150. The two preliminary orchestral rehearsals were held at the Academy of Music in Tenterden St, Hanover Square, Joachim conducting the Symphony and his own Overture. The Symphony gave a great deal of trouble, partly owing to the short and somewhat jerky beat of Joachim, which his own men followed with

[8] C.V. Stanford, *Pages from an Unwritten Diary* (London, 1914) 173–6.

ease but which were enigmatical to English players accustomed to Costa's definite sweep of the baton, and partly owing to the inferior technique of the horn players, who were then the weak spot of British Orchestras. . . .

The London rehearsals attracted every professional and amateur musician within reach, and also many leading literary and artistic notabilities such as Robert Browning, George Henry Lewes, Leighton, Felix Moscheles, and other leading painters. A still more representative gathering came down to Cambridge to witness the conferring of the degree upon Joachim, and to be present at the concert. Amongst the ranks of the musicians there was hardly an absentee, Grove, Manns, . . .Osborne, Dannreuther and many more. Hallé was detained by a concert in Manchester. The performance of the Symphony, as of all the other pieces, was worthy of the work and of the occasion. Joachim wrote to Brahms 'Deine Sinfonie ging recht gut, und wurde mit Enthusiasmus aufgenommen, namentlich das Adagio und mit der letzte Satz taten's den Leuten an. . .Seit Cambridge ist das Schicksal des Werkes für England festgestellt, die Hauptblätter sind alle sehr warm, und je öfter sie nun gehört wird, desto besser fürs Verständniss.' This performance put the crown on Joachim's unceasing and loyal efforts to win for Brahms an abiding place in this country. Never had a composer a more trusty friend. The newspapers to which Joachim referred were represented by James Davison of *The Times*, Joseph Bennett of the *Telegraph*, Gruneisen of the *Athenaeum*, and Ebenezer Prout.

Brahms's withdrawal naturally affected the degree. His correspondence with Gerard Cobb, who acted as mediator between Brahms and the Senate of the University, will ring familiar to those adversely affected by such matters – as well as throwing other light on the subject. Writing from Trinity College, Cambridge on 12 December 1876, he proceeds:

My dear Sir,
I have taken the earliest opportunity of laying before the Council of the Senate the difficulties felt by you with regard to the reception of your Degree in person. I have today received their answer on the subject. The Council would have been fully prepared to have recommended to the Senate that should grant leave to you to receive the Degree in absence, but unfortunately the University *has no such powers* given to it by its Statutes. The only case in which the Statutes sanction such a course is that of a Member of the University who being *already in possession* of a Cambridge degree wishes to proceed to a higher one, and the case of one who has *not* yet taken a Degree here is expressly excluded. The words of the Statute are unfortunately only too explicit on this point and our Statutes are part of the *Laws of the Realm* which nothing short of an Act of Parliament can alter or amend. I am afraid therefore that the wish of the University to confer this honour upon you cannot be gratified in any way except by your

actual presence here to receive it. The Council of the Senate regret exceedingly that this should be the case, but there is no help for it, and they can only hope that your health may sufficiently improve to enable you to undertake the journey, and keep Herr Joachim company on the 8th of March next.
Believe me to remain, My dear Sir, Yours most truly, Gerard F. Cobb.[9]

Brahms's failure to attend elicited a markedly stronger response from the critic of the *Musical Times* for 1 April 1877, which makes it clear that Brahms's reasons had become the subject of considerable speculation and had caused a little hurt, though this held no sway in the face of the manifest musical goodwill created by the Symphony. The work was then given twice in London: by the Crystal Palace Orchestra under Manns on 31 March (List, 48) and by the Philharmonic under Cusins on 16 April. These performances have, however, more than nostalgic interest. A comparison of the respective programme notes with the music led an English writer in the 1940s to posit a different form for the slow movement, with a rondo not ternary structure, and a different first subject structure; that is, one lacking the striking digression at bar 5 of the present score. The recent discovery of some orchestral parts from the Vienna first performance on 17 December taken with English programme notes shows that what Vienna, and Karlsruhe on 4 November, had heard, Cambridge was to hear the following year – the first performed version of the slow movement.[10] Brahms's First Symphony was also to become associated with Cambridge in musical terms; just as Hanslick heard Beethoven's Ninth in Brahms's finale, so Cambridge heard the bell chime of Great St Mary's being rung by the horn at bar 30 of this movement. Whilst there is some substance in the first relationship, however, the second seems to have been entirely fortuitous.

Critical reaction was very favourable. Although reservations about the difficulties of Brahms's language did not disappear, Brahms's stature – his technical mastery and high purpose – were widely acknowledged and, crucially, there is a shift from seeing him only in the perspective of his mentor Schumann to the broader one of the symphony since Beethoven.

'Whether as a whole it will ever be "popular" in the sense in which that term is applied to the Symphonies of Mozart and Beethoven may be doubted; Brahms's style is too reflective, at

[9] Gerard Cobb, unpublished letter to Brahms, reproduced by kind permission of the Gesellschaft der Musikfreunde in Vienna.

[10] S.T.M. Newman, 'The Slow Movement of Brahms's First Symphony', *The Music Review*, 29/1 (1948) 4. See further: R. Pascall, 'Brahms's First Symphony slow movement: the initial performing version', *The Musical Times*, 122 (1981) 664–7.

times too abstruse, to meet with universal appreciation. But the real traces of genius which abound in this symphony, and which become more apparent on each repeated hearing, are such as to secure for this great work a place in the esteem of musicians hardly second to that held by the Symphonies of Schumann, with whom Brahms has much in common.' With the Second Symphony, which the *Musical Times* reviewed in October 1878 following the May review above, the perspective was already shifting: 'Many of the most distinguished German musical critics have spoken of the work as "the greatest symphony since Beethoven"; and although one might perhaps be inclined to dispute the literal accuracy of the statement and to point to Schumann's Symphonies in C and E flat in justification of a different opinion, there can be no doubt that Brahms's C minor Symphony towers above contemporary works like Mont Blanc among the Alps.' And, in acknowledging the quite different character of the later Symphony the trend is confirmed: 'It may be said that the two works occupy toward one another a position somewhat analogous to that held by Beethoven's C minor and Pastoral symphonies.' From this point onwards Brahms's work meets less and less critical resistance and the reception of the *Alto Rhapsody* in June 1877 is the first without essential reservation.

With Brahms's growing acceptance came the development of a younger generation of native English performers inspired by the older German generation. The pioneering Agnes Zimmermann was of German birth, though she settled from early in her life in England. Clara's immense influence on the English scene, not least as effectively the sole advocate of her husband's music for many years, encouraged numerous pupils to travel to Germany. Among her students, Fanny Davies and Leonard Borwick were particularly notable. Fanny Davies is the more familiar; born in 1861, she lived until 1934, leaving us with a tangible link to the Schumann tradition and to Brahms through her recording of the Schumann Piano Concerto and her detailed recollections of the performances of both Clara and Brahms.[11] She gave first English performances of various Brahms works; the D minor Violin Sonata (with Ludwig Straus), the Piano Pieces Opp. 116 and 117, the Clarinet Trio (with Mühlfeld and Piatti) and the Clarinet Sonatas (with Mühlfeld). She is remembered especially in connection with the C minor Piano

[11] The Concerto is recorded on Phoenix Records ALP 1001. See F. Davies, 'On Schumann – and reading between the lines', *Music and Letters*, 6/3 (1925) 214–23 and 'Some personal recollections of Brahms as pianist and interpreter' in *Cobbett's Cyclopedic Survey of Chamber Music* I (London, 1963) 182–4.

Trio, even though it was first performed in England with Clara. Fanny Davies has left a description of a performance of the Trio with Brahms, and her score, with the relevant markings, has survived to the present (List, 24). Borwick was born in 1865 and lived until 1925. In large part, he was associated with the B flat Piano Concerto which he played frequently after his Frankfurt debut with the Beethoven E flat Concerto in 1889. Brahms was particularly impressed with him. Plunket Greene recalls 'when he was little more than a boy he played the Brahms Concerto at Vienna under Richter. Brahms wrote to Frau Schumann (keeping supper waiting in his excitement to do it) that "her pupil's playing had contained all the fire and passion and technical ability the composer had hoped for in his most sanguine moments". Joachim swore by him. He said openly to everyone that he would rather play with Borwick than with anybody,[12] a comment which perhaps reflects on the depth of Borwick's culture as well as his musicianship.[13] Mention should also be made of two other pianists in this context, Ilona Eibenschütz and Frederic Lamond. Though not a native of this country, Eibenschütz was another Clara Schumann pupil who made great contributions to English musical life, notably credited with first performances of his works – in this case of the Piano Pieces Opp. 118 and 119 in a Popular Concert of 7 March 1894. The Glasgow-born pianist Frederic Lamond (a pupil of Bülow rather than of Clara – she would not accept students without a personal recommendation, which he did not have) spoke warmly of Brahms. Noted chiefly as a Beethoven player and for his recorded recollections of Liszt, Lamond was the first after Bülow to give an all-Brahms piano recital in Vienna, in 1886, an unusual form of programming at the time, though very well received.[14]

The attraction of Brahms's music for performers was the most visible aspect of a deep acceptance also apparent in the reactions of the critical fraternity. If it can be rightly said that, as in Germany, there were two camps – supporters and opponents – the opponents were few, and not without considerable sympathy; his music prompted far less contention than in Germany. The prime supporters were the leading figures in then emerging institutions of music education and depart-

[12] H. Plunket Greene, 'Leonard Borwick: Some Personal Recollections', *Music and Letters*, 7/1 (1926) 22.

[13] See, for example, his article 'Rhythm as Proportion', *Music and Letters*, 6/1 (1925), 11–18.

[14] Frederic Lamond, *The Memoirs of Frederic Lamond*, with an introduction by I.T. Lamond (Glasgow, 1949) 51–4.

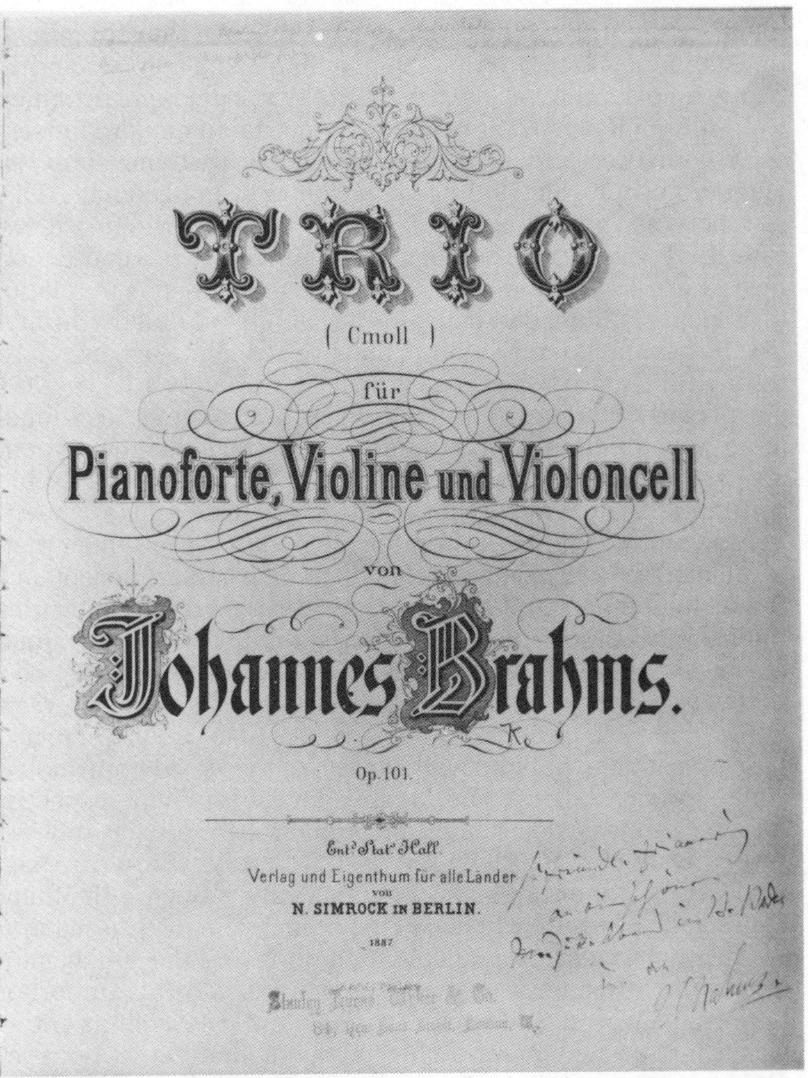

Plate 1 Brahms: Piano Trio in C minor Op. 101. Title page of the first edition (Berlin, N. Simrock, 1887) inscribed to Fanny Davies by Brahms. Her pencil note reads: 'Brahms played from this copy in Baden-Baden – with Joachim and Hausmann. Clara Schumann turned over! An upright piano in a little room at the Deutscher-Hof. Sept. 1890.'

ments of the universities. Yet we should resist the still perceptible tendency to regard these men – Stanford, Parry, Macfarren, Grove, for example – as narrow academics. They were extremely well informed, and their influence was vital in modern musical activity in England. The inherited view that they opposed Wagner and praised Brahms to extremes is not accurate. They saw both as modern masters. If they favoured Brahms it was essentially because he belonged to a tradition. They could more readily assess his work and gauge its characteristics in relation to a deeply understood background which led chiefly through Beethoven to Mendelssohn and Schumann, though also through the more recently absorbed tradition of earlier periods – especially J.S. Bach – and Schubert. Wagner was seen much more as a phenomenon, a composer of immense interest and mastery, though much more difficult to 'place', especially in a country with no comparable tradition of music drama. As with Mendelssohn, Brahms's choral mastery and the assumed piety associated with it were important factors in general acceptance, if not, by the end of the century, for the best informed critics. Indeed, it was those who existed outside the central tradition of music-making and teaching, those with wider aesthetic and – in the case of the most notable, Bernard Shaw – social interests, who did most to promote Wagner's cause. Stanford's reference to Wagnerism as a 'bubble' well expresses the broader outlook of contemporary critics. The balanced view of their respective 'progressiveness' later familiar from Schoenberg is not yet generally apparent, though it is implicit in the writings of some. Parry, for example, found great difficulty with the Piano Quintet in F minor when he first heard it in 1871, a reaction confirming Joachim's judgement in choosing the much more accessible Sextet in B flat, for strings alone, for his important performance of 1867, already noted. An indication of his enthusiasm for the newly appearing works of Brahms is, however, clear from the fact that he was prepared to copy out the A major Serenade for orchestra in its entirety. His later deep admiration was founded clearly on his personal inclinations, both as a composer devoted to the contrapuntal traditions and as an individual responsive to sombre and reflective texts, inclinations which came to strongest expression in his veneration of Bach, with whom he frequently links Brahms, as in the case of the passacaglia from the *St Antoni Variations*. Of more obviously modern features, his references to the speed of Brahms's harmonic digression in main themes – for example, in the openings of the A major Violin Sonata and Rhapsody in

G minor Op. 79 No. 2 – anticipate later and more familiar sources, such as Schoenberg and Schenker.[15] Stanford's interest in the contrapuntal aspect was similar as, for example, in his detailed account of the *St Antoni Variations*,[16] although, as a creative personality, he was broader than Parry and reflects more aspects of the Brahmsian world in his work, as in his Clarinet Concerto, written for, though apparently never performed by, Mühlfeld.

The view of Brahms as a 'modern' continues in the writings of younger critics active from the end of Brahms's life, notably Hadow (*Studies in Modern Music*, 1896) and Fuller Maitland (*Brahms*, 1911), while the older theorist Prout's, best-selling *Harmony* (1901, 16th edn) contains as many references to unusual features in Brahms as in Wagner. The *Handbook to the Entire Works of Brahms* by Edwin Evans, sen., published between 1912 and 1938 reflects just how central a figure Brahms had become, Evans's only other such book being on Beethoven. The critical attitude in turn mirrored the attitude of composers who grew up in the world of 'the modern German school'. Despite the 'Englishness' always observed in Elgar's music, it is, of course, deeply rooted in the German tradition which it richly reflects in its earlier stages, Wagner no less than Brahms. His particular awareness of Brahms as a model of modern symphonic composition is, however, very clear from his enthusiastic and perceptive comments in 1905 on the Third Symphony.[17] His, apparently unique, observation that 'the second theme of the second movement reappears as a subsidiary theme in the finale' (bars 41 ff. and 19 ff.) – the latter the 'tragic outcome' of the former – is surely not without some consequence for his own deeply affecting symphonic transformations across movements.

These men had few opponents in positions of prominence. Yet, contrary to predictable assumption, the most outspoken of them does not appear to have been Bernard Shaw. Rather it was Shaw's friend and fellow Fabian, J.F. Runciman, who committed himself to the greater extremes: 'Much of Brahms's music is bad and ugly music; it is a counterfeit and not the true and per-

[15] See: H. Parry, *Style in Musical Art* (London, 1924) 239–40. Fuller references to Parry's interests in Brahms appear in C.L. Graves, *Hubert Parry: His Life and Work* (London, 1926), 2 vols. I, 129 f. Parry's manuscript of the Serenade in A major is in the Bodleian Library, Oxford.

[16] C. Stanford, *Musical Composition* (London, 1922) 63.

[17] E. Elgar, *A Future for English Music and Other Essays*, ed. P. Scholes (London, 1968) 99–110. It was to Tovey that he remarked 'this is the tragic outcome of the wistful theme in the middle of the slow movement'. See D.F. Tovey, *Essays in Musical Analysis* I (London, 1942) 112.

fect image of life. . .; and it should be buried and cremated (*sic*) at the earliest opportunity.' Yet, as he continues, Runciman points up a seeming ambivalence in outlook: 'But much of it is wonderfully beautiful – almost, but never quite as beautiful as the great men at their best. All his music is irreproachable from the technical point of view. Brahms is certainly with Bach, Mozart and Wagner in point of musicianship. In fact, these four might be called the greatest masters of sheer music who have lived.' And elsewhere: 'If ever a musician was born a happy, careless romanticist, that musician was Brahms.'[18]

This ambivalence can be explained, to an extent, if we look at the much broader spread of Shaw's criticism which, covering the period 1867–1940, remarkably encompasses a large part of our subject. That Shaw repeated so many of his memorable images in condemning Brahms was, of course, part of his self-promotion as a critic. He well knew that openings along the lines of 'it was again my misfortune to have to endure. . .' whetted the appetite. Yet, like Runciman, Shaw was greatly attracted to Brahms's music. However, he seems to reverse completely the values which are so marked in the opinions of the critics forementioned; not a great formal master, but a composer with memorable ideas: '. . .a sentimental voluptuary with a wonderful ear'[19] (Shaw 2/916), a composer of an 'irresistible violin sonata' (Shaw 3/401), of (in the First Symphony) 'such magnificent lumps! such colour! such richness of substance' (Shaw 3/33). What concerned Shaw was not Brahms's ideas, so much as what he did – or failed to do – with them. He sees Brahms as 'a child playing at being grown up' (Shaw 3/402), a composer with a 'commonplace mind' (Shaw 2/440) in relation to the main standard of judgement, Wagner. Yet, Shaw's judgement was not entirely determined by the new values represented by Wagnerian music drama. Thus, the comparison with Hermann Goetz in the context of the latter's Symphony: 'Brahms, who alone touches him in mere brute musical faculty, is a dolt in comparison' (Shaw 1/39). Only in the world of poetic response was Brahms really acceptable to Shaw. The one work in which Shaw's inherent sympathy seems to have survived unimpaired is the *Alto Rhapsody* though, characteristically, it had to be at the expense of someone else: 'his musical power sounded Godlike after a pilgrimage through that hopeless failure, Schumann's Symphony in D minor' (Shaw 3/48). But whenever

[18] Quoted in E. Evans (sen.), *Handbook to the Entire Works of Brahms*, 4 vols (London, 1912–36) 4.

[19] G.B. Shaw, *Shaw's Music*, ed. D. Lawrence, 3 vols (London, 1981) (hereafter Shaw).

Brahms tended towards what Shaw saw as formality, his resistance stiffened. Thus he remained opposed to Brahms's 'dreary Requiem' with its '*point d'orgue*. . .for ten minutes at a stretch' (Shaw 2/376).

Critical as Shaw was of Brahms, however, he was at least involved with him, part of his world. For the anti-Romantic generation of the 1920s and 1930s, greatly influenced by the Russian nationalists and by the neo-Classical development which centred on Paris, Brahms seemed the very embodiment of a vanished world of expression: he was irrelevant. Although Constant Lambert admitted that, 'though entirely lacking in the germinating vitality of Beethoven', Brahms's Symphonies 'at least command respect', he found them, like those of Schumann and Mendelssohn – even, surprisingly, Tchaikovsky – dull and academic.[20] His views recall Shaw when he draws attention to the distinction between the creation of material and its subsequent treatment, which appear to be two separate musical processes. Rather, he found Balakireff's *Thamar*, his favourite work of the Russian school, to be 'more coherent and formally clear than the Brahms Symphonies'. And naturally, Brahms's orchestral language drew much more scorn than from earlier opponents: he refers to the 'drab shades' and 'muddy impastos', an appropriate response in light of his own preferences, though it is well to recall that he also took exception to the character of Stravinsky's scoring. Independence of German tradition came more easily in America. Ives, for example, respected Brahms, but objected to his deification, sharply reacting against the view which he characterizes in the remark that 'music crawled into Brahms's coffin and died',[21] a sentiment paralleled by his great contemporary Carl Ruggles. Many later composers, perhaps most notably Benjamin Britten, have found Brahms's qualities inimical. After early enthusiasm for both Beethoven and Brahms, he turned away from them. As Sir Peter Pears has put it,[22] 'he thought that [they] had "let him down". He had expected so much from both B's – and they faded', playing no part after his study with Frank Bridge: 'His eyes and ears went elsewhere.' Although Britten is known to have played the *Liebeslieder* Waltzes with Josef Krips, and is noted by Sir Clifford Curzon as having been appreciative of a clarification of the – to him – unclear relationship of the themes of the last movement

[20] C. Lambert, *Music Ho!* (Harmondsworth, 1948) 230, 108, 137, 225.
[21] J. Kirkpatrick, ed. *Charles E. Ives, Memos*. (London, 1972) 122.
[22] I am indebted to the late Hans Keller, the late Sir Peter Pears and Sir Michael Tippett for elaborating on their published references to Brahms for the purposes of this essay.

of the Sonata in F minor Op. 5, at Aldeburgh,[23] Sir Peter recalls no interest in or performance of Brahms songs during their long collaboration: 'indeed, Beethoven songs were only sung a few times – "An die ferne Geliebte" and "Adelaide" – where he was nearest to Mozart or Schubert, I dare say'. He has confirmed the apocryphal story that Britten 'made a point of looking at some Brahms scores each year to test his feelings about his music'. Equally, Hans Keller was convinced that, in his last years, Britten's attitude to Brahms mellowed – perhaps because he himself found composing more difficult and sensed greater sympathy with the self-aware quality in Brahms: Keller recalls that Britten 'unreservedly agreed' with Keller's submission that the Clarinet Quintet was 'a profound masterpiece', a view surely not at odds with Britten's lifelong concern for the instrumental aspect of composition and noted aversion to Brahms for what he saw as its denial in his music. Antipathy was also characteristic of the composer so often coupled with Britten in musical interests, Sir Michael Tippett. His earlier view, like so many of his generation, was of Brahms as a symphonist simply filling the Beethovenian mould without realizing its inherently dramatic nature: 'Brahms understood neither Beethoven's nor Wagner's method. The development sections of his sonata forms are often muddled and fail to set up the necessary tension; to borrow the phrase [of] Dr Vaughan Williams, they "live in sin"' – a reference of particular significance in tonal terms at that stage for Tippett.[24] As an aspiring young symphonist, Tippett derived little stimulus from the 'lyrical symphonists', Brahms as well as Schubert, though he recalls benefiting from Adrian Boult's rehearsing of the Third Symphony with the R.C.M. Orchestra, from which time he has always admired the work – an interesting parallel with Elgar. But, like Britten, there has been some shift of attitude of later years, not least concerning the D minor Piano Concerto,[25] the directness of which Britten is also known to have admired; unlike Britten, however, the later experience seems to have borne some positive fruit. Sir Michael acknowledges this work, with the Double Concerto, as 'intriguing', partly as he was preparing to write his own

[23] A. Blyth, *Remembering Britten* (London, 1981) 84, 52.

[24] M. Bowen, ed. *Music of the Angels: Essays and Sketchbooks of Michael Tippett* (London, 1981) 32.

[25] A. Blyth, *Remembering Britten*. Murray Perahia recalls that Britten 'liked the first movement of the D minor Concerto [and] disliked the B flat. He liked the passion and spontaneity of the former; elsewhere he did not find much spontaneity in Brahms. Britten seemed to think that the best Brahms was composed before Schumann, whom he so much loved, died. After that something went out of him'. (171)

Triple Concerto: 'the lyrical invention of these works and their format offered not so much inspiration as a jumping off point'. Indeed, it is not difficult to sense such a relationship in the opening of the Double and Triple Concertos, in the common profusion of improvisatory writing for the string soloists in response to a broad orchestral gesture: the process would seem analogous to the more familiar example of the link from a Vivaldi passage to the opening of Tippett's Second Symphony, the reiterated bass notes of the former suggesting those of the latter and inspiring a completely new conception.

These were the views of creators of a particular generation; they evolved new procedures in response to new stimuli and modes of thought, and were very sensitive to the over-influence of the more recent 'past'. Changing attitudes were much less apparent in the concert hall, where Brahms's acceptance continued, indeed, changed imperceptibly from the context of 'modern' to that of 'classic', though certain works long remained a challenge: in the symphonic sphere, the Fourth Symphony, in the concerted, the Double Concerto. One figure stands out as symbolic of this continuity since his active life spanned the era of Brahms to the year of the composer's sesquicentenary: Sir Adrian Boult. His early Leipzig training belongs to a vanished age, yet he carried his memories of Steinbach and the Meiningen Orchestra, as of Nikisch with their direct contact with Brahms through his life, repeatedly performing and recording Brahms's works and passing his knowledge directly to a younger generation even very recently (List, 61).

In the sphere of criticism, the crucial event to re-orientate attitudes to Brahms was the publication of Schoenberg's essay 'Brahms the Progressive'. Though written for a centenary German Radio broadcast, it was never originally published in German, appearing as one in a collection of Schoenberg's essays titled *Style and Idea* in New York in 1950. Here, in contrast to the by then very firmly established view of Brahms as, in Schoenberg's words, 'the classicist, the academician' (reflecting German as well as English attitudes), he presented him as 'a great innovator', a 'great progressive'.[26] The effect of the essay and its companions, not least in revealing Schoenberg, not as a radical revolutionary, but as one deeply sensitive to the German classics which he saw as his heritage, was profound, if controversial. It sparked off many responses in the younger generation, of which those of Alan Walker were particularly germane

[26] A. Schoenberg, *Style and Idea*, ed. D. Newlin (New York, 1950); second, expanded version, ed. L. Stein (London, 1975) 401.

for Brahms. In two books on analysis and the article 'Brahms and Serialism', he pursued Schoenberg's thoughts to show other 'progressive' aspects of Brahms's language, albeit often in the context of the inherited ideas of his teacher and fellow Schoenbergian, Hans Keller.[27] These writings, together with the translations into English of such important and related texts as Rufer's *Composition with Twelve Notes* and Réti's *The Thematic Process in Music* contributed to the growing attraction of Brahms's music as a prime subject in the emerging academic study of music analysis. Thus, the view of Brahms in England might be seen to have come full circle: from a difficult 'modern' in the 1860s to a re-evaluated 'progressive' about a century later after a period of critical decline. Nor, indeed, has the inevitable reaction against the post-war vogue for Schoenberg ultimately affected this newer attitude, rooted as it is at the heart of Schoenberg's values; like Brahms himself, Schoenberg is now re-emerging from the changes in outlook heralded by Boulez at Schoenberg's death. It may seem ironical to some that such a radical figure as Schoenberg should be the agent of rediscovery, yet that is surely not at odds with the long tradition of German influence on English musical culture. And it is further appropriate that it should fall to an English composer of the present to synthesize a view of Schoenberg's and Brahms's relevance to current concerns with professional associations strong in this essay: the present Professor of Music at Cambridge University, Alexander Goehr. His sesquicentenary broadcast, whilst acknowledging that the modern listener may well empathize with Brahms the man and musician, considers that Brahms the musician may also appear limited in the scope of his compositions, lacking 'individuality of expression and gestural highpoints. In Brahms's work these are intimately connected to and arise out of the formal continuity'. Yet, equally, he observes that there remains in the listener a desire to see gesture made relevant, and accordingly suggests we see Brahms 'as one whose recognition of the legitimate scope of art might help us to curb our slightly sentimental views of what there is to be done now. Certainly, we would do well to remind ourselves that finite means include infinite possibilities. . . .'[28]

[27] A. Walker, *A Study in Musical Analysis* (London, 1962); *An Anatomy of Musical Criticism* (London, 1966); 'Brahms and Serialism', *Musical Opinion*, 81 (1958) 17.

[28] Alexander Goehr, 'A Sense of Proportion', B.B.C. Radio 3, 7 May 1983. Quoted by kind permission of the author.

SIEGFRIED KROSS

The establishment of a Brahms repertoire 1890–1902

I

When Elisabet von Herzogenberg complained to Brahms in a letter of 1 March 1887 about the presumptuous language of the musical press of the day, she immediately received a reply which revealed his attitude in an unusually precise and direct manner:[1]

Newspapers have become necessities for us and I fear that we have even become used to reading musical scandal sheets. Having admitted this, I think that the one by Fritzsch is the most practical, tolerable and, I hesitate to say, the best. The others, from the *Signale*[2] to Chrysander[3] I regard as terrible and I wouldn't look to them for any sense. I don't find the presumptuous language a disadvantage though. The reader who really follows such journals is provoked through it to more intensive reading and even argument. You really wouldn't want to read a blotting paper like the *Signale* and more ambitious attempts. . . ? Fritzsch does not provoke me to any contradiction, probably because he only busies himself with us little people of yesterday and today. I was, however, truly indignant and inspired to protest about Chrysander. . . .But good Fritzsch does not demand any admiration for himself and his journal. . .[4]

Brahms's remarks may perhaps surprise us in revealing a lively awareness of musical journalism which provided such a variety of information about performers and performances, as

[1] *Johannes Brahms Briefwechsel* II: *Johannes Brahms im Briefwechsel mit Heinrich und Elisabet von Herzogenberg*, ed. Max Kalbeck, (Berlin, 41921), 152–3. This letter is wrongly placed in the volume and should appear at page 19. The letter is also available in English. See *The Herzogenberg Correspondence*, ed. M. Kalbeck, tr. H. Bryant (London) 309.

[2] *Signale für die musikalische Welt* (Berlin, 1843–1930). Founded and first edited by Bartholf Senff.

[3] Friedrich Chrysander (1826–1901). The reference is presumably to the *Jahrbuch für musikalische Wissenschaft* which he edited from 1863 to 1867. Brahms had known him since the 1860s.

[4] Ernst Wilhelm Fritzsch (1840–1902). Publisher and, from 1870, editor of the Leipzig *Musikalisches Wochenblatt* (1870–1910), in successor to its first editor, O. Paul, whom he succeeded after only thirteen issues had appeared in the first volume.

well as prevailing attitudes. Indeed, his preference for Ernst Wilhelm Fritzsch's *Musikalisches Wochenblatt* invites us to examine it as a means of tracing the establishment of his own music in Germany and elsewhere, and in illuminating the kinds of difficulties which attend the compilation of reliable statistics to illustrate it. The journal may first be considered generally, then with specific reference to some of the major genres of Brahms's output, providing the background to the table of performances which chart the emergence of a Brahms repertoire during the last decade or so of the nineteenth century.

Despite his enthusiasm, Brahms had not always held Fritzsch and the *Musikalisches Wochenblatt* in such high esteem. On the contrary, he is said to have expressly warned Philipp Spitta against co-operation with it; little imagination is needed to find the reason. Fritzsch was a decided party-liner of the New German School and even the publisher of Wagner's theoretical writings. Wagner had become increasingly aggressive towards Brahms in his later publications – and, in any case, Brahms disliked aesthetic speculations about music. Moreover, Wagner's noted inclination to comment publicly on any topic, however unqualified to do so, was quite against Brahms's nature: one would hardly expect enthusiasm for a publisher who spread these voluminous writings with his own editions. So it speaks well for the objectivity of both Fritzsch and Brahms that they nevertheless appreciated each other's work. Fritzsch strictly separated his financial interest as publisher from his journalistic responsibility for complete but critical news reporting; and Brahms respected Fritzsch's fairness and attempts at objectivity for his own works – in spite of the verdict of the Wagnerians – and honoured it with the quoted judgement. Of course, Brahms's support for Fritzsch was not without provocation: his reply was to a violent tirade against the journal from Frau von Herzogenberg, prompting him to vent his spleen against Chrysander and the Berlin press, especially Eugenio de Pirani. His letter continues by lambasting the latter with their preferences for 'any smut from Paris' and the inadequacy of their response to such great German literary figures as Gottfried Keller and Paul Heyse, with whom Brahms here allies himself: 'Do you believe they would perform a single note of mine in Berlin if today's Frenchmen had a bit more talent?'[5] – in all likelihood a charac-

[5] Eugenio de Pirani (1852–1939). Pianist, composer and correspondent of various Italian and German periodicals.

teristically realistic observation. As for the scholar Chrysander, on the other hand, Brahms had been 'truly inspired to protest' because he found his sober, analytical language – in this instance, his unaffectionate and irreverent attitude to Mozart – inadequate. The artist in Brahms did not want such an idol treated in a detached and critical way under the pretext of 'objectivity'; he wanted inspired language. Fritzsch sought to avoid both extremes as he developed his journal from its small beginnings and resolutely directed it to the events of the day, the only viable field for a weekly publication; hence, Brahms's ironical reference to 'us poor little people of yesterday and today'.

The focus for this was the two regular columns, 'Concert Report' and 'Performances of New Works'. The first listed performances, growing in size until, in the main concert season, it regularly covered six double columns in folio a week; this is a huge but hitherto unanalysed source of information, which clearly chronicles the changes in concert programmes. In identifying first performances, Fritzsch naturally depended on information from the local concert organizers without being able to confirm it himself, for the journal had only a small staff. It is therefore understandable that, occasionally, organizers claimed (carelessly or on their own initiative) to be the first to perform a work in a city, and that Fritzsch printed their report. This editorial concept had the advantage for Brahms that – with a speed of which we may only dream today, despite modern means of communication – he knew about the dissemination of his works, the rapidity with which they were accepted, the centres of performance and the artists involved. Moreover, he always had an essentially reliable picture of the relation of preparation and performance of his work to that of his contemporaries. This had not been the case from the founding of the journal or from the beginning of Fritzsch's editorship, but was the result of tenacious and systematic development. Only in the middle of the 1870s had the concert statistics established themselves to a degree that they provide relevant data. Until he reached this goal, Fritzsch had continually to request the submission of programmes. Having firmly established his 'Concert Report', he could bluntly afford to refuse programmes not sufficiently current: 'Out of date programmes will not be printed!' Even performances in Boston, Cincinnati, Chicago or New York were usually mentioned in the journal within a month. This was not only an organizational and editorial achievement, but an indication of the international prestige of Fritzsch's indexes and their powerful publicity value for concert organizers and artists alike. To what extent the completeness and therefore value of the performance index really depended on him became apparent when Fritzsch's health declined and he died on 14 August 1902. Already, when unable to edit the journal himself, a practice had grown up which he had consistently avoided as editor: the contraction of reports from certain organizers to one for the whole season. Although his son, Willibald Fritzsch, had promised, on behalf of the editorial board, to continue in the spirit of his father (vol. 34, 1903), he was neither willing nor able to do so: 'in the interest of the whole, one must limit the statistical parts and even more the reviews'. Thus Fritzsch's concept of up-to-date reporting was not grasped, and the place the journal had occupied in the market of music publication was simply vacated. The 'Concert Report' became more and more general, unreliable and shorter. Statistics of performances and reviews were mixed. From the manifold events of musical life in Leipzig, for example, only the student performances of the conservatory were listed completely; the reader was referred to the reviews for information on all other performances, which, however, were evidently incomplete too, as a comparison with advertisements and editorial announcements shows. Preliminary announcements may appear, but it is impossible to verify whether the performances took place at all, for cancellations – for example, on account of insufficient ticket sales – were more frequent in those days than they are today. Still more irritating is that, beginning from volume 34, after Fritzsch's death, even the names of composers were sometimes omitted. In an entry like 'Overtures; *Ingwelde*, *Euryanthe*, *Academic Festival*', the latter can be identified as by Brahms; but not always does such a title substitute for the composer's name. Moreover, from the numerous concerts of the Meiningen Court Orchestra conducted by Fritz Steinbach in other cities, only place and time are recorded with the remark, 'works from the tour programme', which makes greater difficulties for the statistics. Traditionally there were always some works by Brahms in the Meiningen Orchestra programme. But which work was performed, and whether it was the first performance in a city, can no longer be ascertained. Given that, in the last volume edited by Fritzsch himself, of the nineteen registered performances of the Fourth Symphony, at least thirteen fell to Fritz Steinbach and the Meiningers, it becomes evident that from volume 34 (1903) onwards, the *Musikalisches Wochenblatt* no longer offers a reliable basis for statistical dating. By chance, in the same year, Steinbach went to Cologne, considerably muting the almost missionary spirit of Brahms promotion by the Court Orchestra as a result. Also during that year, the journal was sold to the publishing house Siegel, and the editor Carl Kipke resigned. By 1906 it had become impossible to continue, and the *Musikalisches Wochenblatt* was merged with the *Neue Zeitschrift für Musik*. The *Neue Zeitschrift* carried 'Musikalisches Wochenblatt' as a subtitle for some time further, probably with a nod to the subscribers, but although it continued its concert statistics, in a reduced form, it is no longer a useful chronicle.

Statistical work from the *Musikalisches Wochenblatt* can only be carried out to the year 1902, at latest including the concert season of 1902–3. It is even more difficult to decide upon the point of termination, since one cannot then avoid drawing on other, biographical data. In those days of public mania for the new, the main criterion in judging a concert promoter or a music association was the speed with which a new work could be presented in the concert hall. As a consequence, a new work could only be presented at the cost of eliminating the same composer's works in order to keep some appearance of balance between composers performed. As long as a composer was productive, his output suffered continuous erosion by his new compositions. A consolidated repertoire could thus only be formed after the entire *oeuvre* was complete.

How far these distortions could go can be shown with the Piano Concerto in B flat major Op. 83. At the time this work was published, Brahms had been specially invited to conduct his own works during the winter concert tours, and he energetically furthered its dissemination. The introduction of a new piano concerto depended above all on the efforts of the composer, before other pianists would take it up, and Brahms projected his new concerto onto the musical scene with almost brute force. After a private test performance with Hans von Bülow in Meiningen, the first performance took place in Budapest on 9 November 1881. After this, the main goal was to get the work accepted: 22 November in Stuttgart, with Max Seifritz as conductor; 27 November, again in Meiningen, in a public performance with Bülow; 6 December in Zürich (with Friedrich Hegar), 11 December in Basle (with Alfred Volkland), three days later in Strasburg, another two days later in Baden-Baden, and 20 December in Breslau. It should not be forgotten that train journeys of twelve and more hours lay between these stops, that intense rehearsals for the conductor and his orchestra were required in order to get acquainted with the unfamiliar work, and that, in addition to the new piece, Brahms usually included an extended programme of other compositions which he conducted himself. Even Brahms's robust nature could not stand this continuous strain. Thus, the second series had a bad start in the two main centres of contemporary musical life: on 26 December in Vienna (with Hans Richter) and on New Year's Day in Leipzig. Those two performances harmed the acceptance of the works more than they helped, because they initiated the familiar catch-phrases 'symphony with obbligato piano' and 'concerto against the piano'. An acceptable performance standard only returned after several later concerts with von Bülow as conductor of the Meiningen Orchestra on 8 January in Berlin, 13 January in Kiel and 14 January in Hamburg. Only three days later, on 17 January, Brahms performed the piece as a favour to his old friend Julius Otto Grimm in Münster; then followed performances in Utrecht on 21 January, The Hague on 24 January, Rotterdam on 26 January, Amsterdam on 27 January, Arnheim on 30 January, and finally, after a short break, in Frankfurt am Main on 17 February. Brahms worked just as intensively in the next season at promoting his new concerto: performances took place in Bonn on 18 January 1882 with Joseph Wilhelm von Wasielewski, Krefeld on 23 January with August Grüters, Koblenz on 26 January with Raphael Maskowsky, Cologne on 31 January with Ferdinand Hiller, and also in Hanover, Schwerin, and Oldenburg in February. Only in the third season does the pace diminish somewhat, with performances in Wiesbaden, on 18 and 22 January 1884, with Louis Lüstner and Elberfeld – on 23 January, with Julius Buths. The first performance in which Brahms contented himself with the conducting, Julius Röntgen playing the piano solo, was on 27 January 1884 in Amsterdam, where this was already the second performance; then followed a performance in Essen, on 2 March with Georg Heinrich Witte. Finally, on 24 November 1884 in Budapest, the concerto started its second cycle from the original performance venue, and slowly found its accustomed place in the repertoire. This was an especially slow process for a concerto; even in the concert season 1886–7, only Brahms himself is mentioned as the soloist, although only a few performances took place with the Meiningen Orchestra under Bülow. Only in the season 1887–8 did Eugen d'Albert start to perform the Concerto, again with this orchestra, though with Brahms as conductor. D'Albert remained its chief performer for a long time; he even introduced it to America, in January 1890, in New York.

As implied earlier, public musical life – whether one views it as a 'market' or not – can support only a small number of works by each composer without distorting the relation of the whole repertoire, especially if the composer, as both promoter and interpreter of his own work, concentrates on a single piece. As long as this happens with new pieces, the frequency of performances, even if based on complete performance information, is of no statistical value for drawing broader conclusions about the repertoire. Shifts in the repertoire have always occurred, but they do not affect the relation between different works of one composer, but rather the entire structure of the programme. This became especially evident both in the Mozart centenary of 1891, and the year 1894 when Anton Rubinstein died. The following underlines the degree to which the repertoire has changed since then. Today, Rubinstein hardly exists in musical life. In 1894, however, the foundation and construction of a special theatre in Bremen for Rubinstein's sacred operas, on the model of Bayreuth, was seriously discussed. In 1896 a peculiar situation arose when Dvořák's Cello Concerto and the *New World* Symphony were first publicly performed. Because of their generally recognized proximity to the style of Brahms, who at that time was no longer producing new pieces, they were simply substituted for his works. The next season was as unusual, beginning as the Schubert centenary year, but ending dominated by Brahms's music after his death in April 1897.

II

In the light of these points, the year 1890 has been chosen to start the inquiry. The first performance of the last orchestral piece, the Double Concerto in A minor Op. 102, was two years before, the first performance of the third Violin Sonata in D minor more than one year earlier. In the time interval under consideration only the second String Quintet Op. 111 and the late clarinet pieces were introduced. Of those, only the Clarinet Quintet Op. 115 caused a minor shift in the repertoire, probably because it was easier for existing string quartets to add a clarinettist than it was to establish the group needed for the Clarinet Trio. Hence, Op. 111 and Op. 114 produce no significant performance statistics. Of the late piano works, only single pieces were played – ignored here statistically, since only performances of entire works have been considered. Such a procedure is necessary because of the very mixed programmes of the day, and especially because of the circumstances of lieder-performance. Songs were performed only as single pieces, usually inserted between symphonies, overtures or solo concertos. The same is true of piano pieces, such as the Rhapsodies Op. 79. The single most popular song was 'Feldeinsamkeit' Op. 86 No. 2; other favourites were 'Die Mainacht' Op. 43 No. 2, 'Meine Liebe ist grün' Op. 63 No. 5 and 'Immer leiser wird mein Schlummer' Op. 105 No. 2. The context in which a song by Brahms was performed can be seen from the following random programme from the second concert of the Concert Association of Zittau in 1894: Liszt: *Mazeppa*, Weber: Overture to *Euryanthe*, Wagner: Prelude to *Parsifal*, Gounod: Aria from *Margarethe*, Brahms: 'Feldeinsamkeit', followed by various other orchestral works. It can be noted, too, that such mixed programmes gave way to programmes concentrating on a particular style or genre much earlier in the main centres of music than in the provinces. In any event, the works of Brahms never achieved the performance-frequency of the most well-known pieces of that decade: the *Wald-Symphonie* by Raff, the *Ocean Symphony* by Rubinstein or the symphonic poem *Ländliche Hochzeit* by Karl Goldmark. Even the popularity of Brahms's *Ein deutsches Requiem* was surpassed for a time by Grieg's *Landkennung*, Bruch's *Odysseus*, and even more by Albert Becker's *Selig aus Gnade*, all of which are now completely forgotten. The second Violin Concerto of Wieniawski, and even the Violin Concerto of Sinding (1901), were played much more often than that of Brahms. Even the Hungarian Dances were only performed in Joachim's arrangement. Brahms's works never approached the prominence of, for instance, Popper's 'Elfentanz' or even Emperor Wilhelm II's 'Sang an Aegir', derisively called 'Kaiserschmarrn' ('Kaiser-trash') by Brahms. A special difficulty arises in evaluating the reports of performances of solo concerts in the *Musikalisches Wochenblatt*. They are not listed under the composer's name, but rather the performer's, reflecting contemporary emphasis on the virtuoso rather than on the composition. The pieces actually performed (apart from one or more concertos, almost always purely solo works) were at best mentioned in parentheses. D'Albert often played both Brahms concertos in one programme, not unusual at the time, but extraordinary to us now. One performance often included several concertos by different composers played by the same soloist. For instance, Teresa Carreño[6] once played Beethoven's

[6] Teresa Carreño (1853–1917). One of the most brilliant pianists of her day, she was also a singer, and composer, and at one time manager of a dance-troupe. She was one of the six wives of Eugen d'Albert, whom she married in 1892.

Concerto in E flat Op. 73, Rubinstein's Concerto in D minor and Grieg's Concerto in A minor in succession in one concert! On the other hand, when the *Musikalisches Wochenblatt* lists solo concerts under first performances, it usually mentions only the conductor's name, not the soloist; this is true, even when we can deduce from independent evidence that the soloist was a famous pianist, such as d'Albert or Busoni.

Of course the statistics of the *Musikalisches Wochenblatt* were never really complete, even during the years of its most extensive coverage; this is easily proven by comparison with similar sources from cities like Berlin or Vienna, where such records exist for a shorter period. After all, Fritzsch was dependent on the information provided by the organizers. Only with a network of correspondents and a large staff could Fritzsch have attained higher accuracy in reporting – but the price would have been less topicality, and a weekly paper lives by just this quality. The total numbers are therefore only minimum estimates. In spite of this, the dissemination of Brahms's *oeuvre* can be traced. The interesting part of these statistics lies less in the pure numbers themselves than in the relationships and shifts which can be found among them. It is obviously noteworthy that, in the period considered here, the first two piano sonatas were performed only 7 and 8 times, respectively – not statistically significant numbers – whereas the Third Sonata in F minor Op. 5 was performed three and a half times more often (27 times). Again, if two contemporary works of the same genre and with the same instrumentation are compared, the Piano Quartet in A major Op. 26 and the Piano Quartet in G minor Op. 25, the numbers of performances are significantly different: the A major Quartet was performed 76 times, and the G minor Quartet 121 times, or around 60 per cent more often. Although the total number of performances was certainly much higher, it probably would not change the ratio of the numbers markedly: the basis of about 200 performances noted is surely sufficient for such a comparison. The data for the performances of Brahms's early works require special interpretation. The relatively high number of performances (73) of the Trio in B major Op. 8, for instance, obviously benefited from its revision and republication in 1891, which falls outside the present timeframe. The Piano Concerto in D minor was performed 68 times in this period, 42 times alone in the year 1897 and after. Of these 42 presentations, Willy Rehberg of Geneva played 16; that is, nearly 40 per cent of all performances since 1897 were played by a single pianist. Identification of the soloist, already difficult in the *Musikalisches Wochenblatt*, is also problematic for other solo concertos. For instance, the Violin Concerto is normally regarded as a Joachim piece; the statistics show a different result, however, noting again the caveat concerning absolute numbers: the violinist with the most performances by far was Hugo Heermann of Frankfurt (1864–1935), with 16, followed by Gabriele Wietrowetz (1826–1927) with 9. Wietrowetz is never mentioned in the Brahms literature, in comparison with Brahms's favourite, Marie Soldat-Röger (1864–1955), though she only performed it 5 times. Joachim only performed the piece on 6 occasions, almost the same number – 5 – as Karl Halir (1859–1909), nearly a generation younger than Joachim. In turn, the work was presented 4 times each by Bram Eldering (1865–1943) and Henri Marteau (1874–1934), and by Franz Kneisel (1865–1926), who performed it at least 4 times in Boston. Even though the statistics are poor, with only 150 documented performances of the Violin Concerto during the period under discussion, the statistics are unlikely to be significantly affected.

Relationships and shifts in the number of performances can best be seen in connection with the orchestral works. This is because the statistics are more complete, arising from their importance in the musical life of big cities. In contrast, chamber music performances might easily be missed in the statistics. In our information about the tours of the Bohemian Quartet for instance, there are gaps which one can only surmise were filled by performances in smaller cities. In principle, this hypothesis could be checked, at least for the most prominent chamber music societies, with a great deal of research. However, the difference would probably not be statistically significant if we reasonably assumed that such concerts corresponded both to the normal repertoire and to the programmes in the bigger cities on the same tour. It is worth noting that the Third Symphony was performed more during this period than today. There is no explanation for this; surely at that time – even more than now – conductors shied away from putting this piece either at the end of a programme, because of its elegiac ending, or at the beginning, because of its weight. The explanation must be that the Fourth Symphony, played so often today, was accepted only slowly during the period under consideration. It can not be explained by the typical gap that occurs after the wave of first performances. The period under consideration begins in 1890, four years after the first performance of the Fourth Symphony. As late as ten years after its premiere, the work was only performed one-third to one-half as frequently as the Third Symphony, in 1894 only one-quarter as often. The relationship between the Third and Fourth Symphonies changes only after 1900 and from around 1902 began the typical sequence in numbers of performances, still valid today, of Second, Fourth, First and Third. It is also very clear how slowly the symphonies of Brahms gained general acceptance. Apart from the years 1893–4, his symphonies were not performed more often than 41 to 46 times per year. During the year of his death, 1897, the number increased to 65, stabilizing again to the old level a little later; only in this century did it rise to 60 and more performances per year. The year 1897 is also interesting in another way: performances of the two minor-key symphonies doubled, whereas those of the major-key symphonies did not change significantly. The minor-key pieces were obviously considered more suitable for mourning and memorial concerts. Especially noteworthy is the jump in performances of the First Symphony, a work generally performed until 1897 only half as often as the symphony most often performed – variously, the Second and Third, until the Second finally established a leading position. At this time, the First Symphony finally exceeded the Third in frequency of performances. This indicates that, in reality, the reputation of the First Symphony as 'Beethoven's "Tenth"' was of no great consequence for its popularity in performance. Among the other orchestral pieces, the Variations on a Theme of Haydn only slowly gained acceptance even though it is probably Brahms's most popular work today. The number of performances was even lower than the least-performed Symphony, the Fourth: only in 1897 was the number of ten registered performances per year surpassed. The piece with the highest number overall is, predictably, the *Academic Festival Overture*, his strongest tribute to the taste of the 'Gründerjahre'.[7] Significantly, the companion, *Tragic Overture*, was performed only half as often. Of those performances, about one-quarter occurred in 1897 and thus only reflect the number of memorial concerts following Brahms's death. The same effect increased performances of both the Serenades, works which otherwise never attained significant performance numbers each year.

A particular problem attaches to statistics of concerto performances. It is by no means clear that we can take the evolution of the number of performances as proof of the 'natural' forma-

[7] The years following the Franco-German War which were characterized by strong national feeling (1871–4).

tion of a repertoire. It can well be argued that the real motivator of this evolution was the performing soloist. Through studying a work for performance, the performer makes an investment in it, and this investment must pay off. This is especially obvious for the Piano Concerto in D minor which was never performed in statistically significant numbers until the year of Brahms's death. Brahms played it occasionally, as did Bülow, Clara Schumann, and also Theodor Leschetitzky, in St Petersburg. In the period under consideration here, from 1890, Robert Freund (1852–1936) and Eugen d'Albert were notable in the work's few performances. D'Albert's feat of playing it with the Second Concerto in one evening was not appreciated by the Berlin critics, as we might assume from earlier comments. After 1897, when two performances by Robert Freund were registered, Willy Rehberg made a speciality of it. Of the twenty verified performances in the 1899–1900 season, at least half were by Rehberg, while Busoni played it only twice in the same period. The situation with the Piano Concerto in B flat Op. 83 was quite different. Despite Brahms's initial efforts, its further evolution can only reasonably be described as that of slow absorption into the repertoire. Although this evolution was mainly determined by d'Albert and Freund, the circle of soloists is larger; Frederic Lamond (1868–1948), Max Pauer (1866–1945), and Dohnányi performed it in England, Leonard Borwick furthered the piece (as he also did in Berlin), and in the United States, Rafael Joseffy (1853–1915) presented it a number of times in East Coast cities. The Violin Concerto found its place in the repertoire much faster, the only setback occurring when Sinding's Violin Concerto Op. 60 appeared in 1901. Brahms's concerto was not only played more often than both his piano concertos together, sometimes it even surpassed them considerably. Perhaps this was influenced by its different nature, since the public conceived of concerto performance in much more virtuosic than symphonic terms. This is revealed not only in the way in which the *Musikalisches Wochenblatt* registered solo concertos, namely as 'solo performance by Herr X', but also in the fact that the public did not object to hearing in a single concert only the first movements of the Brahms and Dvořák Concertos instead of the entire works. Bearing this in mind, it is easier to comprehend Pablo de Sarasate's much-quoted reason for not playing the Brahms Concerto: 'Do you think of me as being so completely without taste that I would stand there with the violin in my hand and listen while the oboe plays the only melody in the entire piece?',[8] a comment in line with early criticism of the Piano Concerto in B flat.

The interpretation of performance data for chamber works is even more difficult – and not only because of the apparent insufficiency of the statistics. It arises from instrumental grouping. There is no plausible explanation for the enormous jump in 1900 in performances of the symphonies. This sharp rise also applied to the 'Haydn-Variations', but not to other orchestral works. It was clearly accompanied by a correspondingly sudden decrease in performances of the chamber music. The numbers of performances both of string quartets and of the works with piano fall to almost half of the long-term average by then established – and the string quintets were not played at all, though they had never attained statistically significant numbers even before. A speculative explanation – though one which would have to be checked carefully for its general usefulness – is that the celebrations for the turn of the century may have led to such a number of more festive concerts that the orchestral musicians who constituted many chamber groups became restricted in their non-orchestral activities. The relationships are clearest in the chamber music with piano. Among the piano quartets, that in G minor Op. 25 clearly dominates; only occasionally does the companion piece in A major surpass it in the number of performances. In contrast, the Third Quartet in C minor Op. 60 was rarely performed. It never attained the performance frequency of even the A major Quartet and from an early stage declined to statistically insignificant performance numbers. For several consecutive years, the *Musikalisches Wochenblatt* registers no performances at all, which illustrates its subsequent failure to develop a solid place for itself in the repertoire. Despite the encyclopaedic tendencies of the modern record industry, discographies confirm this; it appears in complete sets of the chamber music with piano, but rarely by itself, in complete contrast to the G minor work. This observation clearly contradicts the thesis, presented earlier in connection with the Third Symphony, of the advantage in performances accorded the most recent piece of a genre. However, it does not disprove it. The view is supported by a comparison of the string quartets and the piano trios. No new string quartet had been written since 1876, whereas the first performance of the Clarinet Trio Op. 114 was after 1890, and of the C minor Piano Trio as late as 1887. The string quartets were already well established by

[8] See: Andreas Moser, *Geschichte des Violinspiels* (Berlin, 1923) 459.

1890, while the introduction of a new Trio – even the rewritten version of the B major Trio Op. 8 – caused substantial shifts in the trio repertoire. The priority given to a new piece disappears with time – for the Clarinet Trio in only two years – and then the evolution of a repertoire begins and can even end with the exclusion of a piece, as the Clarinet Trio shows. This process may be influenced by the grouping of performers required by a particular work. It is difficult if the violinist of a piano trio has to step back and make room for a clarinettist, even if the player is a colleague from the same orchestra. A performance which cannot use an already existing group is even more difficult to organize. In contrast, the Clarinet Quintet is easier to arrange, because another musician has only to be added to an existing quartet, though it is interesting that this did not happen with the work's dedicatee and first performer, Richard Mühlfeld (with the Joachim Quartet, on 12 December 1891, in Berlin), as often as it is claimed in the Brahms literature. Three months later, Gustav Holländer, the leader of the Gürzenich in Cologne, took the piece on a Rhineland tour with his quartet and the Gürzenich clarinettist, Friede. The Heermann Quartet in Frankfurt, the Skalitzki Quartet in Bremen and the Halir Quartet all obtained Mühlfeld's services in the Quintet. Later, Mühlfeld went alone on tour with the piece and performed it with various quartets. He did so twice in London in February 1895: on the 2nd in the Saturday Popular Concert and on the 4th in the Monday Popular Concert, both times with the violinist Wilma Norman-Neruda.[9] She was involved in many Brahms performances in London and personally contributed to the dissemination of Brahms's works in Great Britain. It may be noted in passing that this was not the first performance in London of the Clarinet Quintet; it had already been performed a number of times, three times alone in December 1892. The work became known in the United States in cities on the East Coast through the efforts of the Kneisel Quartet of Boston, which otherwise furthered Brahms's compositions in America, together with the clarinettist Goldschmidt (on 17 January 1893 in Boston and in the following February in New York).

The string quartets show only insignificant shifts in performance numbers, both in total and in relation to each other: in 1893 and 1899 the Quartet in C minor headed the list, in 1895 and 1898 the Quartet in A minor, and in 1896 and 1901 the Quartet in B flat major. The latter piece was also performed quite often in 1895. Only in 1900 do the performance numbers

[9] Wilma Norman-Neruda (1839–1911), who married Sir Charles Hallé in 1888.

decline, by more than half. At the most, a small increase in the number of performances of the C minor work can be found near the end of the period considered, 1902. In contrast to the piano quartets, which doubled their performances in the year of Brahms's death, 1897, the string quartets show no changes. It seems peculiar that the 50 verified performances of the Clarinet Quintet in the first two years after its first performance did not depress the number of performances of the string quartets, but rather, occurred in addition to them. Perhaps the Clarinet Quintet was considered as an enrichment of the string quartet literature by the additional instrument adding new colour. Yet, at the same time, the string quintets were never widely performed. The String Quintet in G major was performed 18 times in its first year, but only 3 performances are reported in its second year, and it then succeeded the first Quintet to such a degree that the latter, during the next decade, reached a total of only 7. It should be noted that the G major Quintet also received only 2 performances between 1898 and 1902. All this is in sharp contrast to the Clarinet Quintet, which was performed 22 and 28 times in the first two years. The piano trios had a quite different evolution, which led to a clearly established repertoire. The Horn Trio Op. 40 has not been considered here, because it is not apparent from its many performances whether it was played with horn or cello. Initially, the most recent piece of the group, the Trio in C minor Op. 101 led in number of performances. The rewritten version of Brahms's early work in B major, Op. 8, in 1891, resulted in a rapid increase in performances right at the time when the Trio in C minor experienced its post-introduction gap in 1887. Soon the number of performances of the new version of Op. 8 stabilized, in contrast to those of the Clarinet Trio, introduced in 1892, which never really achieved appreciable performance numbers. Only the Trio in C minor was able to maintain its place beside the new version of Op. 8. Both pieces show a similar peak in their respective performance numbers, with 10 of the new version of Op. 8 in 1899 and 12 of the Trio in C minor in 1895. Both pieces then stabilized at 5 to 6 performances per year; in contrast, the Piano Trio in C major Op. 87 never reached statistically significant numbers.

Information has also been extrapolated on the performances of choral works from the 'Concert Report' and 'Performances of New Works' in the *Musikalisches Wochenblatt*. But these numbers contribute little in characterizing the evolution of a Brahms repertoire, since *Ein deutsches Requiem* dominates the entire field, there being no equality, as exists for example, between the four symphonies. Even the *Schicksalslied* and *Triumphlied* cannot sensibly be compared because of their very different texts and, therefore, occasions of performance, in contrast to other pairs of non-texted works; the same observation also applies to the less well-known choral works, *Nänie* and *Parzengesang*. A special case of a different kind is presented by the *Alto Rhapsody*, which has found its way into the repertoire and is widely performed today. Since it employs a male choir, it is difficult to programme with works for a mixed choir; in addition, it has also suffered from the decline in the social role of the all-male choir, as is already reflected in the statistics. These few facts alone demonstrate that, as far as choral works are concerned, the absolute numbers are the more useful, although only with certain restrictions as to minimums. At least, however, the figures clarify the sheer scope of performances of the *Requiem* in the period under consideration. It was the most performed work apart from the *Academic Festival Overture*, with 160 registered performances. And so much were these performances identified with occasion, that it is possible to use them as a calendar for checking the dates of Good Friday and other appropriate festivals for most years. Yet even this association did not entirely predict the context of performance, as in the case of a Palm Sunday concert in St Gallen in 1898, when the *Requiem* was coupled with Wagner's Prelude and 'Good Friday Music' from *Parsifal*. Nor was this as extraordinary as might be thought today, as is shown in Felix Weingartner's programme for the sixth Philharmonic Concert in Bremen in 1897: Brahms, First Symphony; Strauss, *Till Eulenspiegel*; Weber, Overture to *Euryanthe*; Brahms, *Vier ernste Gesänge* (sung by its first performer Anton Sistermanns).

The reports of the *Musikalisches Wochenblatt* provide an important source for information of various kinds. Yet, in conclusion, it can definitely be deduced from the performance statistics which follow that, after a phase of shifting of the stratification by newly-introduced works, which had to gain their places with concert-goers and artists, a Brahms repertoire stabilized in the last decade of the nineteenth century with a canon of certain works which remains essentially valid today.

Table 1 *Number of performances of symphonies*

Year		1890	1891	1892	1893	1894	1895	1896	1897	1898	1899	1900	1901	1902
Opus number	68	12	6	15	11	10	7	9	18	9	9	17	17	14
	73	7	7	15	19	12	16	19	18	18	15	26	17	18
	90	9	12	13	18	19	14	11	14	10	13	14	16	13
	98	7	8	8	10	5	7	8	15	7	4	11	18	15

Table 2 *Number of performances of orchestral works and concertos, excluding symphonies*

Year		1890	1891	1892	1893	1894	1895	1896	1897	1898	1899	1900	1901	1902
Opus number	56	8	6	7	9	7	5	5	13	11	3	13	11	8
	80	13	10	16	14	8	17	14	24	17	13	9	12	13
	81	8	6	7	4	11	8	8	26	7	4	7	7	5
	11	3	4	1	3	2	1	1	4	2	2	3	2	2
	16	2	—	2	—	—	2	—	2	1	2	—	3	1
	15	4	3	3	3	—	5	1	7	8	12	8	—	4
	77	6	14	11	16	6	11	6	14	4	10	12	8	10
	83	4	8	2	3	3	6	8	8	3	4	2	6	10
	102	2	1	4	5	3	2	1	9	2	2	1	2	6

Table 3 *Number of performances of choral works with orchestra*

Year		1890	1891	1892	1893	1894	1895	1896	1897	1898	1899	1900	1901	1902
Opus number	45	14	9	8	8	12	10	8	32	8	8	10	8	13
	50	2	1	—	—	3	1	—	1	2	—	4	—	1
	53	9	4	8	8	10	5	11	9	14	7	10	6	7
	54	4	6	5	10	4	6	11	13	10	5	4	4	6
	55	—	2	1	—	—	1	2	—	1	1	1	1	2
	82	3	2	2	1	5	3	3	5	4	2	—	1	2
	89	4	—	1	2	2	2	1	1	4	1	4	1	—

Table 4 *Number of performances of chamber works with piano*

Year	Opus number	1890	1891	1892	1893	1894	1895	1896	1897	1898	1899	1900	1901	1902
	25	5	9	5	12	10	13	7	14	7	7	4	5	7
	26	3	3	6	8	6	4	7	8	4	9	5	2	8
	60	4	2	3	5	3	1	—	4	2	—	2	—	—
	34	5	8	2	13	8	6	7	13	5	9	3	5	14
		17	22	16	38	27	24	21	39	18	25	14	12	29
	8	2	7[a]	4	6	4	4	6	4	2	10	6	6	6
	87	3	—	4	1	3	5	1	3	—	2	—	2	—
	101	3	4	7	10	1	12	9	3	8	2	4	5	6
	114		1[b]	12	2	1	—	1	3	2	—	1	3	—

a Revised version *b* First performance

Table 5 *Number of performances of chamber works without piano*

Year	Opus number	1890	1891	1892	1893	1894	1895	1896	1897	1898	1899	1900	1901	1902
	51,1	2	3	4	7	3	1	2	4	4	9	5	—	3
	51,2	3	2	5	3	5	8	2	8	7	3	—	2	3
	67	1	3	3	5	2	6	6	2	3	2	1	4	—
		6	8	12	15	10	15	10	14	14	14	6	6	6
	115		1[a]	22	28	7	9	5	11	4	4	6	2	3
	88	2	2	—	1	—	1	1	—	1	2	—	1	—
	111	1[a]	18	3	3	4	7	4	3	1	1	—	—	3
	18	3	—	6	4	1	6	7	5	4	3	1	4	4
	36	2	—	1	2	3	1	5	3	—	1	2	1	1

a First performance

OTTO BIBA

New light on the Brahms *Nachlass*

The fact that difficulties surrounded the dispersal of Brahms's personal estate is well known. Yet the nature of the problems has never been fully explained and scholars in the field have often felt confused by the incomplete and sometimes contradictory information in the literature. The unique holdings of the Gesellschaft der Musikfreunde in Vienna[1] and its intimate connection with the composer, however, provide much information through which a more complete picture may emerge. One is initially taken aback by the lack of attention to the subject in the early writings, where one might expect it most. Kalbeck, normally so well informed on Brahmsian matters of his own time, wastes no words at all; indeed, in the final volume (1914) of his study of the composer, he gives the impression of wishing to dispose of the subject as soon as he can.[2] Nor is there much to learn in the official history of the Gesellschaft der Musikfreunde, which appeared in 1912.[3] Yet this should not cause surprise: for when these two basic works appeared, the fate of Brahms's estate had not been decided – the proceedings were still going on. In fact, the matter of Brahms's estate was to keep the law courts of Vienna busy for no less than eighteen years. The records of these lawsuits are to be found in the archives of the city of Vienna – several thousand pages of them. And there are also related files in the archives of the Gesellschaft der Musikfreunde itself (hereafter referred to as 'the Society'). Important information can also be gained from the files of the Viennese lawyer Dr Ernst Krause, who represented the Society in some of the lawsuits: these files were acquired by the Society in 1979 as a gift from a Viennese antiquarian. The eighteen years of uncertainty over Brahms's estate can be charted through this varied material.

[1] Otto Biba has been Director of the Archive of the Gesellschaft der Musikfreunde since 1979.

[2] Max Kalbeck, *Johannes Brahms* IV (Berlin, ^{2}1914) 227–35.

[3] Richard von Perger and Robert Hirschfeld, *Geschichte der K.K. Gesellschaft der Musikfreunde in Wien* (Vienna, Gesellschaft der Musikfreunde, 1912) 2 parts.

In May 1891, Brahms wrote down his will in a letter from his favourite resort of Bad Ischl to his publisher Fritz Simrock. He himself regarded this letter as his last testament, and it is now generally referred to as the 'Ischl Testament'.[4] In April 1896 he asked to have it back and kept it in the middle drawer of his desk where it was subsequently found after his death. In the letter as originally written, Brahms had named as heirs to his fortune two musicians-assistance associations in Vienna and Hamburg, and had bequeathed various legacies to individuals and his books and musical effects to the Gesellschaft der Musikfreunde. Later he crossed out, in pencil, the two associations, made several changes in the legacies, and added: 'Fortune and library go to the Society. . .' We have the word of Richard Heuberger[5] that Brahms was convinced he had thereby made the Society his chief heir, and he also mentioned this to others. Nevertheless, there must have been some doubt among Brahms's friends as to whether his last will had been drawn up in a manner that was judicially correct. That offers the only explanation for Dr Richard Fellinger[6] drafting a testament for Brahms in the last months of the composer's life, the contents of which Brahms mentioned on several occasions. But this testament was never signed, and so posterity had only the amended letter of 1891 to fall back on. On 5 April 1897, two days after Brahms's death, his estate was taken into the custody of the court until the matter of inheritance could be cleared up. The letter of 1891 was regarded by the court as Brahms's will. But first it had to be decided which court was to have cognizance of the case. On 3 July 1897, the authorities in Hamburg declared that they would give up their claim. Thus Brahms, who had felt himself Austrian but who had never applied for Austrian nationality, was made an Austrian posthumously. On 19 July 1897, proceedings were initiated in a Viennese court in order to resolve the questions pertaining to Brahms's estate.

First of all, there were problems of a formal, judicial nature with regard to the unusual testament in letter-form and its corrections. The Gesellschaft der Musikfreunde insisted that it was to be considered the sole heir, while in Hamburg the Liszt Pension Fund for Musicians and in Vienna the Czerny Foundation for Musicians demanded that the cancellations made by

[4] Kalbeck reproduces the letter in full: Kalbeck, IV, 228–30.

[5] See Richard Heuberger, *Erinnerungen an Johannes Brahms*, ed. K. Hofmann (Tutzing, 1976) 171.

[6] Florence May relates the details as given her direct by Frau Fellinger. See Florence May, *The Life of Johannes Brahms*, 2nd edn. rev. and enl., 664–5, 670.

Brahms in 1896 be ignored and that they be considered joint heirs. If the court were to decide that the will was invalid, it was clear that the legal regulations on inheritance would apply, and this would mean that distant relations would also be declared heirs. A Viennese lawyer, Dr Josef Reitzes,[7] had been making preparations with this end in view; over a period of years, he had succeeded in gaining power of attorney to act on behalf of twenty-two so-called heirs in intestate succession. Only one of the twenty-two went by the possibly more authentic spelling of the name with a 't' – 'Brahmst'.[8] All of them were extremely distant relations, not only from Hamburg and around, but even from Philadelphia, Chicago and Minnesota, where some branches of Brahms's father's family had emigrated. Dr Reitzes's twenty-two would-be heirs believed they would receive sizeable inheritances, for Brahms was considered a wealthy man, but they had no intention of investing anything to his memory or showing their regard for him in any way whatever. Yet heirs have not only rights, but duties. The expenses connected with Brahms's burial had been borne by the Society, which was also prepared to pay for a suitable tombstone. Dr Reitzes stated that erecting a tombstone was his business and that of his 'legal heirs'. It is characteristic of the whole situation, however, that the 'legal heirs' failed to provide the sum needed for a tombstone, and Dr Reitzes was reduced to asking the Society to defray part of the expenses after all.

Dr Reitzes was not at all certain whether the legal contest would end in his favour and whether his 'legal heirs' would in fact be declared sole heirs. This uncertainty was exploited by the Society's lawyers who managed to conclude a special agreement that was signed on 23 June 1900 – before the court had decided whether or not the will was valid and whether or not to recognize the claims of the distant relations collected by Dr Reitzes. Under this agreement the Society received – immediately and irrevocably – Brahms's books and musical effects, including his own and other musical autographs. There was also the sum of 50,000 crowns, most of the interest from which was to go to Brahms's step-brother Fritz Schnack. The Society thus secured, for its archives and for musical scholar-

[7] Dr Josef Reitzes was a member of the governing body of the Deutsche Brahms Gesellschaft. For details of Brahms autographs which he at one time possessed (Opp. 52a, 67, 104) see Margit L. McCorkle, *Johannes Brahms Thematisch-Bibliographisches Werkverzeichnis* (Munich, 1984).

[8] Brahms's father also spelt his name with a 't', though Brahms did not. For his comments on this, see Richard Heuberger, *Erinnerungen an Johannes Brahms*, ed. K. Hofmann (Tutzing, 1976) 63; see further Kalbeck I, 1, 49.

ship, the most important source material for the study of Brahms's work and artistic identity, and kept it from being dispersed. As for Dr Reitzes, he had given a demonstration of goodwill by renouncing all claims to things which were of no interest to the people he represented. It was also a gesture to Brahms's modest and unassuming step-brother, Fritz Schnack (1849–1919), who was the only one of the whole family who had any real understanding and affection for Brahms; hence the bequest in the composer's will. But he was only a step-brother and could therefore not be considered a potential legal heir: on the contrary, he was one of Dr Reitzes's opponents. For Dr Reitzes and the twenty-two in search of an inheritance, legal action over Brahms's fortune and his letters must have seemed a straightforward step. But it was to be a long, drawn-out affair.

The question of the validity of Brahms's testament occupied the Viennese courts on several occasions. On 5 March 1901, the Supreme Court ruled that the corrections made in the letter of 1891, which Brahms regarded as his will, had made it so unclear and contradictory that no unequivocal will could be perceived and thus executed. The next point was to determine which of Brahms's relations were his legal heirs. On 30 March 1901, a few weeks after the testament had been declared void, the twenty-two people represented by Reitzes were recognized as legal heirs by the Supreme Court. A difficult situation thus arose: despite the corrections in Brahms's will, it was more than apparent that he did not want his distant relations, with whom he had had no contact of any sort, as his heirs. This seemed indisputable. Brahms's friends in Vienna now had good reason to fear that people who had no real connection with the composer or his music would be interested only in the purely material side of his estate. Moreover, these distant relations were represented in Vienna by a quite clever lawyer, about whom it must be said in retrospect that he seems to have found them rather than the other way around. At this point Dr Richard Fellinger took a hand in the proceedings. He was afraid that the many extant letters addressed to Brahms might come into the wrong possession; he regarded them not only as personal documents, but also as items of musicological interest. Brahms had ordered in his testament that all these letters should be destroyed; yet his testament had been declared void by the court. One week after Dr Reitzes's 'heirs' had been recognized as legal, on 7 April 1901, Dr Fellinger had a circular sent to the writers of the letters in question or their assignees, in which he stated that it was possible 'that the contents of the letters will be published or that the letters themselves will fall into the wrong hands, against the will of Johannes Brahms'. Fellinger had been made trustee of the Brahms estate in 1897, and he now asked for power of attorney to return the letters or to destroy them. A week later, Reitzes sent out a similar circular. He challenged the right of Fellinger to act as trustee of the estate, now that the court had recognized legal heirs. But Reitzes's success in gaining that recognition did not mean that he could take possession of the letters on their behalf. The Society was not about to give up the struggle. Its lawyers were not fighting so much for its personal advantage as out of respect for Brahms. They were determined that although his will had been declared invalid, as much as possible of what he clearly intended in 1891 should be fulfilled as he had wanted; the letters to Brahms were to be returned to the people who had written them, or be destroyed; on no account were they to pass into the hands of his relations, who, it could be predicted, would immediately turn them into cash with the good offices of their lawyer.

Again the courts got to work, this time for two years. On 26 May 1903, they ruled as follows: the heirs and 'the Society' were to nominate a delegate to open the letters to Brahms, which had been put under seal by the court. He was to examine them and, depending on the outcome of that examination, (1) to destroy them if it seemed that this was necessary because of their personal or confidential nature; (2) to return them to the writers or their nominees; or (3) if it was not necessary to destroy the letters, and not possible or advisable to return them, to deposit them with the Gesellschaft der Musikfreunde and keep them under seal until 1910. Letters which the writers or their nominees expressly stated that they did not wish to have back would be handed over to Brahms's twenty-two 'heirs'. The man appointed to examine the letters was the Viennese lawyer and music lover Dr Erich von Hornbostel.[9] He seems to have gone to work with a sense of duty and without being called into question by either side; but there are no notes of any kind about his work, and we therefore do not know what he destroyed and what he handed over. One example will indicate how complicated was his job. In the correspondence were the letters from Brahms to Hans von Bülow, which Brahms had got back after Bülow's death. The records, by chance, happen to contain some

[9] Dr Erich von Hornbostel (1877–1935). Austrian scholar and music-psychologist. A pioneer in the study of non-European music and in the transcription of field recordings. He knew Brahms in the last years of his life.

information as to what became of them. Hornbostel destroyed one letter because of its quite personal contents. There was a statement of renunciation from Bülow's heirs, so Dr Reitzes claimed the letters for his Brahms heirs, but Hornbostel handed over only twenty-seven of them. He decided that the rest, because of their contents, should be deposited under seal in the Society's archives.

By 1910, only a few of Brahms's correspondents had written to ask for their letters back, and Reitzes sued the Society in 1911 to force it to hand over the letters to the Brahms heirs. This initiated another series of lawsuits. The Society's first step was to inquire of the heirs whether they knew of Reitzes's move and whether they approved. But they knew nothing about it; Reitzes had acted purely on his own initiative. For one of the heirs this was reason enough to take legal action against Reitzes. But after two years, in 1913, Reitzes had got all twenty-two of his Brahms heirs, or their nominees, to the point that he could again bring suit – this time really in their names – for the cession of the letters. The final decision was made on 14 December 1915, after a complicated legal action: the letters were to remain with the Gesellschaft der Musikfreunde. To play safe, the Society decided that the letters would remain under seal, and thus not accessible to anyone, until thirty years after the date of acquisition in 1903 – in other words, until 1933, which happened to be the Brahms anniversary year. This period was chosen because any claim would by then be cancelled by the statute of limitations and there would be no danger of yet another series of lawsuits, however unlikely it might be. This court ruling of 1915, by which the letters were irrevocably awarded to it, was welcomed by the Society, also because of the respect it felt for Johannes Brahms. On the one hand, the Society knew the value of the letters as documents and as objects of musicological research; on the other, it would have been obliged to return or destroy them if Brahms's testament in its final form had been acknowledged by the court. The fact that a large number of Brahms's letters were to be preserved for subsequent research purposes was now legally established.

What, therefore, remains of Brahms's artistic, musical and literary estate, and where is it located? Of letters written to him, there were some 4000 from nearly 400 correspondents. There is no record of how many were destroyed or returned to their writers or their nominees. In the Society's archives there are less than 1500 letters to Brahms from 167 correspondents. Excluded from the estate are some letters which Brahms threw away but which were retrieved, torn up, from his wastepaper basket, by his landlady, Frau Celestine Truxa, who kept them herself. They were acquired with the Truxa estate by the Wiener Stadt- und Landesbibliothek in 1965; a very few found their way into the antiquarian trade.

Of his books and musical effects, Brahms had written in the letter of 1891:

> I leave them to the Gesellschaft der Musikfreunde in Vienna, but before that I wish that my true and worthy friends and acquaintances take something from my estate to remember me by, with the decisions not to be made by the Society management but by yourself [Simrock] and Mr Mandyczewski. (Exceptions, which are to be given to the Society: Mozart's autograph of the G minor Symphony, the manuscripts of the six quartets by Haydn, and all printed and manuscript Scarlatti.)[10] I wish the intended mementos to be bestowed most liberally. . .There are many things that are suitable for this purpose, and Mr Mandyczewski can easily see to it that nothing is chosen which would be of value for the Society's collections. I reserve the right to list individual bequests; for the time being, I have decided that J. Joachim will get the sketches to the three string quartets by Schumann.

Although this will was invalid, it was agreed that Brahms's wishes as expressed here would be respected. In 1904, Joachim did get the Schumann sketches, as the court records prove. Other friends were able to choose, quite freely and discreetly, the mementos they wanted. There are no notes to tell us who chose or received what, which explains why holograph letters and literary manuscripts by Luigi Cherubini, Franz Clement, Emanuel Geibel and Ivan Turgenev, once owned by Brahms, could turn up in 1981 in an auction in London – to everyone's surprise.[11] It must be added, however, that all the important items in Brahms's manuscript collection, his own musical autographs, his musical effects and books, were acquired by the archives of the Gesellschaft der Musikfreunde under the terms of the agreement of 23 June 1900. The printed music and books on musical subjects were incorporated into the library's stocks, with reference to their origin, but not in one piece as, so to speak, a 'Brahms Library'. In his lifetime, Brahms gave away many books and music on many occasions – to the Society's archives, to friends and to acquaintances. They are located

[10] Domenico Scarlatti. Brahms was a great enthusiast for Scarlatti's keyboard music, which he played frequently. The song Op. 72 No. 5 begins with a Scarlatti quote in the keyboard part (Sonata in D, K. 223, L. 214, transposed to A).

[11] See Sotheby's catalogue *Continental Autograph Letters and Manuscripts* (12–13 May 1981).

today in various libraries, but they have nothing to do with his estate. It is, in fact, rather the books on non-musical subjects which have been stored as a separate Brahms collection and it is appropriate here to clarify several points concerning the listing of these books compiled by Kurt Hofmann and published in 1974.[12] Hofmann lists the non-musical books, but not the books on music theory and history that were likewise acquired from the Brahms estate. Although some of these appeared in Orel's catalogue of Brahms's musical effects, which is reproduced in Hofmann, particularly those with many musical examples, the impression is here created that there were few works about music in Brahms's library. Equally, Hofmann does include books that, whilst actually owned at one time by Brahms, were given away by him or found their way into the antiquarian trade via the estates of Miller zu Aichholz and Max Kalbeck; they are today located in various libraries or private collections, or their whereabouts are unknown. That is, Hofmann has taken into his catalogue all the books which were demonstrably once owned by Brahms, though not those which Brahms gave to the Society's archives in his lifetime – a negligible quantity – and, unfortunately, not the works on music which the archive acquired as part of the Brahms library.[13] Of the Brahms musical autographs in the archive, not all are from the estate. He gave the score of *Ein deutsches Requiem* to the Society during his lifetime and other manuscripts were bought or acquired as legacies from, amongst others, Theodor Billroth, Marie Schumann, Eusebius Mandyczewski and the Viennese manuscript collector, Wilhelm Kux.

In conclusion, an examination of Brahms's estate shows that there is more of it extant than the relevant literature would lead one to believe. Equally, considering the vicissitudes through which it has passed, it cannot be assumed that something which is not now present was never present; the mementos chosen by Brahms's friends and the partly dispersed, partly destroyed correspondence addressed to Brahms definitely pose problems for Brahms research. As for the rest of Brahms's estate, his fortune and personal possessions went to the so-called 'legal heirs'. The furniture in the three rooms occupied by

[12] Kurt Hofmann, *Die Bibliothek von Johannes Brahms* (Hamburg, 1974). This book lists the contents of the collection with detailed descriptions in alphabetical order of author. It also reproduces Alfred Orel's listing of Brahms's music library as first published in the *Simrock Jahrbuch* III.

[13] Among a few of the very slight war losses sustained by the Society's archive were a few of the books from this non-musical library.

Brahms in the flat of Frau Truxa was for the most part her own property. Brahms's friends who formed the Deutsche Brahms-Gesellschaft wanted the flat left unaltered as memorial rooms. This was not possible; the house was torn down in 1906. The building of an intended Brahms House in Vienna, as a memorial and documentation centre, came to nothing because of the First World War. The furniture was stored for a few years in the Gesellschaft building and finally went to the Historical Museum of the City of Vienna. With the exception of a few items, it was destroyed in the Second World War. The surviving pieces – a piano chair, a rocking chair and a writing desk are the most striking – are in the Haydn House, Haydngasse, Vienna, in a special Brahms memorial room. And, to judge from his love of this composer, Brahms doubtless feels very good in his company.

IMOGEN FELLINGER

Brahms's 'Way': a composer's self-view

In his final years, Brahms made several very significant comments about his outlook on music, his own compositions and the position of contemporary composers. Of these, his comparison of himself with Schumann and Wagner seems especially pertinent to our understanding of his self-view. In conversation with the composer and music critic Richard Heuberger (1850–1914) on 23 February 1896 he remarked as follows: 'Schumann went the one way, Wagner the other, I the third.'[1] What did Brahms mean by these 'ways'? Did he perhaps think of Schumann as the quintessential German Romantic composer and of Wagner as the greatest theatrical genius of the age? More emerges from the complete context of the remark. Namely, Brahms believed that none of the three composers had passed through a real school of composition. 'Neither Schumann, nor Wagner, nor I learnt properly ['was Ordentliches gelernt']. Talent was the decisive factor. Schumann went the one way, Wagner the other, I the third. Yet nobody actually learnt what is right ['Aber gelernt hat keiner was Rechtes']. Nobody passed through a right school. In truth, it was *afterwards* that we learnt. Actually, it was simply a matter of diligence, the more for the one, the less for the other' (Heuberger, 94). He saw his younger contemporary Dvořák in the same light: 'An individual talent led him spontaneously to do what was right' (Heuberger, 95).

Brahms thus recognized three different paths to self-expression: for himself, representing a younger generation, and for Schumann and Wagner signifying an older order. But it is interesting that he did not merely conceive of different goals for himself and Wagner – as we would naturally expect – but also for himself and Schumann. How, then, did Brahms understand the term 'school'?

[1] 'Schumann ging den einen, Wagner den anderen, ich den dritten Weg': Richard Heuberger, *Erinnerungen an Johannes Brahms*, ed. K. Hofmann (Tutzing, 1971) 94 (hereafter Heuberger).

Several remarks to contemporaries indicate that it seems to have had the meaning of 'standing in a continuity of tradition', in the sense of sharing values and points of historical reference, and he was well aware of the composers he felt to have had such a background. Mendelssohn was an obvious example. As Brahms remarked later to his friend the philologist Gustav Wendt in Karlsruhe, whom he first met in May 1869: 'Mendelssohn had a great advantage compared with us: the excellent school. What indescribable efforts it has cost me to recover this lost ground as a man!' And in 1887 he spoke to Wendt of Mendelssohn's 'incomparable artistic cultivation' ('Kunstbildung').[2] But he was not only sensitive to German traditions. According to Brahms, a school existed in France until the middle of the 1890s as he told Heuberger in 1896: 'Cherubini was the great master from whom everything had proceeded, beside him the excellent Halévy, then Auber, who also mastered his craft to a remarkable degree, eventually even Thomas, who still had good schooling' ('der noch gute Schule besass') (Heuberger, 94–5). Thus, in addition to a general sense of continuity and shared values, the term 'school' also implies for Brahms the mastering of specific musical rules and techniques. Indeed, the emphasis on Mendelssohn and Cherubini directs attention to a particular area of instruction – the tradition of counterpoint and thoroughbass. Cherubini's *Cours de Contrepoint et de fugue* of 1835 connects eighteenth-century traditions of species counterpoint with the goals of extended polyphonic composition of the later nineteenth-century Conservatoire tradition, though it was valued by many others, including Schumann, Mendelssohn and Wagner. And Brahms's reverence for and identity with Cherubini is well known. Recent publication of Mendelssohn's youthful studies vividly reveals the practicalities of a favoured education under Zelter, in its figured bass and counterpoint exercises and chorale harmonizations.[3] Such were the kinds of practical background for which Brahms, like the others, had to compensate.

Brahms's statement must, of course, be placed in the perspective of period. Schumann, Wagner and himself took their points of departure from the quite different historical situations of their own times. That in which the older composers found themselves around the year 1830 was quite another from that twenty years later when Brahms appeared on the musical scene. Each of these situations may be considered in its turn.

[2] M. Kalbeck, *Johannes Brahms* I (Berlin, ^{3}1912) 33.
[3] See: R. Larry Todd, *Mendelssohn's Musical Education* (Cambridge, 1983).

Schumann's special concern was to combat what he regarded as the musical degeneracy of his time – the pure formalism and uncontrolled virtuosity apparent, for example, in the piano works of Henri Herz and Franz Hünten through his demand for the 'poetic idea' of music. 'Poetic' content was primary for him, formal considerations of secondary relevance. The 'poetic' idea and its characterization created in his works a musical language of psychical expression. He emphasized that 'the poetry of art' should again be honoured in order to achieve the desired renewal of musical art.[4] This view predicted important differences in the attitudes of Schumann and Brahms towards the past, a vital dimension for both. Indeed, the extent of Schumann's knowledge of the fruits of research, and the access it provided the young Brahms, has been generally underestimated hitherto. None the less, it was the Romantic aspect which exerted the greatest attraction: for example, Schumann took the fugues of the *Wohl-Tempiertes Klavier* as character pieces in the Romantic sense, 'of which each needs its own expression, its specific lights and shades'.[5] Brahms's standpoint was more historical in its attitude to the identity of the original, as, for example, in his own treatment of Bach's works. He was not alone in recognizing the potential of Bach's Chaconne in D minor for violin: Schumann, like Mendelssohn, had supplied it with piano accompaniment. Yet, in arranging it for piano, left hand alone (1873), he left the structure of the piece untouched.[6] Though Schumann recommended to young people the study of Renaissance vocal polyphony, 'in order to capture the spirit of song', he never undertook such profound studies of the music of the past as did Brahms. The point re-emerges in the comparison of their uses of the traditional devices of counterpoint in instrumental music. In Schumann's instrumental compositions, the fugue is frequently of symbolic importance as in the works of many Romantic contemporaries; it may be used for the expression of an extra-musical idea, notably as a symbol of the sacred, the solemn or the sublime. Thus, in his third (*Rhenish*) Symphony, Schumann characterized the cathedral of Cologne by a solemn movement, consciously recalling the polyphonic tradition in its manipulation of 'learned' devices on its steep, ascending theme. In contrast, such methods in Brahms's

4 R. Schumann, *Gesammelte Schriften über Musik und Musiker* IV (Leipzig, 1854) Introduction.

5 R. Schumann, *Gesammelte Schriften über Musik und Musiker*, ed. M. Kreisig I (Leipzig, ^{5}1914) 354.

6 See I. Fellinger, *Über die Dynamik in der Musik von Johannes Brahms* (Berlin and Wunsiedel, 1961).

instrumental music have exclusively formal function, as, for example, in the finales of the Cello Sonata in E minor Op. 38 or the String Quintet in F major Op. 88, where the first subject area is fugal, thereby recalling classical rather than Romantic antecedents. Attitudes to more recent variation techniques also reveal marked differences. Although Brahms's Variations on a Theme of Schumann Op. 9 are the fruit of his preoccupation with Schumann's pianistic style and variation methods – which he defined in 1856 as 'Phantasie-Variationen'[7] (and are not merely a personal homage) – Brahms subsequently developed a stricter attitude to the principle, which he first realized in the Variations and Fugue on a Theme of Handel Op. 24, composed seven years later in 1861. Generally speaking, Brahms's music is more concentrated in texture than that of Schumann. Schumann strove to reach a balance between homophony and polyphony in much of his music, an integration of the two into a unified equality, but he never really succeeded, in spite of his intensive preoccupation with the compositions of Bach. For Brahms the problem hardly existed at all, for he revealed from the very outset a greater tendency to integration.

Lying behind such apparent differences are fundamental contrasts of attitude towards the creative process. Schumann's statements, reflecting his compositional experience, reveal a preference for a work's first draft. He says of alterations, through the person of Eusebius: 'Often two versions can be of the same value', continuing, through Master Raro: 'The original is mostly the better.'[8] And on another occasion: 'The first conception is always the most natural and the best. The mind may be wrong, but not the feeling.'[9] Thus, not only did he give preference to the original as against later versions, but also the first inspiration, since, as he puts it, the 'feeling, not the mind' is involved. Schumann's manuscripts reveal that the basic conception of a composition, as a rule, was left untouched. Besides the alteration of single notes, a certain smoothing of melodic lines in single phrases and supplying of expression marks, as can be demonstrated, for example, in piano pieces and likewise in lieder, do not have any decisive influence on the direction of the original conception. Cases are also to be found in which Schumann returned to the first conception after several alterations, for instance formal alterations.[10] This more intuitive and

[7] *Brahms Briefwechsel VIII: Johannes Brahms im Briefwechsel mit J.V. Widmann, E. und F. Vetter, A. Schubring*, ed. Max Kalbeck (Berlin, 1915), 218.
[8] Schumann I, 28.
[9] Schumann I, 25.
[10] I. Fellinger, 'Unbekannte Entwürfe zu Robert Schumanns Klavierstücken Op. 99 und Op. 124' in *Kongressbericht* (Leipzig, 1966; Kassel, Leipzig, 1970) 313–17.

spontaneous aspect of the creative process is the very opposite of the more self-aware, constructive procedure of Brahms. This becomes clear from Brahms's comparatively detached attitude to the first, spontaneous musical ideas, as he explained in his familiar though invaluable remarks in 1876 to the singer Georg, later Sir George, Henschel (1850–1934).

There is no real creating without hard work. That which you would call invention, that is to say a thought, an idea, is simply an inspiration from above, for which I am not responsible, which is not merit of mine. Yes, it is a present, a gift, which I ought even to despise until I have made it my own by right of hard work. And there need be no hurry about that either. It is as with the seed-corn: it germinates unconsciously and in spite of ourselves. . . .Nothing, however, is lost. If afterwards I approach the subject again it is sure to have taken shape; I can now really begin to work at it.[11]

Thus, for Brahms, the elaboration of a musical idea is far more important than its invention.[12]

If the outward character of their music might disguise important differences in attitude between Brahms and Schumann, there is no disguising the differences between Brahms and Wagner, so different were their essential natures and views on music. For Wagner's all-consuming ideal lay in the achievement of a combination of drama and music through a concept of *Gesamtkunstwerk*, an ideal of the development of the arts in which all previous achievements were seen as preparatory stages, with even composers of Beethoven's stature seen as precursors. In turn, Wagner's characteristic development emerged as a natural consequence of his double literary and musical talent, a feature which links him to some extent to Schumann, though not to Brahms. How did Brahms interpret Wagner's gradual realization of his aims, in which Brahms took such a keen interest? He clearly recognized that Wagner's early compositions showed no individuality. A case in point is his Symphony in C major, which Wagner composed and performed in Leipzig at the age of nineteen, and which was found again in 1882 by pure chance and performed by him at Christmas of that year in Venice. Brahms commented on it to Heuberger in 1887:

Wagner was always angry that Mendelssohn did not say a word whilst looking through his Symphony. And hardly surprising, by God! By that time, Mendelssohn had reached a high level of mastery, had written his chief compositions; from this position, the work must

[11] G. Henschel, *Personal Recollections of Johannes Brahms: Some of His Letters to and Papers from a Journal* (Boston, 1907) 22.

[12] See also I. Fellinger, 'Tendencies in Brahms's Compositional Process'. Paper read at the International Brahms Congress (Detroit, Michigan, 1980) published as 'Tendenzen in Brahms' Schaffensprozess' in *Wege der Forschung: Johannes Brahms* (Darmstadt, 1986).

have seemed to him very insignificant. The Symphony is routine in execution, hastily written down, [it is] well scored but shows no feature typical of Wagner. One could take it for Reissiger,[13] yet each work by Reissiger is actually better. No individuality! Nobody in the whole world could have expected or hoped that there would one day arise: a Wagner! (Heuberger, 34)

Of interest for Brahms's deep respect and understanding of Wagner is the following statement from his discussion with Heuberger on 5 March 1888 concerning the recently published Wagner-Liszt correspondence: 'Wagner had long known in which direction he and he alone wanted to go, but he was not always able to make this fact intelligible to everyone else, so that often something by Wagner looks a little pretentious, even though it was natural to his disposition' (Heuberger, 36). In discussing *Die Meistersinger*, Brahms touched on another vital aspect of the Wagner phenomenon, stressing how necessary it was for Wagner to force the public to his views 'by writing, words and action' in order to realize them (Heuberger, 39). In recognizing the importance of Wagner's writings for his compositions, he acknowledged him as possessing 'one of the clearest heads the world has ever seen' (Heuberger, 16). He saw him as a 'theatrical genius' (Heuberger, 16) but observed that, as a consequence, his music is implicitly attached to the scene, as for example in the funeral march of *Götterdämmerung*. Accordingly, in contrast he praised the higher quality of the funeral march from Handel's *Saul*, since, unlike Wagner's march, 'it also has its value without the scene' (Heuberger, 23), a distinction as reflective of aesthetic outlook as of personal taste. Yet, the striking fact that Brahms offered his services, through Cornelius, in the copying of parts for the partial performance of *Die Meistersinger* in Vienna in 1863 was a kind gesture towards him, nothing more, probably due to Brahms's friendly relations with Cornelius in these years. There can hardly be seen any causal connection with the Manifesto, initiated by Brahms in March 1860,[14] because this was only directed against Liszt and the New German School, not, as Brahms emphasized more than

[13] Karl Gottlieb Reissiger (1798–1859). German composer, conductor and teacher, whose prolific output 'embodied the dying tradition of the Kapellmeister-composer' in the assessment of *The New Grove*. See John Rutter, 'Karl Gottlieb Reissiger', *The New Grove Dictionary of Music and Musicians*, ed. S. Sadie, 15 (London, 1980) 729–30.

[14] As might be concluded from Michael Musgrave's observation: 'This was a significant gesture in view of the embarrassment he had suffered through the debacle of the Manifesto three years earlier'. See 'The Cultural World of Brahms' *Brahms: Biographical, Documentary and Analytical Studies* ed. R. Pascall (Cambridge, 1983) 18.

once in letters to Joachim, against Wagner and Berlioz.[15] On the contrary, Brahms mentioned to Heuberger in 1888 that he received letters from Wagner, Berlioz and others obviously agreeing at that time. None of these letters seem to have survived, however.[16] He also told Heuberger that he had been present when, in 1863, Wagner advised Cornelius and other composers that they should work along other lines than his (Heuberger, 50). Such advice could hardly have influenced Brahms, since his own goals were clearly envisaged about ten years before. Already in June 1853, that is, before he met Schumann, he had decided not to follow Liszt and the New Germans because he could see his own way forward, if perhaps more instinctively than consciously at this stage.[17] None the less, his arrival in Vienna in the autumn of 1862, as well as his personal acquaintance with Wagner in December of that year gave him additional insight beyond his earlier views of Liszt and Schumann.

The generation which separates the emergence of Brahms from his predecessors placed him in an entirely different situation: one dominated not only by Liszt and his school – focused as it increasingly was towards extra-musical literary subject matter – but also, to a great extent, by the epigones of Schumann, who used music increasingly and sometimes completely for the expression of a subjective emotional mood. The difficulty which Brahms encountered as a composer in the second half of the nineteenth century – not only in his attitude to the masters of the past, especially the Viennese classics, but also to the dominating tendencies of his own epoch – forced him to develop his own compositional personality. Yet Brahms was his own person from the very beginning. As his statement makes quite clear, he was never, in essence, a follower of Schumann. Moreover, neither did Schumann see the young Brahms as such, whether in the article 'New Paths' ('Neue Bahnen')[18] or in other remarks. Rather, this was the view projected into the world by music critics, notably Adolf Schubring (1817–93) and by the musical public of the time, who considered Brahms as belonging to the 'Schumannsche Schule'. Schubring meant by this term composers who were 'either

[15] *Brahms Briefwechsel V: Johannes Brahms im Briefwechsel mit Joseph Joachim*, ed. Andreas Moser (Berlin, ²1912) 273–4, 279.

[16] See: I. Fellinger, 'Brahms und die Neudeutsche Schule' in *Johannes Brahms. Symposion Brahms und seine Zeit* (Hamburg 1983) (=*Hamburger Jahrbuch für Musikwissenschaft* VII, ed. C. Floros, H.J. Marx and P. Petersen) (Laaber 1984) 169, n. 35.

[17] See I. Fellinger, 'Brahms und die Neudeutsche Schule', 159–60.

[18] *Neue Zeitschrift für Musik* (28 October 1853).

actual pupils of Robert Schumann or who at least continue in his sense and direction'.[19] From this point of view, Schubring identified Brahms as 'the greatest living master of the School of Schumann',[20] an evaluation which stood in total contradiction to Brahms's own intentions as a composer. In fact, the remarks made by Schumann or, for example, Joachim stress again and again the individuality and originality of Brahms's first compositions, which prophesied still greater works in the future.[21] Had Schumann seen in Brahms only his successor, the title 'New Paths' would have been unsuitable – indeed wrong – for his essay. It was precisely the characteristic originality of Brahms's early compositions, as well as their youthful elan, by which Schumann instantly was so deeply impressed. He recognized the quite distinctive quality of Brahms's music as compared with his own. 'Here you shall hear music such as you have never heard before' said Schumann to Clara during Brahms's first visit to Düsseldorf on 30 September 1853.[22] We may well conjecture that he observed in Brahms's compositions a constructive force missing in his own.[23]

None the less, there were already far-sighted contemporaries who saw in Brahms the 'real opener of new paths'. Hermann Deiters (1833–1907) emphasized in his biography of 1880 the difference between Schumann and Brahms, which, in his opinion, was 'to a large extent the result of a heterogeneous musical education in their youth'.[24] Friedrich Chrysander emphatically underlined Deiters's view in his criticism of the book. In Chrysander's view, 'Brahms persisted much more continuously with the essential elements of music than Schumann. This can be demonstrated in four disciplines. . .Besides variation, it was the dance, the folklike secular and spiritual song and polyphonic church music which are to be seen as basic elements of Brahms's education in his early years.'[25] In 1892, Philipp Spitta emphasized that 'the strangest thing one could hear about

[19] *Neue Zeitschrift für Musik*, 55/7 (1861).

[20] *Leipziger Allgemeine musikalische Zeitung*, 3 (1868) 51.

[21] Joachim spoke as follows of his first meeting with Brahms in Hanover in April 1853: 'Never in my artistic life was I more overwhelmed by happy astonishment than when the almost shy looking, fair-haired accompanist of my compatriot, with a noble face, played me his sonata-movements of a fully unexpected originality and force. It touched me like a miracle as the song 'O versenk' dein Leid' sounded towards me then.' Festival Speech during the Second Brahms Festival in Meiningen, 17 October 1899. See A.v. Ehrmann, *Johannes Brahms: Weg, Werk und Welt* (Leipzig, 1933) 27.

[22] M. Kalbeck, *Johannes Brahms* I (Berlin, ^{3}1912) 115.

[23] See I. Fellinger, 'Grundzüge Brahmsscher Musikauffassung' in *Beiträge zur Geschichte der Musikanschauung im 19. Jahrhundert* (Regensburg, 1965) 117.

[24] H. Deiters, *Johannes Brahms* (Leipzig, 1880).

[25] *Allgemeine musikalische Zeitung*, 16 (1881) 337–9, 353–7.

Brahms is that he is a successor of Schumann. He is as wholly different from Schumann as any artist with fundamentally sympathetic views could be at all.'[26]

That, in his own words, Brahms went 'the third way' was decisive for his whole compositional development and thus for his eventual historical position. His single-mindedness emerges from his recollections of his youth and confirms how diametrically opposed he was to Liszt and his world. Years later he recalled to Heuberger his visit to Liszt at the Altenburg in Weimar in June 1853: 'I was already at that time an energetic fellow and knew what I wanted to do' (Heuberger, 61). This determination was little influenced by his background. He realized that the instruction he had received from Eduard Marxsen was not profound and comprehensive enough to support his ambitions to become an artist of first rank, given the musical climate in which he began. Marxsen's instruction, which reflected certain traditions from Bach and Beethoven, was apparently applied in a more dogmatic than artistic way and his role has long been discussed (despite Brahms's dedication of his Piano Concerto in B flat to Marxsen), most notably by his pupil Gustav Jenner.[27] Only through Brahms's assiduous studies, in the second half of the 1850s, of musical form and texture, especially canons and fugues – as well as theoretical writings of the eighteenth century, mainly by Marpurg, Kirnberger and C.P.E. Bach – did he acquire his high level of compositional mastery. In such kinds of studies Brahms recognized the basis for all compositional activity. In looking through the compositions of Gustav Jenner for the first time at the end of December 1887, Brahms emphasized that Jenner had not learnt properly ('nichts ordentliches gelernt'), dismissing his studies in harmony, his attempts at composition, instrumentation and the like and advising him as follows: 'First you must look for a teacher to instruct you in strict counterpoint. . .it is absolutely necessary to see the world through these spectacles for a good while. Here you will have enough to do for the next few years.'[28] As mentioned, interest in the past was common to many composers of the period. Even Wagner as well as Schumann incorporated it in various ways. In addition to Schumann's marked historical inclinations, Wagner too took the past as a vital but precursory part of his heritage – albeit a more recent past for the

[26] P. Spitta, 'Johannes Brahms' in *Zur Musik* (Berlin, 1892) 390.
[27] G. Jenner, 'War Marxsen der rechte Lehrer für Brahms?', *Die Musik* (1912/13) 77–83.
[28] G. Jenner, *Johannes Brahms als Mensch, Lehrer und Künstler. Studien und Erlebnisse* (Marburg, 1905) 12–13.

most part, especially the Beethoven symphonies, culminating in the Ninth – in the formulation of his vast world of ideas.

Yet, it can well be argued that, of the three composers, Brahms appreciated the music of the past for its own sake to a much greater extent.[29] He was the only one who, consistent with his view of a missing school, restored a kind of continuity of tradition by going back to the great masters of the past, in whom he found a form of substitute school through which to further his own compositional abilities, and, more broadly, to enhance the future of the art of music as he understood it. Nor were his endeavours lost on his successors who sought more fully to explore the workings of the tradition of which he was a part. Not only the youthful Schoenberg, but also Schenker recognized the contrapuntal techniques and the role of variation which permeate his work, frequently explored by Schenker in his emerging speculations on tonal coherence and especially reflected in his editing and publication of Brahms's autograph study of consecutive octaves and fifths and similar progressions in the works of a wide variety of predecessors from the sixteenth to the nineteenth centuries.[30] Brahms's great sense of responsibility towards his own works and towards the tradition he respected, his strong combination of emotional and constructive elements, made it possible to pursue a path to high mastery and to create works of validity for the future, which at the same time contain progressive elements. His reassessment of the nature of music in the second half of the 1850s through studies of compositional methods and practices has to be understood as an important phase in his self-development, which he fulfilled with an individual selectivity towards past traditions. In absorbing himself in earlier music and the values it enshrined, he was able to reinterpret it in his own compositions with a new and individual spirit. He thus formed the basis for his mature art and outlook and, in time, for the achievements of musical art in the future. Thus, for the history of music, Brahms represents not only a point of culmination, but at the same time a turning point. His music reveals features which later generations took up – perhaps to a more profound extent than has yet been fully charted.

[29] See also I. Fellinger, 'Brahms und die Musik vergangener Epochen' in *Die Ausbreitung des Historismus über die Musik* (Regensburg, 1969) 163.

[30] *Johannes Brahms. Oktaven und Quinten u.a.*, ed. H. Schenker (Vienna, 1933). For a modern transcription and commentary, see Paul Mast, 'Brahms's Study, *Oktaven u[nd] Quinten u[nd] A[nderes]*', in *The Music Forum*, 5 (New York, 1980) 1–196.

GEORGE S. BOZARTH

Brahms's posthumous compositions and arrangements: editorial problems and questions of authenticity

I

Johannes Brahms left little doubt about the fate he intended for those of his original compositions which remained unpublished at the time of his death: in the letter to his friend and publisher Fritz Simrock of May 1891 known as the 'Ischl Testament' he stated unequivocally, 'I wish that all I leave behind in manuscript (unpublished) be burned. I am now taking care of this as best as possible, particularly with respect to music; you will find little on which you will be able to fulfil my wishes. . .if I should leave behind something which is undoubtedly ready for printing, then I herewith give it to you. I am scrupulously taking care that nothing superfluous is left!'[1]

The only unpublished compositions 'ready for printing' that were found in Brahms's apartment in Vienna at the time of his death in 1897 were eleven chorale preludes for organ, composed in May and June of the preceding year, and arrangements for four-hand piano, dating from 1854, of Joseph Joachim's Overtures to Shakespeare's *Henry IV* and Hermann Grimm's *Demetrius*. In 1902, after several years of delay caused by legal problems with Brahms's will,[2] the firm of N. Simrock of Berlin exercised its rights and issued the chorale preludes, as Op. 122, and the *Henry IV* Overture. Since then, however, numerous additional compositions attributed to Brahms have appeared in print; what fell outside the purview of the testament was a substantial number of compositions and arrangements extant in

[1] Max Kalbeck, *Johannes Brahms*, IV (1912–21; reprint edn, Tutzing, 1976) 230; a full facsimile of this document appears in Alfred von Ehrmann, *Johannes Brahms: Weg, Werk und Welt* I (Leipzig, 1933) 440–1.

[2] See Otto Biba, 'New light on the Brahms *Nachlass*', pp. 39–47 of this volume.

Key:	
A	Autograph manuscript
S	*Stichvorlage* (manuscript used as engraver's model)
MS	Manuscript, in a hand other than that of Brahms
Sop.	Soprano
Vln	Violin
Vla	Viola
Vc	Violoncello
A-Wgm	Gesellschaft der Musikfreunde, Vienna
A-Wn	Oesterreichische Nationalbibliothek, Vienna
A-Wst	Stadt- und Landesbibliothek, Vienna
CH-Private	Switzerland, Private Collection
D-brd-F	Stadt- und Universitätsbibliothek Frankfurt
D-brd-HS	Staats- und Universitätsbibliothek Hamburg
D-brd-Private	Bundesrepublik Deutschland, Private Collection
D-ddr-Bds	Deutsche Staatsbibliothek, Berlin
D-ddr-LE	Universitätsbibliothek Leipzig
GB-Ob	Bodleian Library, Oxford
J-Musashino	Musashino Academia Musicae, Tokyo
PL-Kj	Biblioteka Jagiellońska, Cracow
US-NYpm	Pierpont Morgan Library, New York
US-PHu	Van Pelt Library, University of Pennsylvania, Philadelphia
US-Smith College	Sophia Smith Collection, Smith College, Northampton (Massachusetts)
US-Wc	The Library of Congress, Washington, DC
DBG	Deutsche Brahms-Gesellschaft
JBSW	*Johannes Brahms Sämtliche Werke*
WoO	Werk ohne opuszahl number as given in Margit L. McCorkle, *Johannes Brahms Thematisch-Bibliographisches Werkverzeichnis* (Munich, 1984)

WoO	Title	Editor	Edition/Date	Type	Sources Previous and present owners
	11 Choralvorspiele, Op. 122	Anon. (Mandyczewski)	N. Simrock, 1902	A	Brahms estate; A-Wgm
				A (#11)	Kalbeck(?); US-Private
	Joachim, Overture to Shakespeare's *Henry IV* (2 piano)	Anon.	N. Simrock, 1902	S	D-brd-HS
				A	Brahms estate; A-Wgm
2	Scherzo for Violin and Piano, from the 'F.A.E. Sonata'	Anon. (Mandyczewski)	DBG, 1906	A	Joseph Joachim; D-ddr-Bds
	Schubert, 'Ellens zweiter Gesang', Op. 52 No. 2 (Sop., women's choir, winds)	Anon.	DBG, 1906		?
12	2 Cadenzas for Beethoven's Concerto in G, Op. 58	Anon.	DBG, 1907	A	Paul Wittgenstein; Ernest Walker; Margaret & Helena Deneke; GB-Ob
23	'Regenlied' (Groth)	Stange?	DBG, 1908	A	Klaus Groth: Hermann Stange, Annemarie Waetzoldt, Helmut Brauss; J-Musashino (facsimile)
5	2 Sarabandes	Friedlaender	DBG, 1917	A	?; Haas Kat. 33; ? (facsimile)
				A	Fr. Octavia Maria Otten; D-brd-HS
				A	Clara Schumann; Jerome Stonborough; US-Wc
32, 35	32 New Folksongs	Friedlaender	DBG, 1926	A	Clara Schumann; Deutsche Staatsbibliothek; PL-Kj
4	2 Gigues	Mandyczewski	JBSW 15, 1927	A	Clara Schumann; Jerome Stonborough; US-Wc
	Theme & Variations from Op. 18	ditto	ditto	A	ditto

WoO	Title	Editor	Edition/Date	Type	Sources Previous and present owners
	Cadenzas for:				
11	Bach, BWV 1052	ditto	ditto	A	ditto
13	Mozart, K. 453	ditto	ditto	A	ditto
14	K. 466	ditto	ditto	A	ditto
15	K. 491	ditto	ditto	A	ditto
	Beethoven, Op. 37	ditto	ditto	MS	Boerner Kat. 92; Viktor von Miller zu Aichholz; Wiener Brahms-Gesellschaft; A-Wst
	Schubert, Impromptu, Op. 90 No. 2 (arr. by Brahms)	ditto	ditto	MS	A-Wgm (lost?)
9, 10	2 Preludes & Fugues for Organ	ditto	JBSW 16, 1927	A	Clara Schumann; Jerome Stonborough; US-Wc
16	Kleine Hochzeitskantate (Keller)	ditto	JBSW 20, 1927	A	Sigmund Exner; Heinz Hauser; CH-Private
20	'Dem dunkeln Schoss' (Schiller)	ditto	JBSW 21, 1927	A	?; Jerome Stonborough; US-Wc
35	Deutsche Volkslieder, Nos. 15–22	ditto	ditto	A A	Score & parts: A-WSingakademie (Nos. 15–20) Parts: A-Wgm
	Canons:				
24	'Grausam erweist'	ditto	ditto	A	?
27	'In dieser Welt'	ditto	ditto	A	Numerous
30	'Zu Rauch'	ditto	ditto	A	A-Wgm
29	'Wann? wann?'	ditto	ditto	A	A-Wgm
	12 Trumpet Studies	Schmeisser	Leichsenring, 1928	MS?	?
		Goldman	Mercury, 1947		
		Zimolong	Polski Wydawnnictwo Muzyczne, 1957		
		Leloir	Henn-Chapius, 1964 (arr. for horn)		
		Whitwell	The M-F Co., 1966		
		Zimolong	Sikorski, 1973		
		Bialimtchev	Edition Ka We, n.d. (arr. for horn)		

WoO	Title	Editor	Edition/Date	Type	Sources Previous and present owners
22	5 Ophelia Lieder (Shakespeare)	Geiringer	Schirmer, 1934–5; Schönborn, 1960	A	Frau Olga Lewinsky; ?
	Orchestrations of Schubert Lieder:				
	'Memnon'	Hadow	Oxford, 1933	A	Julius Stockhausen; Wilhelm Heyer; D-brd-F
	'An Schwager Kronos'	ditto	ditto	A	Julius Stockhausen; Wilhelm Heyer; Mary Flagler Cary; US-NYpm
				A	Viktor von Miller zu Aichholz; A-Wst
	'Geheimes'	ditto	ditto	A	Julius Stockhausen; Wilhelm Heyer; Margaret & Helena Deneke; GB-Ob
	'Gruppe aus dem Tartarus'	Deutsch	Oxford, 1937	A	Viktor von Miller zu Aichholz; A-Wst
	Trio in A for Vln, Vla, Piano	Bücken, Hasse	Breitkopf & Härtel, 1938	MS	Erich Prieger; Ernst Bücken; ?
	Liebeslieder Walzer, Opp. 52, 65 (arr. for orchestra)	Weismann	Peters, 1938	A	CH-Private
19	'Dein Herzlein mild'	Drinker	University of Pennsylvania, 1938	MS	Partbook of Hamburg Frauenchor; Henry Drinker; US-Smith College
				A	J. Rieter-Biedermann; Edmund Astor; Wilhelm His; Jerome Stonborough; US-Wc
36	7 Folksongs	Drinker	University of Pennsylvania, 1940	MS	Partbooks of Hamburg Frauenchor; Henry Drinker; US-Smith College
	'Dar geit en Bek' (Groth)		Groth Sämtliche Werke, 1952	A	Klaus Groth, Hermann Stange; Annemarie Waetzoldt, Helmut Brauss; J-Musashino (facsimile)
18	Benedictus	Mueller von Asow	Doblinger, 1956	A	Mary Sefton Thomas Lux; Heineman Foundation; US-NYpm
				A	?; GB-Ob

WoO	Title	Editor	Edition/Date	Type	Sources Previous and present owners
37, 38	Folksongs	Kross	*Die Musikforschung* 16 (1964)	MS	Partbooks of Hamburg Frauenchor; Henry Drinker; US-Smith College
			Bärenreiter, 1965		
		Helms	Diss., Berlin, 1968		
		Gotwals-Keppler	Smith College, 1968		
	Sonata, Op. 78, arr. Vc, Piano	Starker, Marcus	International, 1975	1st edition?	
	Hymn for the Glorification of the Great Joachim	Stahmer	Schuberth, 1976	A	Joseph Joachim; D-brd-HS
3	2 Gavottes	Pascall	Doblinger, 1979	A	? (Facs. in Hoboken Photogramme Archiv, A-Wn)
	Piano Piece (B flat)	ditto	ditto	A	
	Canon for piano (F minor)	ditto	ditto	A	A-Wgm
	Cadenza to Mozart, K. 466	Badura-Skoda	Doblinger, 1980	MS	Kurt Taut; D-ddr-LE
	Die Müllerin (Chamisso) (fragment)	Draheim	Breitkopf & Härtel, 1983	A	D-brd-Private
17	Kyrie	Biba	Doblinger, 1984	MS	Julius Otto Grimm; US-Private; A-Wgm
18	*Missa canonica*	ditto	ditto	ditto	ditto

autographs which Brahms had given away to friends[3] or in manuscripts which others had prepared from his autographs.

The table presents a complete list of the posthumous works attributed to Brahms, cited in order of publication. These entries fall into three phases. From 1906 to 1926 the Deutsche Brahms-Gesellschaft issued six publications of works found in the manuscript collections of Joseph Joachim, Klaus Groth, and Clara Schumann, among others: a Scherzo for violin and piano composed in October 1853 as part of the 'F.A.E.' Sonata, a work using Joseph Joachim's motto 'Frei, aber einsam' and dedicated to him, with an opening Allegro by Albert Dietrich and Intermezzo and Finale by Robert Schumann; an arrangement for solo soprano, women's choir, four horns, and two bassoons of 'Ellens zweiter Gesang' by Schubert, prepared for and performed in a concert of the Gesellschaft der Musikfreunde in Vienna in March 1873; two cadenzas for Beethoven's Fourth Piano Concerto, Op. 58, probably composed in late 1855 for a performance of this concerto with the Gewandhaus Orchestra of Leipzig on 10 January 1856; Brahms's first setting of Klaus Groth's 'Regentropfen aus den Bäumen', sent to the poet in manuscript in midsummer 1872 (Brahms's second setting was published as Op. 59 No. 4),[4] two keyboard Sarabandes from the mid 1850s;[5] and thirty-two folksongs with piano accompaniments by Brahms, extant in an autograph which Brahms had given to Clara Schumann in 1858. These publications were followed in 1927 by Eusebius Mandyczewski's editions for the *Johannes Brahms Sämtliche Werke* (hereafter, the *Brahms Werke*) of a number of keyboard pieces preserved in manuscripts once owned by Clara Schumann and, by 1927, part of the vast collection of Brahms autographs assem-

[3] For a compilation and discussion of the dissemination of Brahms's manuscripts, see George S. Bozarth, 'The First Generation of Brahms Manuscript Collections', *Notes* 39 (1983) 239–62.

[4] Cf. the letter from Doris Groth, wife of the poet, to Brahms, 22 August 1872, published in Volquart Pauls, ed. *Briefe der Freundschaft Johannes Brahms-Klaus Groth* (Heide in Holstein: Westholsteinische Verlagsanstalt Boyen and Co., 1956) No. 16; also, Imogen Fellinger, 'Zur Entstehung der "Regenlieder" von Brahms', *Festschrift Walter Gerstenberg zum 60. Geburtstag*, ed. Georg von Dadelsen and Andreas Holschneider (Wolfenbüttel and Zürich, 1964) 55–8. The autograph of this song, which was published in facsimile in the DBG edition, bears no date, but cannot have been prepared before September 1871, for it contains a form of natural sign: ♮ which Brahms only began using sometime between that date and July 1873. In all likelihood, Brahms wrote out this autograph not long before sending it to Groth (and not in the 1860s, as Hermann Stange suggested in his 'Vorbemerkung' to the DBG edition). In bar 18, though, there occurs one natural of the pre 1871 variety: ♮ This suggests that the change in type of natural in fact occurred during the summer of 1872.

[5] Cf. Robert Pascall, 'Unknown Gavottes by Brahms', *Music and Letters* 57 (1976) 404–11.

bled by Jerome and Margarete Stonborough in Vienna (now in the Whittall Collection at the Library of Congress): two Gigues, dated 'January 1855'; an arrangement for solo piano of the variations from the String Sextet in B flat major, Op. 18, presented to Frau Schumann in September 1860 as a birthday present; several cadenzas for keyboard concertos by Bach and Mozart, stemming from the 1850s and early 1860s; and two preludes and fugues for organ (1856–7). The *Brahms Werke* also released a cadenza for the first movement of Beethoven's Third Piano Concerto, Op. 37; an arrangement of Schubert's Impromptu, Op. 90 No. 2, with the rapid passagework assigned to the left rather than right hand (published as 'vermutlich Johannes Brahms'); a short wedding cantata on a humorous parody by Gottfried Keller of the closing lines of Goethe's *Rinaldo*, composed at Keller's request in July 1874 for the nuptials of Sigmund and Emilie Exner; 'Dem dunkeln Schoss der heil'gen Erde', a brief choral setting of lines from Schiller's *Lied von der Glocke*, composed by 1880;[6] eight additional choral arrangements of folksongs, found amongst vocal parts in the archives of the Wiener Singakademie and the Gesellschaft der Musikfreunde in Vienna; and a few vocal canons, preserved on various *Albumblätter*.

Since 1927, previously unpublished compositions and arrangements attributed to Brahms have continued to appear periodically. Most notable are the Trio in A major for violin, violoncello, and piano, edited by Ernst Bücken and Karl Hasse; orchestrations of several of the *Liebeslieder Walzer*, Opp. 52 and 65, and of four more Schubert songs; a version for violoncello and piano of the Violin Sonata in G major, Op. 78, released by Gottfried Marcus and Janos Starker; a few more short keyboard pieces, edited by Robert Pascall; and another cadenza for Mozart's Piano Concerto in D minor, K. 466, edited by Paul Badura-Skoda.

At this late date, few would dispute the right of scholars to contravene Brahms's final wishes and publish the compositions and arrangements which they have discovered. After all, many of the works released so far might well be considered 'finished',

[6] Brahms mentioned this brief work in a letter to Joseph von Wasielewski, dated 'February 1880' and written in response to Wasielewski's request for music from Brahms for the unveiling of the Schumann monument in Bonn in May 1880: 'I have of course composed the verses from the *Glocke*, "Dem dunkeln Schoss der Erde", for such purposes. But they are hardly "for all times and occasions"! The chorus "Schlaf nun und ruhe" from [Schumann's *Das Paradies und die*] *Peri* [Op. 50], which can easily be adapted for winds, would seem to me possible and very appropriate. . . ' (*Stargardt-Versteigerungs-Katalog* 595, 16 and 17 February 1971, item 549).

even though Brahms did not supervise their publication, because they were either performed in public by Brahms or his friends, or given away in fair-copy autographs. And surely even such 'unfinished' works as the second Gavotte among the keyboard pieces edited by Pascall should be made available in print for the purpose of study, if not for public performance. Yet in a sense, one can still appreciate the composer's qualms about allowing such publications, for, as Brahms the experienced editor must have anticipated, a fair number of these editions are significantly flawed, and, what is more, some of the compositions and arrangements published with attribution to Brahms are not authentic.

II

Editorial problems begin already with the 1902 Simrock edition of the eleven Chorale Preludes, Op. 122. Brahms completed the initial seven preludes at Bad Ischl in May 1896, shortly after the death of Clara Schumann; the autograph, in which the preludes appear in the order 1, 5, 2, 6, 7, 3, 4, is twice inscribed 'Ischl/ Mai 96' (at the end of Nos. 2 and 4), and in Brahms's pocket calendar book for 1896, the page for May bears the entry:

Wien 4 ernste Gesänge für Bassstim̄e
20t † Clara Schumann
Ischl 7 Choralvorspiele.

Brahms sent these seven preludes to his copyist William Kupfer, who prepared a manuscript which Brahms then proofread and corrected. The final four preludes Brahms composed in June, also at Bad Ischl, according to the inscription he entered on the autograph at the end of No. 11. There is no evidence, though, that the copy of these pieces which Eusebius Mandyczewski added to the end of the Kupfer manuscript and which served as the engraver's model was prepared at Brahms's request and under his supervision: this portion of the manuscript contains no entries in Brahms's hand, and may indeed have been prepared by Mandyczewski only in 1902, in order that the autographs themselves need not be sent to the engraver. Thus, the first edition of preludes Nos. 1–7 was prepared from a primary source, a copy commissioned and, to some extent, controlled by Brahms, while the first edition of Nos. 8–11 was based on a secondary source, a copy probably prepared after Brahms's death.[7]

[7] The autograph of the eleven chorale preludes belongs to the Gesellschaft der Musikfreunde in Vienna (A 115); the Kupfer-Mandyczewski manuscript is in the Staats-

Ironically, though, the quality of the Simrock edition varies inversely to the pedigree of the sources, for Mandyczewski proved a more accurate copyist than Kupfer, and a more precise editor than Brahms. Indeed, in the first edition the final four preludes contain far fewer errors than the initial seven. Neither Brahms's notation of the autograph nor his proofreading of Kupfer's copy was entirely without error. For example, twice in the autograph of the first prelude, at bars 13–14 in the soprano voice and at bars 27–8 in the alto, Brahms failed to continue his slurs past the end of one brace and on to their proper conclusions on the next brace. At both places Kupfer terminated the slurs with the end of the initial measure, Brahms neglected to correct these errors, and the first edition adopted the incorrect readings. Furthermore, in these same two passages Kupfer deleted slurs present in the autograph (bars 11–13, alto; bars 28–9, soprano) and terminated others slightly too early (bars 10–12, tenor; bars 26–7, tenor). Brahms also neglected to correct these oversights, and they too found their way into the first edition (Example 1).

Example 1. Chorale Prelude 'Mein Jesu, der du mich', Op. 122 No. 1, bars 10–14 (editorial revisions indicated with dotted lines)

und Universitätsbibliothek Hamburg. Brahms's calendar books are owned by the Wiener Stadt- und Landesbibliothek (Ia 79.559); on these documents, see George S. Bozarth, 'Brahms's Lieder Inventory of 1859–60 and Other Documents of his Life and Work', *Fontes Artis Musicae* 30 (1983) 104–5.

A number of other inaccuracies and omissions in Kupfer's copy escaped Brahms's scrutiny, and, even when he did notice Kupfer's mistakes, the 'corrections' he introduced were not always consistent with or superior to the readings in the autograph. In a few passages, Brahms subsequently revised both autograph and manuscript copy, but the two readings do not match; either Brahms did not notate the articulation as fully in the copy as in the autograph, or Mandyczewski, when preparing fair-copy 'paste-overs' for these passages, failed to carry over onto these 'Zetteln' all of the slurs Brahms had indicated (blame cannot be assessed because the 'paste-overs' are all still firmly attached). Again, these errors were carried on into the first edition, as in the third prelude at bars 5–8 (Example 2). And of

Example 2. Chorale Prelude 'O Welt ich muss dich lassen', Op. 122 No. 3, bars 5–8 (editorial revisions indicated with dotted lines)

course, in the process of preparing the plates, the engraver allowed other errors to creep in. All in all, the first edition of the initial seven preludes was not carefully prepared, nor have subsequent editions fared any better.[8] According to a contemporary

[8] Despite Mandyczewski's claim that his edition of the *Choralvorspiele* for the *Brahms Werke* was based on the autograph as well as the first edition (which should not, of course, have been considered as having any authority, since it was not a primary source), his 1927 edition matches the first edition in nearly all details. Furthermore, he made no mention of the Kupfer manuscript. A list of revisions for the *Brahms Werke* edition of Op. 122 appears in Appendix A. A new edition of the complete Brahms organ works, prepared by the author, will be published in 1987 by G. Henle Verlag, Munich.

account of the publication of these pieces, Mandyczewski gave both the autograph and the manuscript copy to Simrock.[9] But Simrock's interest in the autograph was merely in having it photographed as proof that these organ works were by Brahms, and apparently no attempt was made to reconcile the variant readings between the two manuscript sources or to check for errors.

The editorial quality of the publications issued by the Deutsche Brahms-Gesellschaft is uneven. Of the compositions for which primary sources are still extant and accessible,[10] the most accurately edited are the two Sarabandes prepared by Max Friedlaender; the only unequivocal error occurs in the last bar of the opening section of the Sarabande in B minor.[11] The edition of Brahms's first 'Regenlied' is also reasonably good, containing only about a half-dozen minor mistakes, as well as the usual misplaced dynamic signs.[12] Most problematic is Mandyczewski's edition of the Scherzo from the 'F.A.E.' Sonata.[13] Assessment of even just the opening section yields a long list of errors:

— the addition of ties in the left hand of the piano, between g′-g′ at bars 2–3, 3–4, and 4–5;
— the deletion of the '3⌢' signs in both parts at bars 8 and 23–5;
— the misinterpretation of '<=>' for '< >' in the violin at bars 11–12, 12–13;
— the omission from the violin of a crescendo hairpin at the end of bar 14, of accent signs (>) on beat 1 of bars 16 and 24, and of a bar-long slur in bar 23;
— the deletion from the piano of ' ⌢. . . ' above the right hand at bar 23 and, from both parts, of crescendo hairpins extending from bar 19, beat 4, to the end of bar 15;
— the revision of ♩̣ ♩̣ | ♩ to ♩̣ ♩̣ | ♩ (slurred) in the violin at the final cadence.[14]

[9] Ludwig Karpath, 'Der musikalische Nachlass von Johannes Brahms', *Signale für die musikalische Welt* 60 (1902) 353–5; quoted in part, in English, in Vernon Gotwals, 'Brahms and the Organ', *Music, the A.G.O. and R.C.C.O. Magazine* 4 (April 1970) 51.

[10] I have not been able to locate primary sources for Brahms's orchestration of 'Ellens zweiter Gesang' by Schubert, and have not had access to the autograph of the 32 Volkslieder. For the two Sarabandes and the 'Regenlied' I have worked from the excellent facsimiles published together with the first editions of these pieces.

[11] Bar 8: the *b* on beat 1 should be a crotchet, i.e., not stemmed with the *d′* above it. For information on the *Brahms Werke* edition of the two Sarabandes, see Appendix D.

[12] The *Brahms Werke* corrected about half of these errors; see Appendix B for a list of revised readings for the *Brahms Werke*.

[13] Although Mandyczewski is not cited as the editor of this work, the engraver's model for this edition, 'copied from the autograph, with Joachim's consent' (statement written on the title page and signed by Mandyczewski) and preserved in the archive of the Gesellschaft der Musikfreunde in Vienna (XI 38372), is in his hand.

[14] Working only from the inaccurate DBG print and from Mandyczewski's manuscript copy, which was indeed the source for most of the errors in the first edition (the autograph itself, by 1926 in the Deutsche Staatsbibliothek, Berlin, was not consulted),

The editions of works first issued in the *Brahms Werke* under the editorship of Eusebius Mandyczewski are also highly variable in quality, even though the *Brahms Werke* was supposed to have been a carefully prepared 'critical edition'. The number of errors in these editions is all the more surprising because for each of these compositions Mandyczewski needed to control only a single primary source.

Not all of the editions of posthumous compositions in the *Brahms Werke* are poorly done. Virtually error-free are those of the Gigue in B minor, the cadenzas for Bach's *Klavierkonzert* in D minor, BWV 1052, and Mozart's Piano Concerto in C minor, K. 491, and the short wedding cantata on Keller's parody of Goethe's *Rinaldo*. The accuracy and quality of editing for other works, however, is only fair: the errors in the organ Prelude and Fugue in G minor include one missing chord, one missing and three incorrect pitches, several missing or misplaced slurs, and a number of variants in stemming of contrapuntal voices and in beaming, while one set of pitch errors, a series of incorrect or overlooked ornaments, and a few missing accent signs, rests, and slurs mar the edition of the Prelude and Fugue in A minor. Similar errors and omissions occur in the editions of the cadenzas to Mozart's Piano Concertos in G major, K. 453, and in D minor, K. 466.[15]

The cadenza to the first movement of K. 453 presents a particular problem which Mandyczewski failed to elucidate: it ends with a deceptive cadence, which, of course, will not connect the cadenza to the concerto proper. In his *Revisionsbericht* Mandyczewski made no mention of this incongruity; in a note that accompanies the autograph manuscript he simply remarked that 'at the end of the first cadenza Brahms erroneously placed a deceptive close, analogous to the deceptive close *before* the cadenza'.[16] It hardly seems possible that Brahms would have inadvertently written such a cadence. But what other explanations account for this action? Tovey has termed

Hans Gal perpetuated in his edition of this Scherzo for the *Brahms Werke* virtually all of the errors of the DBG edition. Hans Otto Hiekel has recently re-edited this composition, working directly from the Berlin autograph, and has corrected most of the errors and omissions of the DBG and *Brahms Werke* editions (see Appendix C for a list of minor revisions for the Hiekel edition).

[15] For details about the editorial errors in these and other posthumous works in the *Brahms Werke*, see Appendix D. In this paper I am not including discussion of the *Deutsche Volkslieder a 4* and the canons first published in the *Brahms Werke*, because I have not had access to the primary sources for these works.

[16] There is no explanation of why, in his *Revisionsbericht*, Mandyczewski cited the Stonborough manuscript of this cadenza as an 'Abschrift der Originalhandschrift von Brahms'; on the note that accompanies the autograph, Mandyczewski accurately described this source as an 'Original Handschrift'.

this high-spirited concerto 'one of Mozart's richest and wittiest',[17] and it is possible that Brahms, the perennial prankster, wrote this musical 'noch einmal' as a private joke for Clara Schumann, for whom this cadenza was composed, as a 'dodge' to throw her off the track of a tonic resolution, as Mozart had thrice done in the course of the movement (bars 49, 184, and 319). Or perhaps his intentions were more serious: to include in his cadenza all of the dramatic incidents with which Mozart had tempered his otherwise joyously exuberant movement – the 'wistful cantabile' (Tovey) which had served as the second subject, sung over a 'Brahmsian' descending bass line (Brahms bar 10 ≈ Mozart bar 35); the sudden tonal shift to parallel minor that began the modulatory exploration of 'flat-side' keys (Brahms bar 17 ≈ Mozart bar 126); and the deceptive cadence to ♭VI – thereby signalling to Frau Schumann the affinity of his cadenza to the most 'Romantic' moments in Mozart's concerto.

Editorial errors of a more serious nature include Mandyczewski's decision to reject the revised reading Brahms had entered in pencil at the beginning of the second part of the Gigue in A minor (vol. 15, pp. 53f.: see Example 3a). Brahms's intent, I believe, is clear: to limit all *Vorimitation* to the five-note 'head' motive and to reserve the fuller entrance of the soprano voice until the complete melody is sounded. Mandyczewski also ignored Brahms's pencil revision of the left-hand cadential pattern at the end of the Gigue (Example 3b), even though he did accept the pencil revisions at bars 15, 31, 41, and 42 as

Example 3. Readings for Gigue in A minor, according to revisions in the autograph

[17] Donald Francis Tovey, *Essays in Musical Analysis*, 5 vols. (London, 1935–9) 3, 33.

representing Brahms's final wishes. One senses that in this instance Mandyczewski considered the work 'unfinished' and therefore felt free to choose subjectively from amongst the various readings present; the quality of his decisions, though, is dubious.

Also problematic is Mandyczewski's revision, without editorial comment, of the text underlay and dynamics in the short choral work 'Dem dunkeln Schoss der heil'gen Erde' (vol. 21, pp. 155f.). In bars 5–8 he deleted the 'hairpin' dynamics, applicable to all voices, and recast the tenor and bass lines to accommodate the entire line of text instead of the portion which Brahms, by his use of vocal slurs in the tenor, had unequivocally allotted to these voices (Example 4a); in the tenor, at bars 22f. he delayed the second syllable of 'köstlicheren' for three beats, from bar 22/3.0 to bar 23/2.0, thereby improving the declamation slightly, but at the same time thwarting the imitation (Brahms's vocal slur from bar 22/3.0 to 23/2.5 (bar 22, beat 3 to bar 23, beat 2, third crotchet) [*e′*-*a*] leaves no doubt about the underlay of text he intended); and, in the final two lines of text (bars 34ff.) he completely revised Brahms's explicit and meaningful dynamics (Example 4b) – why do we need the crescendo and decrescendo on 'dass er aus den Särgen', and why should the crescendo for the last line of text not begin at bar 36/4 and peak at the first rather than the second 'schönerm'?

The poorest editing by far occurs in Mandyczewski's edition of the *Thema mit Variationen* from the Op. 18 String Sextet (vol. 15, pp. 59ff.), the sole source for which was the fair-copy autograph that Brahms gave to Clara Schumann in 1860 and

Example 4. Readings for 'Dem dunkeln Schoss der heil'gen Erde', according to the autograph

Ex. 4 (*cont.*)

from which she performed this work in Frankfurt in November 1865. Neither musical nor editorial reasons can explain the many arpeggiation signs, staccato dots, slurs, fingerings, and dynamic markings missing or incorrectly placed in this edition, nor is there any need for the many adjustments made to standardize the placement of the 'hairpin' dynamics. The errors are too numerous to list here, but the reader can see them for himself by comparing the *Brahms Werke* edition with the facsimile of this autograph published by the Robert Owen Lehman Foundation.[18] Note, for example, in just the theme and first variation, the incorrectly placed slur in bar 7; the missing arpeggi-

[18] *Johannes Brahms, Opus 24, 23, 18, 90* (New York, The Robert Owen Lehman Foundation, 1967).

ation signs in bars 13, 28, 32, 37, 41, and 45; the missing staccatos in bars 25, 27, 28, and 32; and the missing fingering and slurs in bars 22, 42, 44, and 48.

III

For a number of the compositions published since 1928 – the five *Ophelia Lieder*,[19] the Trio in A major, the *Trumpet Studies*, and the orchestration of several of the *Liebeslieder Walzer* – the primary sources are either lost or inaccessible, making it impossible to verify their musical texts.[20] The quality of most of the remaining editions has been reasonably high.[21] The greater problem that has arisen with these works is questionable attributions. Into this category fall four works, plus two others first published in the *Brahms Werke*. The authenticity of three of these – the 'left-hand' arrangement of Schubert's Impromptu, Op. 90 No. 2, the twelve trumpet etudes, and the Trio in A major for violin, violoncello, and piano – must remain disputed, at least for the time being. Mandyczewski attributed the Schubert

[19] Although in 1934–5 G. Schirmer issued Karl Geiringer's edition of the *Ophelia Lieder* in both low (36534) and high (36535) keys without designating which was the original and which the transposed reading, there can be no doubt that the version in the lower keys is the original one (as Schirmer's plate numbers would suggest): the manuscript which Schirmer submitted for copyright in 1934 (now in the Library of Congress) used the lower keys, and in a letter to Brahms dated 18 November 1873, Joseph Lewinsky, who commissioned these songs for his future wife, the actress Olga Precheisen, noted that she was a mezzo-soprano and recommended settings in a low register (unpublished letter, offered for sale in *Hauswedell Auktion 146* [Hamburg, 23 May 1966], lot 23). The 1960 Schönborn-Verlag edition presents the songs only in the low keys.

[20] I have not examined the many arrangements of folksongs edited by Drinker, Kross, Helms, and Gotwals-Keppler, because the numerous primary sources for these pieces have only recently been organized (see Margit L. McCorkle, *Brahms Thematisch-Bibliographisches Werkverzeichnis* (Munich, 1984) 552–609), and many are not readily available for study. Given the simplicity of these pieces, I would not, however, expect to find serious problems in these editions.

[21] In the humorous *Hymn to Joachim*, the editor has eliminated the effect of all three musicians counting beats together at the end of the introduction (the correct version is clear in the extant violin 1 and contrabass parts) by giving this comic incantation to just the first violinist; also, the chords in bars 2–4, violin 2, should be tied, a few articulation and dynamic markings present in the sources need to be added, and passages clearly implied in the autograph score, such as the viola in bars 50–63, should be realized. The editor rectified some of these problems in his set of parts for performance, but copious editorial markings in these parts make it impossible to determine which indications are by Brahms and which are by the editor.

In Pascall's edition of the Sarabande in A minor, which is a variant version of the A minor Sarabande published by the DBG in 1917, I would only suggest that the slur in b. 4 should end on beat 3.0, the *piano* in b. 4 should appear at b. 5/1.0, the hairpin crescendo at b. 7 should begin at b. 6/3.33, and the slurs in the left hand on the third beat of bars 5 and 6 are articulation slurs which function with the staccato dots, and not as part of the triplet sign.

arrangement to Brahms because the manuscript copy he found in Brahms's estate (Gesellschaft der Musikfreunde in Vienna) bore no name of arranger and 'no work by another composer was found in his estate on which the composer was not identified'. Moreover, the faulty Italian used to indicate a dal segno repeat, Mandyczewski argued, 'is evidence in favour of authorship by the youthful Brahms, whose Italian was very poor and in whose manuscripts similar linguistic errors are frequent enough', and 'internal study of the piece speaks entirely for his authorship' (*Brahms Werke*, vol. 15, p. xi). One might also note that Brahms made an arrangement for left hand (alone) of Bach's Chaconne for Violin. But the weakness of these bases for attribution is manifest, and since no autograph has been located, and even the manuscript copy Mandyczewski used has been lost, it is impossible to verify this arrangement as the work of Brahms. Similarly, the manuscript source from which Otto Kurt Schmeisser prepared the first edition of the trumpet etudes (Verlag Leichsering, Hamburg) is not to be found,[22] and the story reported in the 1973 Zimolong edition – that Brahms composed these studies for a trumpeter who played in the same pub as the young Brahms, but whose embouchure and technique were not up to Brahms's standards – cannot be confirmed.[23]

To assess properly the authenticity of the A major Trio would require a full-length analytical study of this work in relationship to the stylistic characteristics of Brahms's music through the early 1860s, and such an undertaking necessarily exceeds the scope of the present investigation. Attribution to Brahms, or to anyone else, will have to rest on style-analytical grounds, for once again the manuscript copy, discovered by Ernst Bücken in 1924 in the estate of Erich Prieger and used as the model for the Breitkopf und Härtel edition (1938), cannot be found.[24] The

[22] Frau Liselotte Schwartz of Sikorski Verlag, Hamburg, reports that the Verlag Leichsering was taken over, probably by 1929, by Musikverlag Viegener, whose archive was destroyed during the Second World War. I would like to thank Frau Schwartz, as well as Kurt R. Schmeisser, David Whitwell, and Max Zimolong, for answering my inquiries about these pieces.

[23] Professor Zimolong recounts in private correspondence that he obtained these etudes in a Hamburg edition (Schmeisser's, no doubt) 'in 1930 in Bayreuth from a Hamburg colleague, Weschke, who knew Brahms personally and well'. According to Frau Schwartz, it was Weschke who related to Zimolong the account of their origins.

[24] Quite apart from questions of style, the performance indications in the Trio differ greatly from Brahms's practices in his early instrumental music: the number and variety of indications are considerably less; Brahms's strong predilection for compound indications of volume plus mood (e.g., 'p dolce poco scherzando') is not manifest in the Trio; and the term 'cantabile' is used quite often in the Trio, but never in early keyboard and chamber works (Opp. 1, 2, 5, and 8).

authenticity of the three remaining works, however, can successfully be challenged.

In addition to the cadenzas for piano concertos published by the DBG and the *Brahms Werke* already discussed, two others – for Beethoven's Concerto in C minor, Op. 37 (*Brahms Werke*, vol. 15, pp. 120ff.), and for Mozart's Concerto in D minor, K. 466 (Doblinger, Vienna) – have been published. The Beethoven cadenza has been discussed in some detail elsewhere. To summarize, this cadenza is by Ignaz Moscheles, not Brahms, and was published in 1845 or 1846 in London by Cramer, Beale and Co., and in Paris by Maurice Schlesinger/Brandus.[25] The attribution of this work to Brahms stemmed from an auction by C.G. Boerner in 1908, at which a manuscript of this cadenza was offered for sale.[26] Boerner's catalogue described this manuscript as a Brahms autograph dating from between 1845 and 1848 (thus, composed between the ages of twelve and fifteen) and noted that it had been discovered in 1901 in the possession of a Hamburg junk dealer ('Trödler'). Despite the dubious pedigree of this item, Dr Viktor von Miller zu Aichholz, a close personal friend of Brahms and president of the Viennese Brahms-Gesellschaft, purchased it, and, after passing through the hands of at least two Brahms experts, Max Kalbeck and Eusebius Mandyczewski, this manuscript finally came into the collection of the Wiener Stadt- und Landesbibliothek in 1922. Though Mandyczewski did properly devalue the manuscript from autograph to copy when writing about it in the *Revisionsbericht* for the *Brahms Werke*, apparently neither he nor anyone else questioned the authenticity of this work.

The cadenza for the first movement of Mozart's Concerto in D minor, edited by Paul Badura-Skoda (1980), was discovered by the late Professor Dr Johannes Müller in the estate of Dr Kurt Taut, once librarian for the Musikbibliothek Peters, who reportedly owned other Brahms manuscripts, including an autograph of 'O schöne Nacht', Op. 92 No. 2, and both Müller and Badura-Skoda took the manuscript of the K. 466 cadenza, which bears no attribution, to be in Brahms's hand.[27] The

[25] Richard Davis, 'Moscheles Brahms', Letters to the Editor, *The Musical Times* 118 (1977) 1006, and George S. Bozarth, 'A Brahms Cadenza by Moscheles', Letters to the Editor, *The Musical Times* 121 (1980) 14.

[26] *C.G. Boerner-Versteigerung-Katalog 92 von 8. und 9. Mai 1908: Katalog einer kostbaren Autographen-Sammlung aus Wiener Privatbesitz; Wertvolle Autographen und Manuskripte aus dem Nachlass von Joseph Joachim, Philipp Spitta und Hedwig van Holstein*, lot 51.

[27] On this cadenza, in addition to the Preface to the Doblinger edition, see Paul Badura-Skoda, 'Eine ungedruckte Brahms-Kadenz zu Mozarts D-moll-Konzert KV 466', *Österreichische Musikzeitschrift* 35 (1980) 153–6.

handwriting, however, is clearly not Brahms's – most strikingly different are the G clefs (see Example 5)[28] – and thus there is no reason to attribute this work to Brahms.[29]

Example 5. (a) G clefs in the manuscript of the Cadenza to Mozart's Piano Concerto K. 466 (Universitätsbibliothek, Leipzig); (b) Brahms's usual symbol

The final composition whose attribution to Brahms does not bear up under scrutiny is the violoncello transcription, in D major, of the Violin Sonata in G major, Op. 78. With much ado, and just as much inaccuracy, a report of this 'uncovered masterpiece' appeared in *Time* in 1974.[30] According to this story, a 'manuscript' of this arrangement had 'for some 60 years . . .been filed and forgotten in the library of the Vienna Municipal Conservatory'. Then, in February 1974, the late Gottfried Marcus, an Austrian pianist and scholar, found this source, and the work was performed on Austrian television and, by Janos Starker and Rudolf Buchbinder, at the Ravinia Festival in Chicago. The following year this transcription was published by the International Music Company, with Starker cited as editor and with a short preface by Marcus. Since then, this arrangement has been recorded at least four times and has begun to enter the violoncello repertoire as a genuine Brahms work.

Testifying against the authenticity of this arrangement are two uncontestable pieces of evidence. To begin with, the source in the Vienna Conservatory library is not a manuscript, but merely a copy of the 1897 Simrock edition, on which the name of the transcriber is not given.[31] Furthermore, in Simrock's 1903 *Thematisches Verzeichnis sämtlicher in Druck erschienen Werke von Johannes Brahms*, this arrangement is attributed to Paul Klengel. Citing Brahms's amply documented insistence on anonymity as arranger of his own works, Professor Marcus

[28] I have also never seen in Brahms's autographs hairpin dynamics shaped like some of those in this manuscript (><), nor am I aware that Brahms ever used the type of pedal indication present here ('Ped *' vs. Brahms's 'ped ⊕').

[29] The version of this cadenza in the Taut manuscript is only a rough sketch, and Badura-Skoda has completed it, publishing both rough and finished readings. I wish to thank Herr Badura-Skoda for kindly providing me with a photocopy of the Taut manuscript.

[30] *Time* (5 August 1974) 77–8.

[31] I wish to thank Margit McCorkle, Otto Biba, and Flynn Warmington for independently verifying that no manuscript exists.

maintained that the absence of an attribution in the 1897 edition of Simrock's Brahms catalogue pointed to the composer as arranger (he did not mention the attribution to Klengel in the 1903 catalogue). Marcus believed, moreover, that only Brahms could have made the decision to transpose the sonata down a fourth and introduce the more than two hundred alterations (Marcus's count) which this transposition necessitated, revisions whose 'mastery. . .leaves no doubt that they were done by the composer himself'. *Time* suggested that Brahms made this transcription for his friend Robert Hausmann; two writers of record notes have cited Clara Schumann's wish that 'the last movement would accompany me on my journey to the next world' and suggested that this arrangement is a 'quiet memorial' to Frau Schumann, who had died in May 1896, a memorial in which, by transposing the work into a lower key, Brahms transformed 'hope. . .into resignation'.[32]

Beguiling as such hypotheses might be, they have no foundation in fact, since, as shown, all documentary evidence unequivocally points to Paul Klengel, not Johannes Brahms, as the arranger. More likely, Klengel, an accomplished violinist and pianist (as well as choral conductor) whom Simrock employed in the 1890s to prepare more than a dozen transcriptions of works by Brahms, conceived and executed this arrangement for his brother Julius, a virtuoso cellist with whom Paul had performed duo-recitals in earlier years and about whom Brahms remarked, after hearing him perform Paganini's *Perpetuum mobile* in transcription, 'I have already heard about your phenomenal technique, but I would not have thought such marvels ['Wunderdinge'] possible on your instrument'.[33] True,

[32] Notes to Phillips-Blumenthal recording, Gasparo GS-208, and Lewis-Lewis recording, Orion 79338. If this arrangement were by Brahms, such speculation would not be idle. Clara Schumann had been particularly fond of the last movement of this Sonata; she confided to her diary that, although she felt there were unfortunately a few unpleasant passages in this Sonata, the last movement was 'a piece full of charm and rapture, and of wonderful harmonic beauty. . .' (Litzmann, *Ein Künstlerleben*, III, 404). At the intimate musical commemoration that followed Clara Schumann's funeral, Brahms, together with Richard Barth, was to perform the G major Sonata, but in the midst of the Adagio, Brahms suddenly stopped, with difficulty uttered 'Es ist doch nichts mit den Duos, wir wollen Trio spielen', and hastily left the garden where they had been playing, in order to conceal his agitation (reported in Kalbeck, *Brahms* IV, 436–7). Kalbeck felt that Brahms had been overcome by memories of both Clara Schumann and her son Felix, who had been Brahms's godson, whose poems Brahms had set to music, and after whose early death (15 February 1879) Brahms had instructed Simrock anonymously to give the honorarium from his recently completed G major Sonata to the 'Ehrensolde' being collected for Frau Schumann (Kalbeck, *Brahms* III: 192, n. 2, and *Johannes Brahms Briefwechsel X: Johannes Brahms Briefe an P.J. Simrock und Fritz Simrock*, ed. Max Kalbeck (Tutzing, 1974) 130.

[33] Kalbeck, *Brahms* IV, 383.

Klengel's name does not appear on the title page of the 1897 Simrock edition, just as Brahms's name does not appear as arranger on the cover of the 1895 Simrock edition of his transcription of the Op. 120 Clarinet Sonatas for violin and piano.[34] But by 1903 the firm of N. Simrock revealed the true authorship of both of these transcriptions, citing in its catalogue the availability of Op. 120 in an 'Ausgabe für Violine und Pianoforte vom Componisten. 1895' and Op. 78 in a version 'Für Pianoforte und Violoncello (D dur) bearbeitet von Paul Klengel. 1897'.[35]

External evidence aside, this issue could have been decided on musical grounds. Though some have seen in the alterations made to accommodate cello and piano 'the unmistakable mark of the master's hand',[36] one must side with the reviewer who had trouble getting used to 'so much keyboard figuration above instead of below the melody' and to whom 'the opening piano chords sound almost subterranean'.[37] Yet at least in the opening passage the elimination of bass notes and the revoicing of the right hand of the piano are handled skilfully. But how can one attribute to Brahms such static moments as the 'vamping' piano at the end of the first theme of the first movement (bar 19) and the halt of the cello just before the onset of the second theme (bar 35), while the piano vacantly reiterates its bass note (see Examples 6a and b)? Equally disconcerting is the sudden octave drop of the cello at bar 25, just as it approaches the climax of the phrase, and the reiteration of the second theme with the cello playing in unison with the piano (bars 40–3). And then there are muddy passages like bars 66ff., where the cello must cut through a piano tremolo wrapped around it, or the beginning of

[34] Brahms is undisputably the arranger of the violin-piano version of the Op. 120 Sonatas. The printed copy of the Clarinet Sonatas on which Brahms made his revisions for violin and which served as the engraver's model in 1895 is now on deposit in the library of the University of California at Riverside (Oswald Jonas Collection; cf. Oswald Jonas, 'Eine privat Brahms-Sammlung und ihre Bedeutung für die Brahms-Werkstatt-Erkenntnis', *Bericht über den Internationalen Musikwissenschaftlichen Kongress Kassel 1962*, ed. Georg Reichert and Martin Just (Kassel, 1983) 212–15).

[35] Subsequent to the preparation of this essay, it has come to my attention that even in the 1897 Simrock *Brahms Verzeichnis* the violoncello arrangement of Op. 78 is attributed to Paul Klengel, not in the main entry for Op. 78, as it is in the 1903 edition, but in the *Anhang* which lists available arrangements (p. 171). I would like to thank Margit McCorkle for pointing this out. Other works cited in this 'Anhang' as being arranged for violoncello and piano by Klengel include the Intermezzi, Opp. 116 No. 4 and 117 No. 1; Klengel also arranged these two pieces for full orchestra (!), as well as for violin and piano and for clarinet or viola and piano.

[36] Teri Noel Towe, Notes for Moye-Vetrano recording, Columbia MX 35173 (as mentioned above, this was Marcus's opinion too).

[37] Joan Chissell, Review of Sellheim-Sellheim recording, CBS Masterworks 76816, in *The Gramophone* 57 (1979) 66.

Example 6. Arrangements for cello and piano of Brahms's Violin Sonata Op. 78

(a) First movement, bars 18–21a

(b) First movement, bars 34–6

the development (bars 80ff.), where the revoiced string chords are quite pointless and the whole section would sound much less disagreeable were the cello and piano to play an exact transposition of the original violin-piano reading, only with the lower octave note deleted from the left hand of the piano for the second chord in each bar (a procedure Brahms typically used in the transposed versions of his songs).

Throughout the transcription similar problems occur, as the arranger tries to contain the two instruments within the narrow range mandated by the lower key. The overall effect is claustrophobic, and all too often Klengel has merely coped with rather than solved his problems.

For the sake of comparison, we might look at how Brahms converted the Op. 120 Clarinet Sonatas into violin works. Here we find passages with simple problems of range altered simply by deletion or transposition, and passages with more serious problems recomposed, rather than rearranged, with great skill. To be sure, Brahms's task was less difficult than Klengel's, for he did not have to contend with severe registral problems in the piano. Yet when he encountered difficulties, he consistently turned adversity into advantage. Consider the transformations shown in Examples 7a and b, made near the end of the second movement of the first sonata, to avoid exceeding the violin's lower limit. The revised readings may differ slightly in effect from the original, but their musical validity is unquestionable.[38]

Example 7. Brahms's arrangement for violin and piano of his Clarinet Sonata Op. 120 No. 1

(a) Second movement, bars 52–5
Version for clarinet and piano

[38] The IMC edition must be used with caution. Except for minor alterations, probably to secure copyright, this publication is a direct photoreproduction of the 1897 Simrock edition and, as such, perpetuates the errors of that edition, errors which are easily corrected by comparing the IMC edition to a good edition of the original violin sonata (for example, the Hiekel edition published by G. Henle Verlag). Also, the IMC edition has not included the two 'Ossia' readings for the cello (movement 1, bars 150/5.0–160/1.0, an octave lower; movement 3, bars 52/4.0–69, an octave higher) which many may find preferable to the readings in the score.

Ex. 7 (*cont.*)

(b) Second movement, bars 67–72
Version for clarinet and piano

IV

This long after the death of Johannes Brahms, the chances of additional unpublished works emerging from obscurity would seem slim. Yet this is exactly what has been happening during the past few years. In 1980 a manuscript copy of Brahms's long-lost Kyrie and *Missa canonica*, composed in the mid 1850s, suddenly appeared in private hands in Massachusetts. This manuscript, prepared from Brahms's autograph by his close friend Julius Otto Grimm, has been acquired by the Gesellschaft der Musikfreunde in Vienna.[39] These pieces were performed in Vienna during the sesquicentennial year and have recently been published. Similarly, a fragment of a heretofore unknown setting of Chamisso's 'Die Müllerin', for voice and soprano, was recently discovered by Joachim Draheim in a private collection in Karlsruhe,[40] and the searches of Margit McCorkle have yielded an autograph manuscript of Brahms's unpublished orchestral arrangement of Schubert's 'Greisengesang'.[41] Discoveries such as these provide encouragement for scholars to continue searching for 'lost' works. Although it is only the most optimistic of spirits that can still hope for the recovery of such compositions as the symphonic version of the First Piano Concerto or the string quintet version of the Piano Quintet – the manuscripts of these works probably met the same fate as the two chests full of early compositions which Brahms burned in the 1880s[42] – perhaps someday items like the autograph violin part for Brahms's early Violin Sonata in A minor, seen by Albert Dietrich in the 1870s in the possession of Joseph von Wasielewski,[43] or the engraver's model for the Violoncello Sonata in

[39] The Kyrie is for SATB with basso continuo; the other Mass movements are for a cappella groupings: Sanctus (SSATB), Hosanna (SSAT), Benedictus (SSAT), Agnus dei (SSATB), and Dona nobis pacem (SSATB). The manuscripts of these movements were sold at auction by J.A. Stargardt (*Katalog 624*, 24 and 25 November 1981), together with manuscripts for Brahms's songs, Op. 3, and choral pieces, Opp. 12 and 37. A second auction (*Katalog 626*, 8 and 9 June 1982) sold the rest of this collection. On this pair of auctions, see George S. Bozarth, '"New" Brahms Manuscripts', *The American Brahms Society Newsletter* 1/1 (1983) 4–5; on the Grimm collection, see Bozarth, 'The First Generation', 248–9, 257. The Mass movements are now available in print from Doblinger Verlag, Vienna and Munich, in an edition by Otto Biba. A discussion of this edition by Daniel R. Melamed and Virginia Hancock appears in *The American Brahms Society Newsletter* 3/1 (Spring 1985) 3–5.

[40] Cf. Christiane Jacobsen, ed. *Johannes Brahms: Leben und Werk* (Wiesbaden, 1983), where a facsimile, with lengthy caption, appears on pp. 141–2; this piece has now been published by Breitkopf und Härtel, completed and edited by Joachim Draheim.

[41] The autograph of this arrangement is in a private collection in Great Britain. A manuscript copy of it is preserved in the library of the University of Pennsylvania.

[42] Kalbeck, *Brahms*, I, 132–3.

[43] In 1853 Brahms played this sonata in May with Reményi in Göttingen, for the Schumanns that autumn in Düsseldorf, and in December with Ferdinand David in Leipzig, and we know that he considered publishing it as his Op. 5 (Kalbeck, *Brahms* I, 73, 139; B. Litzmann, *Ein Künstlerleben*, II 280; B. Litzmann, *Clara Schumann-Johannes Brahms Briefe* I, 2, 3; A. Moser, ed. *Johannes Brahms Briefwechsel V: Johannes Brahms im Briefwechsel mit Joseph Joachim* (Berlin, 1912) 13–14; Albert Dietrich, *Erinnerungen an Johannes Brahms* (Leipzig, 1898) 8). During his stay in Leipzig, though, he lent the autograph to Franz Liszt, from whom Reményi subsequently borrowed this manuscript, apparently unbeknownst to Liszt. It has long been thought that Brahms never saw this sonata again, despite the efforts of Joachim and Liszt to recover the autograph (Moser, *Brahms-Joachim* V, 40, 42, 44; Florence May, *The Life of Johannes Brahms*, 2nd edn, rev. and enl. 149–50). An unpublished letter from Brahms to Clara Schumann, however, sheds new light on this situation. From Düsseldorf on 20 March 1855, Brahms wrote: 'On Sunday

E minor, Op. 38, catalogued in the 1930s as part of the Simrock collection and described as containing an Adagio which Brahms subsequently deleted,[44] will resurface, offering us fresh insights into Brahms's development as a creative artist.[45]

evening I again had a presentiment! At 9 o'clock I went to the train station! There I saw [J.P.] Klems [a piano builder in Düsseldorf], Breunung, and Reinthaler from Cologne. Imagine, through this presentiment I found my lost Violin Sonata! Liszt obtained it from Reményi in England and entrusted it to Breunung. He will now send it to me' (letter owned by the Staatsbibliothek Preussischer Kulturbesitz, Berlin). Thus, Brahms most likely regained possession of the autograph of this sonata in 1855, and it may well have perished together with his other early works. The autograph of the violin part which Dietrich reported seeing at the home of the violinist Joseph von Wasielewski in Bonn in 1872 may, however, have survived (Dietrich, *Erinnerungen*, 68–9).

44 Catalogued and briefly described by Julius von Kromer, whose card file of Brahms manuscripts was prepared in the mid 1930s and is preserved at the Library of Congress.

45 I would like to thank the following archivists for responding to my inquiries and for allowing me to consult materials in their collections: Dr Otto Biba and Mr Peter Riethus, Gesellschaft der Musikfreunde in Wien; Dr Ernst Hilmar and Mr Johann Ziegler, Wiener Stadt- und Landesbibliothek; Dr Bernhard Stockmann, Staats- und Universitätsbibliothek Hamburg; Dr Evelin Bartlitz, Deutsche Staatsbibliothek, Berlin; Mr Peter A. Ward Jones, Bodleian Library, Oxford; Mr. J. Rigbie Turner, Pierpont Morgan Library, New York; and Mr Donald Leavitt and Ms Elizabeth Auman, The Library of Congress, Washington. Financial assistance from the Graduate School Research Fund of the University of Washington and the American Council of Learned Societies made the archival research for this essay possible. I would also like to thank the University of Washington for the travel grant which allowed me to present this paper at the London Brahms Conference.

APPENDIX A

Revised readings for the *Brahms Werke* edition of the *Choralvorspiele*, Op. 122 Nos. 1–7 (based on readings in the two primary sources, the autograph [A-Wgm] and the engraver's model [D-brd-HS])

I. 'Mein Jesu, der du mich'

Pitch at b. 43/4.5, Alto, should be ♯a′ (?; ♯ added in pencil in engraver's model by?).

'Forte' in b. 34 should begin on beat 2.25.

Whole rest should be added at b. 35, Alto.

Slurs should be added or adjusted as follows:

b. 10/4.5–12/1.0, Tenor (g-e)
11/4.5–13/1.0, Alto (♮ d′-b)
13/2.5–14/3.0, Soprano (g′-e′)
26/3.0–27/3.0, Tenor (d′-b)
27/3.0–28/3.0, Alto (g′-f♯′)
28/4.0–29/4.0, Soprano (d″-b′)
31/4.0–4.5, Tenor (b-♮c′)
37/2.25–3.0, Alto (♯c′-♯c″)
39/4.0–4.5, Tenor (b-B)

Slur at bars 35/4.25-36/1.0, Tenor (A-a) is not present in the primary sources and should be deleted (the slur at b. 36/1.0–1.5, Tenor [A-d] is present in the primary sources).

II. 'Herzliebster Jesu'

Add 'f' below tenor at b. 1/3.5 (added by Brahms in engraver's model).

Slur b. 14, Soprano, should begin beat 1.0 (d♭″).

III. 'O Welt ich muss dich lassen'

Slurs should be added or adjusted as follows:

b. 1/3.0–3.25, Tenor (b♭-a)
4.5–4.75, Tenor (b♭-a), editorially
2/3.0–3.25, Alto (d′-e′)
3.5–3.75, Alto (e′-f′)
4/2.0–2.25, Baritone (d-g)
5/1.25–1.75, Tenor (a-♮b)
2.0–2.25, Tenor (d′-c′)
5/4.75–6/2.5, Baritone (a)
7/2.25–3.75, Alto (♮b-♭a)

8/1.0–1.75, Alto (g-b♮)
2.0–2.75, Alto (c′-d)
1.0–1.75, Tenor (d-f)
2.0–2.75, Baritone (e-f)
17/2.0–2.75, Soprano (g′-a′)

Tie at b. 1/3.25–3.5, Alto (c′-c′), and slur at b. 4/1.0–1.75, Baritone (d-d), are editorial and should be deleted; tie at bars 14/4.5–15/1.0, Alto (♮f′-f′), and slurs at bars 6/5.5–7/1.0, Tenor (b♭-b♭), is also editorial.
Tie should be added at b. 10/3.0–3.25, Tenor (d′-d′).
Rests (𝄽 𝄾) should be added at b. 13/3.0–3.5, Soprano.

IV. 'Herzlich tut mich erfreuen'
Pitch at b. 28/6.0, Alto, should be d′ (instead of b).
Slurs should be added or adjusted as follows:
Anacrusis, Tenor (a-♯g)
b. 4/4.0–5.5, Tenor (g-e)
8/6.0–6.5 (a-c♯′)
10/1.0–3.5, Baritone (g′-♮c′)
22/6.0–23/2.0, Alto (d′-d′)
24/4.0–26/5.0, Soprano-Alto (e′-e)
Tie at b. 28/1.0–3.0, Alto (g-g), and slur at b. 31/3.0–5.0, Soprano, are editorial.
Rests should be added in the Alto from the anacrusis through b. 3/6.5 and bars 8/6.0–11/6.5 to match those in the Soprano.

V. 'Schmücke dich, o liebe Seele'
In the autograph, Brahms used beaming and stem directions in the bass line to indicate articulation; the *Brahms Werke* has eliminated this through 'standardization'.
No other revisions necessary.

VI. 'O wie selig seid ihr doch, ihr Frommen'
No revisions necessary.

VII. 'O Gott, du frommer Gott'
'Man.' indications absent in autograph; added by Brahms in engraver's model at b. 3 only.
Ties should be added at bars 26/2.75–27/1.0, Alto (c′-c′) and Tenor (a′-a′).
Slurs should be added and adjusted as follows:
b. 25/1.0–1.75, Soprano (e′-f′)
26/2.75–27/1.75, Tenor (a′-b′)
31/1.0–2.0, Alto (b′-g′)
33/2.25–35/1.0, Soprano (e′-c′)
42/1.75–2.0, Alto (f″-d″)
46/2.25–47/1.75, Alto (g-a)

Slurs at b. 54/2.25–2.5 and 55/1.25–1.5, Alto, are editorial.
Rests (𝄾) should be added at b. 21/2.75, Alto, 47/1.75, Soprano, and 54/1.75, Alto and Bass.
Rests at b. 22/1.75, Bass, 31/1.0–1.5, Bass, and 1.5–2.0, Soprano, and 54/1.0–1.5, Bass, are editorial.
Both 'forte' signs in b. 58 should be on beat 2.0.

Note: The performance edition of the *Choralvorspiele* prepared by W.E. Buszin and P.G. Bunjes and published by C.F. Peters Corporation (New York, 1964) is a careful replica of the version in the *Brahms Werke*, and as such reproduces virtually all of the errors of that edition.

APPENDIX B

Revised readings for the *Brahms-Werke* edition of 'Regenlied', WoO 23 (based on readings in the autograph [J-Musashino])

Slurs should be added at b. 23/2.0–2.5, Piano lh (c-A) and b. 39/1.0–1.5, Piano rh (a-g).
At b. 10 the 'poco f' should begin on beat 2.0; at b. 37/2.0 a 'poco f' should be added.
The hairpin dynamics should be adjusted as follows:
< at bars 8/2.0–9/1.0; 10/2.5–11/1.75; 23/2.0–26/1.5; 32/1.5f.;
> at bars 9/2.5–10/1.75; 16/2.0f.; 34/1.75f.; 36/2.0–37/1.0; 38/2.0–39/1.0.

APPENDIX C

Revised readings for the Hiekel edition (G. Henle Verlag) of Brahms's Scherzo for Violin and Piano for the 'F.A.E.' Sonata, WoO 2 (based on readings in the autograph [D-ddr-Bds])

The following additions and adjustments should be made (bar numbers taken from Hiekel edition):

b. 8	Vn, Prh, Plh	‘$\overset{\frown}{3}$’ for full bar; also, at b. 17, 23–5, 86, 92–4, 143, 152, 158–60, 221, 227–9
12–15, 147–50	Plh	<> are editorial additions (cf., b. 3f., Vn; b. 87, Plh)
13, 148	Vn	<, as in b. 11, 12, 146, 147
23/1	Prh	Staccato dot
31/3, 166/1	Piano	> for rh only
34, 35, 45, 46, 169, 170, 180, 181	Vn	> ends slightly before beat 6.0
41/1–3, 176/1–3,	Prh	Slur (g′-g′)
47, 181	Prh	Place slur *over* chord
52f., 187f.	Piano	> begins at barline of b. 52–3, 187–8 (cf., b. 58, 193)
77, 112	Vn, Prh	‘$\overset{\frown}{3}$’ in autograph, which probably means ‘triplet plus slur’ (cf., b. 8 and similar passages, where ‘$\overset{\frown}{3}$’ denotes ‘triplet’)
87/1, 222/1	Vn	> for g‴
113/1	Piano	p
124/1	Prh	> over d″ + d′ (rather than >)
127/1–2.5, 130/1–2.5	Vn	<

Note: The edition prepared from the autograph by Erich Valentin and Otto Kobin and published by Heinrichshofen's Verlag (Amsterdam and Wilhelmshaven, 1935) also represents a great improvement on the *DBG* and *Brahms Werke* editions, but is not as accurate as the Hiekel edition.

APPENDIX D

Editorial problems in the *Brahms Werke* edition of the Sarabandes in A minor and B minor (WoO 5), the Gigue in B minor (WoO 4), the Preludes and Fugues in A minor and G minor (WoO 9 and 10), and the Cadenzas for the Mozart Concertos, K. 453, 466, and 491 (WoO 13–15)

Sarabandes in A minor and B minor (vol. 15, pp. 57–8)
The quality of Mandyczewski's edition of the Sarabandes for the *Brahms Werke* is much poorer than the *DBG* edition. The length and placement of almost all the hairpin dynamics in the A minor Sarabande have been altered, and the version of the B minor Sarabande printed is a hybrid, pieced together from elements of Friedlaender's autograph and readings in a second autograph, dated 'Feb. 55' (then owned by Jerome Stonborough in Vienna, now in the Library of Congress). As an example of the problems with the *Brahms Werke* edition of the Sarabande in B minor, in bar 8 Mandyczewski took his beaming for the first beat from the Stonborough autograph, but added the c′ on the second beat from the Friedlaender manuscript; on the other hand, at the final cadence he adopted the reading in Friedlaender's autograph for both beats. The result is a version of bar 8 that never existed in any source, and cadences which are consistent with each other in each of the two autographs but not in the *Brahms Werke* edition. It is startling to read in Mandyczewski's *Revisionsbericht* that he considered such differences between his sources to be 'ganz unwesentlich'. The Staats- und Universitätsbibliothek Hamburg owns a third autograph of the B minor Sarabande, dated 'Dec. 55', which the Hamburg Brahms-Gesellschaft published in facsimile, with a reasonably accurate transcription, in 1972.

Gigue in B minor (vol. 15, pp. 55–6)
Slurs present in the autograph have been omitted from the alto voice at bars 26/3–7 (b′-f♯′) and 26/9–27/1 (f♯′-c♯′); one might also question the editorial naturals added in the soprano voice at bars 16/11 (g′) and 37/10 (g′).

Prelude and Fugue in A minor (vol. 16, pp. 1–6)

The reading for bar 14 of the Prelude should follow the one which Brahms gave when queried by Joseph Joachim (*Johannes Brahms Briefwechsel* V, VI: *Johannes Brahms Briefwechsel mit Joseph Joachim*, ed. Andreas Moser [1912–21; reprint edn., Tutzing: Hans Schneider, 1974], V: 149): until beat 4.0 c should be sharp, where a ♮c″ should sound against ♯d′. The pitch at bar 28, beat 3.75, alto, in the Prelude should read d″ instead of c″. Accent signs (v) should be added below the three pedal notes in b. 23 of the Prelude, and the pedal should join the bass in playing an a in b. 31. Slurs need to be added above the descending thirds in the right hand of b. 26 of the Prelude and at the following points in the Fugue: alto, bars 28/2.0–29/3.0 (g′-c♯′) and 29/3.0–31/2.0 (c♯′-a♯); bass, bars 31/3.0–32/4.5 (d-f♯). Furthermore, the one slur above bars 26–9 should be two slurs, the first ending and the second beginning at b. 27/2.5 (b♯). In the Fugue the application of ornaments is garbled: a trill should be added to the statement of the subject in b. 30 (alto) and cadential mordents (~), not trills, should appear in bars 12 (soprano), 13 (tenor), and 17 (soprano); the dynamic indication at bars 42/1f. should be a single statement: *forte, sempre più forte*; and, there should be no tie between the bass notes at bars 68–9. I would also restore the beaming for the initial twelve bars of the Prelude to the version found in the autograph, which parallels and at times indicates the proper articulation. All of these revisions need to be made in the Buszin-Bunjes edition (New York: C.F. Peters Corp., 1964) which was derived from the *Brahms Werke* edition.

Prelude and Fugue in G minor (vol. 16, pp. 7–16)
Pitch errors occur in the Prelude at bars 1/6.0–6.5 (g″-d″, not d″-b♭′) and 31/4 (g + b♭ missing from chord), and in the Fugue at bars 60/1.0 (b♭′ missing from chord) and 68/4.75 (alto: a instead of b♭). Variants in stemming and beaming occur in the Prelude at bars 10ff. and 42, and in the Fugue at bars 48ff., 51f., and 60ff.; for example, at b. 64/1–2 the middle voices should read  instead of 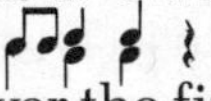 . The hold signs in b. 6 of the Prelude should be over the first beat, with no tied chord present on beat 7, thereby indicating a suspension of metre, and there should be no crotchet rest on the top brace at the end of b. 6. In the Fugue a slur should be added to the middle voice in b. 29 (d′-g♯); the slur in the preceding bar should begin on beat 1.5 (c♯′) and end at b. 29/1.0 (f); the slur in the soprano at b. 67 should end on beat 3.0; and at bars 74–8, in the alto voice, one slur should extend from b. 74/1.5 to b. 76/1.0 (g′-e♭) and the slurs

which end at b. 77/4.0 and 4.5 should both be extended to b. 78/1.0 (the slur in the tenor, bars 74–5, is editorial). Also, in the Fugue the *forte* in b. 70 should begin on beat 1.5, and rests need to be added at bars 3 (soprano, semibreve rest), 31/3 (alto, crotchet rest), 51/2 and 52/2 (soprano, crotchet rests), 64/4 (tenor, crotchet rest) and 75/2 (tenor, crotchet rest). These same revisions need to be made in the Buszin-Bunjes edition which was derived from the *Brahms Werke* edition.

Cadenzas for Mozart's Piano Concerto in G major, K. 453 (vol. 16, pp. 102–4)
In the cadenza for the first movement of K. 453, the stress signs in bars 1–2 should be staccato dots; a slur should be added at b. 16/4.0–4.5 (b♭′-a′); the chord at b. 19/1.0 should read c♭″ + e♭′ + c♭′ and the chord at b. 20/1.0 should read c♭″ + a♭′ + c♭′; the pair of ⟩ in b. 21 are editorial additions, as is also the extension of the hairpin in b. 24 from beat 3.0 to 4.75; and slurs should be added to the left hand at bars 26/1.0–27/1.0 (f♯-D), 27/1.0–28/1.0 (D-𝄾), and 28/1.25–4.75 (f♯-d).

In the cadenza to the second movement of K. 453, the chord at b. 2/3.5 should read d♭′ + b♭ + g; all the slurs in bars 4–11 are editorial additions; the rhythm for the right hand in bars 7 and 8 (and bars 7a and 8a) should read, and in bars 9ff., 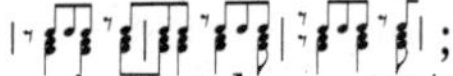 ; quaver rests should be added for the tenor voice at bars 12/1.0, 12/3.0, and 13/1.0; the articulation of the right hand at bars 13/3.5ff. should read  ; the symbol '÷' should be added below the alto chord at b. 7/3.5 (and editorially at b. 8/3.5) and above the left-hand chord at b. 13/3.5; the hairpin in b. 17 should be below the left hand on beats 2.5–3.5; the hairpin in b. 18 should extend from beats 1 to 3; an arpeggiation sign should be added to the left-hand chord at b. 9a/3.5 and the arpeggiation sign at b. 10a/1.5 should extend downward to the bottom of the left hand; and bars 11a–13a should be filled out editorially to match bars 17–19.

Cadenza for Mozart's Piano Concerto in D minor, K. 466 (vol. 16, pp. 105–80)
In the cadenza to the first movement of K. 466, the right hand at b. 9 should read: 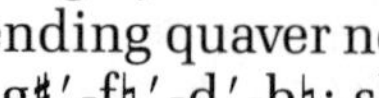 and the arpeggio at b. 35/2–4 should probably outline a simple G♯7 chord, d♯‴ down to f♯, followed by e-d♯; there should be no barline, bars 65–6, the left-hand chord (d′ + f♮′ + g♯′) should be a breve, held for all eight beats, and the descending quaver notes in the right hand should read g♯″-d″-c♯″-b♮′-g♯′-f♮′-d′-b♮; slurs should be added at bars

13/1–4 (alto, f″-e″) and 14/4–15/4 (alto, d″-f″), and the slur in b. 16 (soprano) should begin at b. 15/4 (b♭″); the slur in b. 39 (alto) should begin on beat 3 (a′ + c♯″), the slurs for the left-hand arpeggios, bars 39, 41, 45, 47, and 49, should all end on beat 3 (as in b. 36), and there should be one long slur between bars 52/1.0 and 53/4.75; the hairpins in b. 42 should peak on beat 4.0 (not beat 3.0), and the decrescendo hairpin should end at b. 43, beat 1.75, with the *piano* on beat 2.5; a missing *fortissimo* should be added at b. 75, beat 1; staccato dots are missing from the left hand at b. 79, beats 2, 3, and 4; and a number of other hairpins need to be adjusted. (Several slurs are editorial additions, but all of these are sensible.)

It should be noted that this cadenza is not entirely by Brahms. Mandyczewski issued it as a Brahms cadenza 'mit Benutzung einer Kadenz von Clara Schumann' (without designating which portions are by Frau Schumann, which by Brahms), but more accurately it should be entitled 'a cadenza by Clara Schumann with passages revised by Brahms'. Together with the Brahms autograph of this cadenza is a fair-copy manuscript, in Frau Schumann's hand, of a cadenza that is virtually identical to the 'Brahms' one, with the exception of two passages (Library of Congress, ML96.W56S4 Case). Berthold Litzmann's interpretation of the situation is, I believe, correct: 'The cadenza originated with Clara, who at the time [mid 1850s] gave it to Brahms, with the request that he alter a few things, and he did this only for a pair of passages; but because of this he wrote out the whole cadenza once again.' (Berthold Litzmann, ed., *Clara Schumann: Ein Künstlerleben nach Tagebüchern und Briefe*, 3 vols., rev. edns. [Leipzig: Breitkopf & Härtel, 1902–10] III, 543, n. The variant passages are the equivalent of bars 11b–21 and 54–66 of the Brahms version. In each passage Brahms's version uses the same melodic fragments and textures chosen by Frau Schumann, but avoids her rather Romantic tonal and harmonic schemes, employing instead a simpler tonal language more consistent with Mozart's own.

In 1891 Clara Schumann published a version of her cadenza for K. 466 which varies at certain points from both of the earlier versions, and at that time she noted in her diary (Litzmann, *Ein Künstlerleben*, III, 543) and in a letter to Brahms (Berthold Litzmann, ed., *Clara Schumann-Johannes Brahms Briefe*, 2 vols. [Leipzig: Breitkopf & Härtel, 1927] II, 461–2) that upon looking at his autograph of the earlier version she was horrified to see that, although she thought she had only used 8–10 bars of his cadenza in her own, in fact she had borrowed extensively from him. On the blank front page of the Brahms autograph she even noted: 'Cadenz z. D moll Concert v. Mozart v. Brahms/mit Benutzung einer Cadenz von mir./Wiederum benutzte ich in meiner später/herausgegebenen Cadenz einige Stellen aus/der Brahms'shen Cadenz, und habe diese/in den hier beiliegenden Exemplaren/unter 'A-B C-D' bezeichnet./In der 2ten Cadenz (z. letzten Satze)/ist die Stelle von A-B von Brahms./Meinen Kindern dies Notiz zur Vermeidung/etwaiger Irrungen./Clara Schumann./1891.' Unfortunately, the 'beiliegende Exemplare', no doubt copies of the 1891 edition which she had annotated, are no longer to be found with the manuscript sources. But comparison of the two earlier manuscripts with the engraver's model, in Frau Schumann's hand, for the 1891 edition (also Library of Congress) suggests that in fact she no longer remembered exactly who had composed which passages (this was Litzmann's assumption too). In the Brahms autograph she entered letters 'A' and 'B' at bars 11b and 35, probably to designate one of the portions she thought to be by Brahms, but the version of bars 22–35 is almost exactly the same as the equivalent bars in Frau Schumann's earlier manuscript. The loss of her annotated copy of the 1891 edition also prevents us from seeing which portion of her cadenza for the third movement she attributed to Brahms.

I would like to thank Gordana Lazarevich, who presented a paper on Brahms's Mozart cadenzas at the 1980 International Brahms Congress in Detroit, for calling my attention to the Clara Schumann manuscripts of the K. 466 cadenza and for sharing with me her ideas about these pieces.

Cadenza for Mozart's Piano Concerto in C minor, K. 491 (vol. 15, pp. 109–11)

In the cadenza for K. 491 the slurs in bars 2, 4, 6, 8, 9, 31–2, and 74 are editorial; slurs are missing in the right hand at b. 47/1.0–3.75, and similarly in bars 49 and 51, and in the left hand at b. 50/1.0–3.5; in the right hand at bars 63–4 the autograph has two slurs, one over each measure; the *piano* in b. 15 should be on beat 1.33 (g); the crescendos in bars 31 and 33 should begin and end slightly later (beat 2.66 to beat 1.0 of the following bar); the *cresc.* in b. 37 should begin on beat 3.0; and a crotchet rest should appear in the soprano at b. 32/1.0 (as in bars 28 and 30).

VIRGINIA HANCOCK

Brahms's links with German Renaissance music: a discussion of selected choral works[1]

Music historians investigating the life and works of Brahms have traditionally complained about the difficulty of coming to grips with the thought processes of a composer who was so reluctant to share his secrets. But one unusually valuable source of information does survive: Brahms's personal library, preserved in the Archiv of the Gesellschaft der Musikfreunde in Vienna.[2] The development of his interest in German Renaissance music may be traced in this collection – not only printed books and music, but also manuscript copies (Abschriften), some made himself and some given him by friends (a list of the material is given in Table 1);[3] at the same time, some possible effects of this development can be observed in a small sample of the choral compositions he wrote during the early part of his career, up to about 1864.

Brahms's interest in specifically German Renaissance music began with a rather naively patriotic enthusiasm for folk song, similar to that of the early Romantics who were seeking the 'authentic' voice of the people; it progressed to a desire to know more about the more sophisticated settings of the old songs

[1] This Paper was originally given with the music examples sung by a choir drawn from Conference participants and the Goldsmiths' College Chamber Choir, conducted by the present writer, as follows:

Insbruck, ich muss dich lassen	Heinrich Isaac (c.1450–1517)
Übers Gebirg Maria geht	Johannes Eccard (1553–1611)
Marias Kirchgang, Op. 22 No.2 from the *Marienlieder*	Johannes Brahms
Die Sonn, die ist verblichen	Stephan Zirler (c.1518–68)
Schein uns, du liebe Sonne	Antonio Scandello (1517–80)
Morgengesang, 'Wach auf, mein Kind' *Deutsche Volkslieder*, No. 12	Brahms
O Heiland, reiss die Himmel auf Motet, Op. 74 No. 2	Brahms

[2] For an account of the legal manoeuvring which took place after Brahms's death, see the article by Otto Biba elsewhere in this volume.

[3] A catalogue of Brahms's library of Renaissance and Baroque choral music is given in Virginia Hancock, *Brahms's Choral Compositions and His Library of Early Music* (Ann Arbor, 1983) 9–101.

Table 1 *German Renaissance Music In Brahms's Library*

Abschriften made by Brahms [year copied]	
Tenorlieder [1862–3? – copied from Nottebohm (see below)]	
Greitter	Es wollt ein Jäger jagen
Senfl	Ich stund an einem Morgen
Stoltzer	Entlaubet ist der Walde
Zirler	Die Sonn, die ist verblichen
Calvisius	Josef, lieber Josef mein (transcription from partbooks) [1862–3?]
Hassler	Mein G'müth ist mir verwirret [1857–60?]
Isaac	Insbruck, ich muss dich lassen [1857–60?]
Lasso	Aus meiner Sünden Tiefe [1862–3?]
Praetorius [?]	Maria zart von edler Art [1857–60?]
Scandello	Schein uns, du liebe Sonne [1862–3?]
plus many miscellaneous chorale settings, folk songs, transcriptions from lute and organ tablatures	
Abschriften made by others [year given to Brahms]	
Eccard	Übers Gebirg Maria geht (Clara Schumann) [1858?]
various	Tenorlieder (transcribed by Gustav Nottebohm) [1862–3 (loaned?) or 1882]
Forster (many composers)	Ein aussbund schöner Teutscher Liedlein. . . (five volumes transcribed from partbooks published 1553–60) [1869]
Published collections (year published) [year acquired by Brahms]	
Arnold, ed.	Das Locheimer Liederbuch (1867)
Becker, ed.	Lieder und Weisen vergangener Jahrhunderte (1849–50) [1854?]
Becker, ed.	Mehr-stimmige Gesänge berühmter Componisten des sechzehnten Jahrhunderts (n.d.) [1856?]
Becker and Billroth, eds.	Sammlung von Chorälen aus dem XVI. und XVII. Jahrhundert (1831) [1856?]
Böhme, ed.	Altdeutsches Liederbuch (1877)
Eccard	Geistliche Lieder auf dem Choral (ed. Teschner, 1860) [1863?]
Eccard and Stobaeus	Preussische Festlieder (ed. Teschner, 1858) [1863?]
Kretzschmer and Zuccalmaglio, eds.	Deutsche Volkslieder mit ihren Original-Weisen (1838–40) [1856]
Liliencron, ed.	Die historischen Volkslieder der Deutschen vom 13. bis 16. Jahrhundert (1869)
Meister, ed.	Das katholische deutsche Kirchenlied in seinen Singweisen (1862) [1862]
Tucher, ed.	Schatz des evangelischen Kirchengesangs im ersten Jahrhundert der Reformation (1848) [1854?]
Wackernagel, ed.	Das deutsche Kirchenlied (1841) [1862]
Wackernagel, ed.	Kleines Gesangbuch geistlicher Lieder (1860) [1864]
Wüllner, ed.	Chorübungen III (1880) [1880]
plus more collections of chorales and folk songs	
Books not owned by Brahms, but used as source for Abschriften [year copied]	
Corner	Gross Catolisch Gesangbuch (1631) [1862–3?]
Winterfeld	Der evangelische Kirchengesang (1843–7) [1854–60?]

as art music. His other route to German Renaissance music stemmed from his interest in the history of the Lutheran chorale, working backwards from the settings of Bach.

There are surviving copies of folk songs Brahms made when he was a teenager,[4] but the first evidence of a fairly thoughtful and systematic approach to their study comes from the period of Robert Schumann's illness, when Brahms spent a great deal of time working in Schumann's library. His manuscript copies of folk songs and chorales from this period, a few dated 1854, include a number taken from the collections of C.F. Becker, Gottfried von Tucher, Carl von Winterfeld, and Kretzschmer and Zuccalmaglio; they show evidence of an emerging critical attitude to the material. For example, Brahms made several copies of different editors' versions of Hassler's 'Mein G'müth ist mir verwirret', the secular Lied which later became the most familiar of the Passion chorales, 'O Haupt voll Blut und Wunden'. In those taken from Tucher and Winterfeld, he noted the different decisions about metre made by the two editors – Tucher's unvarying duple metre, and Winterfeld's more logical combination of triple and duple.[5]

Brahms eventually acquired his own copies of all these collections except Winterfeld's, and used them to pursue his investigations. The volumes are full of his annotations, including many cross-references to different versions of texts, tunes, and settings, along with notes about which ones were authentic.[6] He continued to be concerned about editors' interpretations of rhythm in particular, providing revised barlines in some cases.

His interest in polyphonic settings of these folk songs and chorales seems to have remained at most academic, except for the obligatory reverence for Bach's chorale settings, up to the time in 1856 when the Schumann household was broken up by Robert's death. In fact, Brahms's study of early choral music before this date was probably limited to the sacred music of Palestrina and a few of his contemporaries and successors – widely circulated during the first half of the nineteenth century with the support of the Roman Catholic church – and the contents of the first volumes of the Bach *Werke*, together with what he had learned from Winterfeld's *Der evangelische Kirchen-*

4 Max Kalbeck, *Johannes Brahms* I (Berlin, [3]1912) 184, facing, in facsimile; Kalbeck dates the manuscript, which is now in the Library of Congress, 1848–50.

5 See Hancock, *Brahms's Choral Compositions*, Ex. 40, 161.

6 Much has been written on the issue of authenticity. See especially Werner Morik, *Johannes Brahms und sein Verhältnis zum deutschen Volkslied* (Tutzing, 1953); and Walter Wiora, *Die rheinisch-bergischen Melodien bei Zuccalmaglio und Brahms* (Bad Godesberg, 1953).

gesang. His own choral writing consisted almost entirely of a few canons, some of which later found their way into his published compositions. However, within a year of leaving the Schumanns', Brahms was faced with the need to find repertoire for the choir at Detmold, which he agreed to conduct beginning in the autumn of 1857. He wrote to Joachim that he was 'making experiments with folk songs'[7] – his early, simple four-part settings. Most of the tunes come from Kretzschmer and Zuccalmaglio, and the settings are distinguished from hundreds of others only by some more interesting part writing in the lower voices. During the three years he spent each autumn at Detmold, Brahms also began to work with the Frauenchor in Hamburg; for them he wrote more folk-song settings and arranged a number of works of early music.[8]

At this time he must still have had access to a copy of the first volume of Winterfeld's history, which contains music from the first century of the Reformation, because it was his main source of German Renaissance polyphony.[9] Among other things, he copied from it the full settings of Isaac's 'Insbruck, ich muss dich lassen' and Hassler's 'Mein G'müth ist mir verwirret' (both of which he already knew from his earlier investigations of chorales), as well as a Praetorius setting of 'Maria zart von edler Art'. Clara Schumann made an Abschrift of Eccard's 'Übers Gebirg Maria geht' for him, and she probably also gave him Becker and Billroth's collection of late Renaissance chorale settings, mostly by Calvisius and Schein, which had been in Robert Schumann's library.

Heinrich Isaac's 'Insbruck' probably attracted Brahms's attention in the first place because it is a well-known setting of a tune which became a famous chorale, 'O Welt ich muss dich lassen', used twice by Brahms in the Chorale Preludes for organ Op. 122; and it became a kind of early music trademark for him – he not only arranged it for the Frauenchor, but also put it on the first programme of each of the two choirs he conducted in Vienna. His Abschrift from Winterfeld (the text after the first verse comes from Becker) shows that he noticed the metric ambiguities in the tune: he copied the regular $\frac{4}{2}$ barring used by Winterfeld, but marked the soprano line in red pencil to show the real $\frac{3}{1}$ metre determined by the text accents at the beginning.

7 *Johannes Brahms Briefwechsel V: Johannes Brahms im Briefwechsel mit Joseph Joachim*, ed. Andreas Moser (Berlin, 1912) 191.

8 Sophie Drinker, *Brahms and His Women's Choruses* (Merion, Pa.: privately published, 1952) esp. 103–4.

9 See references in Hancock, *Brahms's Choral Compositions*, Appendix III.

Example 1. Heinrich Isaac: 'Insbruck ich muss dich lassen', opening as notated by Brahms

The other voices do not have the same pattern, however; and in the performance copies prepared in 1872 under his supervision at the Gesellschaft der Musikfreunde, all the parts are barred in $\frac{4}{2}$. Other features which he may have found attractive include the treatment of dissonance in suspensions and passing tones, and the series of first-inversion sonorities in the last phrase.

Brahms was much attracted by the tradition of Marian legend in German poetry and song; he marked many examples in his library, and sought out the poems he set in his own *Marienlieder* Op. 22. An especially appealing example of the genre is Eccard's 'Übers Gebirg Maria geht', which he not only owned in Clara Schumann's Abschrift but also presumably knew from Winterfeld; then he acquired a published version of his own in Teschner's edition of the *Preussische Festlieder*. He arranged the piece for the Frauenchor,[10] and in 1872 conducted the original version for mixed voices at the Gesellschaft der Musikfreunde, preparing the parts from Teschner's edition with some changes in the text from Clara's copy. Apart from its text, the work probably appealed to Brahms for its particularly beautiful treatment of dissonance; and his own dynamic markings in Teschner's edition and in the parts in the Archiv are clearly intended in some places to emphasize the dissonance in suspensions. He added pencil dynamics to Clara's copy as well; these include an accent on the word 'Heiland', the textual and musical climax, which Eccard set with one of the expressive flat-side chords so characteristic of Renaissance music.

Brahms originally composed six of the seven *Marienlieder* in 1859 for the Frauenchor; later he added another, arranged them for mixed voices, and published the entire set in 1862 as Op. 22.[11] Although he used old texts, his own tunes have little resemblance to those found in early music. For example, in 'Marias Kirchgang', the second of the set, the two melodies are entirely modern in the concentration and sophistication with

10 The Frauenchor version was published in 1938 by Henry Drinker (Univ. of Pennsylvania Choral Series no. 75A). This edition is marred by a number of errors in notes and text underlay.

11 Siegfried Kross, *Die Chorwerke von Johannes Brahms*, 2nd edn, (Berlin-Halensee: Max Hesse, 1963) 96–101. Kross gives detailed information on the circumstances and chronology of composition of all Brahms's choral works.

which their motivic fragments are combined.[12] For six of the seven verses the first of these melodies is set in the alto – here the next lowest of four voices (the sopranos are divided and the basses silent); this position in the effective 'tenor' may be a consciously archaic feature, as may the Dorian flavour of the setting. At the same time, the harmonization, apart from several open fifths, is far from archaic, moving rapidly from the tonic E flat minor to the relative major to the dominant minor; this is so quickly and firmly established that the C flat chord bringing back E flat minor has a Neapolitan effect, made still more surprising because of its $^{6}_{4}$ position. The sixth verse, different from the others, is a naive and joyous illustration of 'all the bells' ringing. A new E flat major melody, related motivically to the minor melody, appears in the soprano and is immediately repeated in the tenor; the basses join in with a tonic pedal in a complementary rhythm that maintains the resonance of bells throughout the verse.

The development of Brahms's interest in Tenorlieder was a natural consequence of his investigations of the history of the Lutheran chorale and of German folk song. Their collection and study was a relatively late development in the nineteenth-century Renaissance revival, partly because so much of that revival was devoted to sacred music. German Lutherans were occupied with the Baroque period and especially with Bach, and therefore earlier sacred music in German attracted relatively little notice. Even for those who were especially interested in 'early music', a concern for anything written before the late Renaissance was unusual; the only recently published editions were the oldest chorale settings included by Winterfeld, and a few other randomly collected pieces appearing in mostly mixed anthologies.

The folk-song collectors were also slow to develop a taste for early polyphonic settings, even though these were of many of the same tunes they were collecting. As late as 1877 the foremost 'scientific' collector, Franz Böhme, published a statement in the introduction to his *Altdeutsches Liederbuch* (which Brahms marked with an exclamation point) to the effect that fifteenth- and sixteenth-century settings were so foreign to modern tastes as to have no real value.[13] The few musicians who did find these early settings attractive had for the most part to learn them either by making their own transcriptions from surviving sets of partbooks, or by making their own copies of other people's

[12] Kross, 104.

[13] The passage is quoted by Hancock in *Brahms's Choral Compositions*, 79.

transcriptions. The first good collection was finally published in 1869 by Liliencron.

Until Brahms went to Vienna in 1862 and met Gustav Nottebohm, one of the few established music historians of the day, he was essentially self-taught in music history. The only transcription from original partbooks still in his library which he had already made himself is Gallus's 'Ecce quomodo moritur justus'. Probably quite early in his acquaintance with Nottebohm, Brahms borrowed a large manuscript collection of early folksong settings that Nottebohm had presumably transcribed from partbooks during his years as a student in north Germany, and made Abschriften for himself of Tenorlieder by Greitter, Senfl, Stoltzer, and Zirler.[14]

When Brahms copied Zirler's 'Die Sonn, die ist verblichen', he made only a few minor changes in Nottebohm's transcription: he used different clefs from those Nottebohm had taken directly from Forster, and moved the text from the soprano to the tenor (Forster's partbooks have text in all voices). He kept Nottebohm's editorial accidentals. Zirler's setting is a good example of tightly organized Renaissance imitation: the tune in the tenor is G Dorian, and its striking beginning, covering a seventh upward in only three notes, is preceded by exact *Vorimitation* in the soprano; the alto and bass, also imitating, span a sixth. The texture is a constant overlapping of voices and phrases; only once, at the beginning of the second phrase of the Abgesang, is there a well-defined halt for all the voices – and then the alto and bass continue immediately with exact imitation of the next melodic phrase. In the tenor, the end of each phrase is given a short decorative flourish.

Example 2. Stephan Zirler: 'Die Sonn, die ist verblichen', first line

14 Nottebohm's transcriptions are now part of the Brahms collection in the Archiv. I am grateful to Dr Hedwig Mitringer for having called them to my attention and to Dr Otto Biba for having identified Nottebohm's hand.

Ex. 12 (*cont.*)

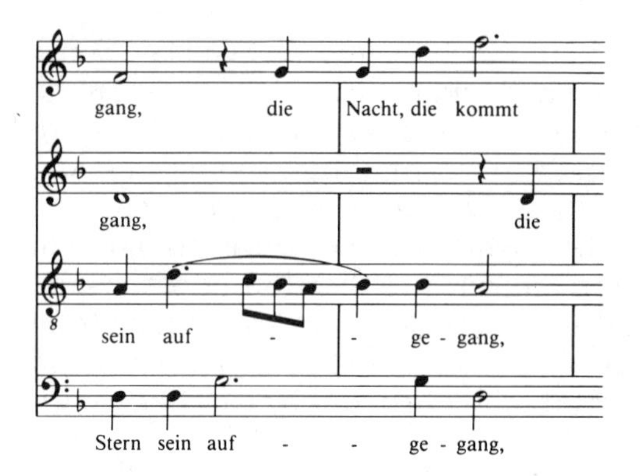

A later Tenorlied, published in 1567 by Antonio Scandello, also appears among Brahms's Abschriften, on a sheet which also contains Lasso's 'Aus meiner Sünden Tiefe'. Both pieces follow the conclusion of Senfl's 'Ich stund an einem Morgen', one of the four Tenorlieder Brahms had copied from Nottebohm's collection; because there is no published source for either, it seems most likely that they were also taken from transcriptions by Nottebohm. In Scandello's setting of 'Schein uns, du liebe Sonne', the tune in the tenor is again ornamented at the phrase endings and anticipated exactly by the soprano, but the alto and bass participate in the imitation in only a very limited way. The remarkable features of the setting are harmonic and rhythmic; both aspects have echoes in some of Brahms's choral writing.

Scandello's harmonic richness stems largely from his treatment of dissonance, which is similar to Eccard's in 'Übers Gebirg', and to many memorable moments in Brahms's music, in the warmth and sweetness resulting from its almost completely diatonic behaviour. Semitone clashes are avoided except on unaccented passing tones and in suspensions (in the less carefully controlled dissonance of Zirler, for example, they occur also on accented passing tones and neighbour notes); whereas wholetone clashes occur quite frequently on strong beats or accented syllables, as suspensions, restruck suspensions, or accented passing tones.[15] The rhythmic complexities of Scandello's setting, especially at the beginning, make attempts at editorial barring seem even more feeble than those in 'Innsbruck'.

[15] Schoenberg's setting of 'Schein uns, du liebe Sonne' exhibits dissonance treatment remarkably similar to Scandello's.

Example 3. Antonio Scandello: 'Schein uns, du liebe Sonne', first line

Brahms reaches a similar level of complexity in choral music only in some of the later secular choral songs.

Brahms acquired his largest collection of German Renaissance music some years after the composition of the latest choral works discussed here. However, his work with it, and especially his annotations about its musical contents, can still be helpful in understanding something about the way his mind worked: it is possible to see what features attracted his attention, and to be confident that he would have been aware of them when he used them himself.

The collection is Georg Forster's *Ein aussbund schöner Teutscher Liedlein*,[16] all five volumes of which were given to Brahms in 1869 to commemorate the first performance of *Ein deutsches Requiem* in Karlsruhe. His friends there, knowing of his interest in early music, commissioned a copy of a complete set of transcriptions from the partbooks that had been made two years earlier by a local music teacher; the series of events is explained in volume 1. Brahms obviously appreciated the value of the five volumes, studied them carefully, and annotated them copiously – often with cross references to other settings in Forster and to tunes and settings in other collections he owned.

His musical markings include a series appearing in three Zirler settings of the same tune, 'Mein selbs bin ich nicht gewaltig mehr'. In each, the melody is in a different voice: first the tenor, next the bass, and finally the soprano. Brahms's notes to himself, beginning 'N.B. die Cadenzen', show that he was interested in the fact that regardless of the position of the cantus firmus, the cadential patterns never change; the ending of the tune itself is altered rather than the conventional behaviour of each voice as it comes to the cadence.

[16] The collection is more generally known by the title *Frischer Teutscher Liedlein*, from the first edition. Brahms's copies were made from later editions in most cases; this title is the one appearing in the tenor partbook of the 1560 edition of Volume I.

Plate 2 A page from Leon. Heydhammer's quodlibet 'Der Winter kalt ist vor dem Haus' from Georg Forster's *Ein aussbund schöner Teutscher Liedlein* showing Brahms's annotations

In a long quodlibet by Heydhammer, Brahms marked the appearance of each new cantus firmus, and consistently added editorial accidentals. The majority are cadential leading tones, but in the G Dorian setting several E flats also appear – some in places where they are needed because of coinciding B flats, but three in the bass line which cancel the modal identity of the setting for short periods. Brahms's notes on rhythmic features in this piece include a marked cadential hemiola (see Plate 2), and N.B.s and numbers pointing out a brief passage of sesquialtera two against three.

One additional series of annotations by Brahms in his Forster volumes has no immediate relevance to his early choral writing, but is interesting in connection with some of his later music – works such as the secular choral songs 'Waldesnacht', 'Dein Herzlein mild', the first 'Nachtwache', and 'Letztes Glück', as well as the *Fest- und Gedenksprüche*. In all of these the voices are sometimes divided, implicitly or explicitly, into two choruses that often work against each other in imitation, and sometimes nearly in canon. Forster's volume 5 includes a piece by Paminger in which one five-voice chorus is written out, and a note at the beginning explains the canon: a second chorus enters at the sign and repeats the material of the first exactly. For the first three pages, Brahms filled in the empty staves left for the second chorus only after page turns (so he could see what was happening without turning back); but after that he wrote in all the missing parts, checked the result for parallels and chord positions, and marked a missing clef change and an error in the notes.

In 1863, when Brahms returned to Vienna to conduct the Singakademie, he had already had one successful long visit there, but had also been seriously disappointed by his failure to secure the conducting position in Hamburg he so badly wanted. He looked forward to his work with the Singakademie, however, even though it was not his first choice, because in spite of its many difficulties, it was certainly the largest and best choir he had yet conducted. He was stimulated by its possibilities, and by his discovery of still more sources of old music in the Viennese libraries and in collections owned by friends like Nottebohm, to write several new choral works.

An old Hamburg friend of Brahms, Theodor Avé-Lallement, had been responsible for many additions to his library over a period of about eight years. One of his last gifts to Brahms was a copy of a newly published collection, Karl Severin Meister's *Das katholische deutsche Kirchenlied in seinen Singweisen*. In addition to its main content of texts and tunes, it contained an appendix of polyphonic settings and an exhaustive index of sources. Brahms marked sources in the holdings of libraries he could visit easily – in Hanover and Vienna, for instance – and probably learned for the first time of the existence of David Gregor Corner's *Gross Catolisch Gesangbuch* (Nuremberg, 1631), a copy of which was in the Vienna Hofbibliothek. From Corner he made a series of Abschriften of texts and tunes, and then used them, in conjunction with supplementary material from Meister's collection, as the source for a number of the folk songs he arranged at that time, as well as for the motet 'O Heiland, reiss die Himmel auf' Op. 74 No. 2.[17] At about the same time, presumably, he made the copies of Tenorlieder from Nottebohm's transcriptions.

The group of folk-song settings Brahms made during this early period in Vienna are all of genuinely old tunes, taken with relatively little alteration from his sources. The settings are his most elaborate ones, clearly affected by his acquaintance with Renaissance practice; and in fact the few surviving sketches show that he was actively looking for ways to use such techniques as *Vorimitation*. For 'Wach auf, mein Kind', Brahms took Corner's unbarred original (which appears as 'Auff auff mein Kind') and at first tried to devise a logical barring for the tune – an impossible task because the note lengths of the melody are at times simply not compatible with the iambic metre of the text. He also sketched out an approach to the setting, starting with the tune in the soprano, and writing in fragments of direct imitation at various intervals, inversion, and augmentation. All these procedures eventually appear in the setting, though not always as originally sketched. The result is a contrapuntal *tour de force* – and also, in an unusual departure for Brahms, a piece in which he hides the tonality for two bars under *Vorimitation* of both the original and inverted forms of the opening phrase, appearing at unexpected intervals. The barlines in the lower voices have no more connection with the metre of the text than did Brahms's first attempts to find a solution to the metric problem of the melody; in performance, the best solution seems to be to try to ignore them – as one does with much Renaissance music.

The motet 'O Heiland, reiss die Himmel auf' may have been composed at about the same time as these folk-song settings,

[17] George Bozarth, 'Johannes Brahms und die Liedersammlungen D.G. Corners, K.S. Meisters, und F.W. Arnolds,' *Die Musikforschung*, 36 (1983) 177–99. See also Hancock, *Brahms's Choral Compositions*, 15–16 and 119–26.

1863–4. There is, however, no firm evidence beyond two facts: Brahms must have been in Vienna, because his sources for the text and tune were Corner and Meister; and the first reference in the correspondence does not appear until 1870, in a letter Brahms wrote to Max Bruch about the latter's setting of the Latin version of the same text, 'Rorate coeli'.[18] Brahms finally published the motet in 1879 as Op. 74 No. 2 with the much better-known motet 'Warum ist das Licht gegeben dem Mühseligen?' The 'Warum' motet has received so much justly deserved attention in accounts of Brahms's choral music that 'O Heiland, reiss die Himmel auf' has been largely neglected and often underrated. In the present author's opinion, it is also very much worth study and performance, and it is also a particularly rewarding example of the composer's assimilation of techniques that appear in Renaissance and Baroque music he had studied or performed.

The motet is a set of five chorale variations, each a different setting of one of the verses. Brahms took the tune and first verse from Meister, and copied the second through seventh verses from Corner. For the motet, he left out verses four and five, perhaps because they provided fewer opportunities for text illustration than those he chose to set. The overall structure of the motet bears resemblances to two Bach works Brahms had studied, Cantata 4, 'Christ lag in Todesbanden', and the motet 'Jesu, meine Freude'.[19]

The first verse of Brahms's motet is a straightforward setting in four points of imitation of the F Dorian tune in the soprano. The setting is Dorian as well, with a key signature of three flats, and added D flats only when the tune leads to A flat major. The dissonances are all suspensions, and the last chord is an open fifth; the metre is $\frac{3}{2}$ – the minim unit an obviously archaic feature. With constant imitation and overlapping of phrases very like those in Tenorlieder such as Zirler's 'Die Sonn, die ist verblichen', this verse is Brahms's closest approach to his Renaissance models.

In verse two the process of intensification that gives the motet its overall shape begins.[20] The tune is still in the soprano

[18] *Johannes Brahms Briefwechsel III: Johannes Brahms im Briefwechsel mit Karl Reinthaler, Max Bruch. . .*, ed. Wilhelm Altmann (Berlin, ²1912) 98. For more complete details of the chronology see: Margit L. McCorkle, *Brahms Thematisch-Bibliographisches Werkverzeichnis* (Munich, 1984) 314–15.

[19] For Brahms's study of the music of Bach, see Hancock, *Brahms's Choral Compositions*, esp. 84–8. His decisions as conductor of Cantata 4 are described by the same author in 'Brahms's Performances of Early Choral Music', *19th-Century Music*, 8/2 (1984) 125–41.

[20] Hans Michael Beuerle, 'Untersuchungen zum historischen Stellenwert der A-cappella-Kompositionen von Johannes Brahms' (PhD dissertation, Johann Wolfgang Goethe Universität, Frankfurt am Main, 1975) 130–1.

and is unchanged, but the pace of the three lower voices is now doubled, perhaps as an image of the plentiful flow of salvation down from heaven. In contrast to the first verse, where the imitation in each phrase was based on its own melody, here the accompanying material comes principally from the first phrase of the melody ('O Gott ein Tau'). Beginning with the second phrase, where the cantus firmus ascends against the meaning of the text ('im Tau herab'), the music from the first phrase, sung by the accompanying voices, is inverted, so that it does follow the text. For the rest of the verse the same material is used in both directions. Harmonically the setting is still nearly all in the Dorian mode, but the quickly moving lines contain much more passing dissonance, and the effect is a great deal more restless than the first verse. Again the final chord is an open fifth.

The third verse is a charming extravaganza of text painting. The tune, moved to the tenor, begins at the same pace as before, but at the end of each phrase breaks into ornamented hemiola flourishes, rather in the manner of Zirler's or Scandello's tenors but much less restrained. The decorative triplets of the tenor cadences reappear in the other parts to depict the flowering of nature, with many resulting two-against-three patterns; and the accompanying voices also have ascending arpeggios for mountains and valleys, and the image of the Saviour springing from the earth. The D natural of the key signature gives a Lydian flavour to the A flat major middle part of the verse, but for the F minor sections the Dorian mode disappears completely. The verse ends on a complete F minor triad.

The mood and setting change abruptly in the fourth verse: the tempo is adagio; the metre becomes duple, $\frac{4}{2}$; the cantus firmus moves to the bass, in C minor. Alterations in the cantus firmus at cadences to give the bass V-I patterns are similar to those Brahms later marked in the Zirler Tenorlieder in Forster; and his addition of chromatic passing tones to the melody foreshadows the famous case in which he is said to have added a similar note to the chaconne bass of Bach's Cantata 150 for the finale of the Fourth Symphony.[21] The contrapuntal interplay of the three upper voices resembles the methods Brahms sketched and carried out in 'Wach auf, mein Kind', but with loftier expressive purposes: the tenor begins with *Vorimitation* of the ascending line of the cantus firmus, broken up in a way whose

[21] The source of this anecdote is the reminiscences of the conductor Siegfried Ochs, *Geschehenes, Gesehenes* (Leipzig, 1922) 299–300. It is quoted, without citation, by Richard Specht in his *Johannes Brahms* (Dresden, 1928) tr. Eric Blom (London, 1930) 270.

purpose immediately becomes clear when the sopranos enter with its inversion (the two parts have a mirror canon for the first phrase) – in the descending pattern, the interpolated notes are appoggiaturas, and the entire line exemplifies the Baroque sighing figure expressive of suffering, perfectly matching the text 'Hie leiden wir die grösste Not'. The harmony continues the theme with its sharp dissonances – many resulting from appoggiaturas – and intense chromaticism. This part of the verse culminates in the one spot where Brahms made a significant change in the text he had taken from Corner; he substituted 'der bittre Tod' for 'der ewig Tod', probably for the hard sound of the word 'bittre' and perhaps also for its evocation of bitter dissonance.

With the change in character of the text in the second half of the verse comes a change in the character of the setting. The counterpoint is as thick as before, but the chromaticism is relieved except for a return with the word 'Elend'. 'Ach, komm, führ uns' is set with a series of entrances in E flat major, each one diatonic step higher than the last; for this series the cantus firmus is changed again so that the bass can also participate. Another change in the last phrase of the cantus firmus introduces an E natural which leads to the C major final chord of the verse.

After the expressive climax of the fourth verse, the fifth can be anticlimactic. On the surface it seems rather stodgy: the key is F minor again; the metre is allegro $\frac{4}{4}$; the chorale melody, in a slightly ornamented version, is back in the soprano; and the text is a straightforward song of praise. However, this surface covers one of Brahms's most dazzling contrapuntal displays. The soprano and bass have a mirror canon which is carried on for the entire verse; and for the Amen, the free imitative counterpoint of the altos and tenors becomes a second mirror canon, identical to the first in its first phrase, but then taking its own course. Musically the result is convincing enough that only a few awkward moments give it away, to the extent that some writers on Brahms's choral music have altogether failed to notice it. His friend Franz Wüllner, writing to thank Brahms for a copy of the motet sent to him in 1877, commented, 'Nobody could do the double canon in contrary motion at the end as you do. To write a double canon isn't so hard; what's hard is to write one that sounds as if it weren't!'[22]

[22] *Johannes Brahms Briefwechsel XV: Johannes Brahms im Briefwechsel mit Franz Wüllner*, ed. Ernst Wolff (1922) 80.

Brahms continued for all of his career to write choral music in which elements of what he learned from earlier periods in the German tradition can be traced. In no other work, though, are so many of these ideas combined in so compact a musical structure. At the same time, the listener is never in any doubt that what he is hearing, ultimately, is not a pallid imitation of outdated practices, but the voice of Brahms himself.

ROBERT PASCALL

Brahms's *Missa canonica* and its recomposition in his Motet 'Warum' Op. 74 No. 1

I

'Yesterday I wrote a small Benedictus (canonic) for four voices, which I think is rather beautiful.'[1] In his letter to Clara Schumann of 26 February 1856 Brahms thus announced what seems to have been his first setting of any part of the text of the Ordinary of the Latin Mass, and what was certainly the first piece to be composed of his later *Missa canonica*. There is however no evidence that the *Missa canonica* was a compositional project at this time, though such a project had coalesced by about the middle of the year. This kind of genesis, a bigger project growing out of an already composed piece (or pieces), is to be found in the case of the Suite in A minor for piano (now mostly lost), which was finished in September 1855 and had formed itself around separately composed dance-movements from mid 1854 and early 1855.

In June 1856 Brahms began copying Palestrina's *Missa Papae Marcelli*,[2] and that same month, during their famous mutual correspondence-course in counterpoint, he sent Joseph Joachim three additional settings of his own of texts from the Ordinary of the Latin Mass – a Kyrie, Sanctus and Hosanna, Agnus Dei and Dona nobis pacem. He wrote in the accompanying letter: 'The Kyrie which I am sending you is simply an exercise. The other pieces belong to a (forthcoming) Mass in C major for five voices. The Agnus Dei follows after the F major Benedictus which you know. Before the Sanctus the Amen of the Credo is in C major. . .Is there not too much modulation for a Mass, when the Sanctus and Osanna are in A flat, the Benedictus in F, the Agnus Dei in F to A minors, and the whole Mass is in C major?'[3] In his extensive reply, Joachim offered a far-reaching

1 *Clara Schumann-Johannes Brahms: Briefe aus den Jahren 1853–1896* ed. Berthold Litzmann (Leipzig, 1927) (hereafter *Schumann-Brahms Briefe*) I, 178.

2 Virginia Hancock, *Brahms's Choral Compositions and His Library of Early Music* (Ann Arbor, 1983) (hereafter Hancock) 43.

3 *Johannes Brahms Briefwechsel V: Johannes Brahms im Briefwechsel mit Joseph Joachim*, ed. Andreas Moser (Berlin, [3]1921) (hereafter *Briefwechsel V*) 149–51.

appreciation of the Kyrie, which he described as 'certainly more than an exercise'.[4] He thought it perhaps too compressed, and he criticized some of Brahms's declamation. Likewise he criticized also the declamation of the words 'Peccata' and 'pacem' in the Agnus Dei and Dona nobis pacem, and marked musical passages he did not like. Of all the pieces, he preferred the 'wonderful Sanctus' but was again somewhat worried by the declamation. He advised Brahms to consult Dr Hasenclever or Dietrich concerning proper Latin declamation.

In the middle of that July Brahms wrote again to Joachim: '. . .a half-finished Credo I shall let rest. . .I am delighted that you like my Sanctus and by everything that you wrote about the other pieces. All will be put in order in the matter of word-setting; I am seeing Hasenclever often at present.'[5] Brahms let the Credo rest for some time, and it was not finished until mid 1861. By comparing Joachim's comments in his letter with the later version of Brahms's music which has come down to us, we may readily see that Brahms did indeed revise his declamation of the Latin in many places. This revision had been done before Brahms sent the music to his friend Julius Otto Grimm about the end of April 1857.[6]

Brahms's letter accompanying the package to Grimm is unfortunately lost, but on 4 May 1857 Grimm wrote an appraisal of the same music as Joachim had seen in the previous year.[7] He liked the music greatly, but criticized the vocal ranges; he thought Brahms had written impossibly low for altos, especially in an unaccompanied Mass. He proposed revising the setting in the Sanctus himself, from Brahms's original SSATB to SATTB, leaving the Hosanna, Benedictus and Dona nobis pacem, and transposing the alto entry in the Agnus Dei up an octave. Brahms replied on 8 May with some agitation: 'What is to be done with the impossible alto part in my religious pieces? I was so immersed in enthusiasm for the low alto, without thinking that they no longer exist. I do not want to continue

[4] *Briefwechsel V*, 152–4.

[5] *Briefwechsel V*, 155–8.

[6] A letter from Joachim to Brahms, No. 73 in the first edition of the correspondence between them, 74 in the third edition, and dated editorially in both as 'End of March 1855', refers to a performance of Brahms's Hosanna and Benedictus. But this letter belongs at the very earliest after June 1856, at which time Joachim had not yet heard any of the music of the *Missa canonica* (see his letter of that month quoted above), and probably after mid 1857, by which time Grimm himself had got to know this music (Joachim refers casually to sending the parts to Göttingen).

[7] *Johannes Brahms Briefwechsel IV: Johannes Brahms im Briefwechsel mit J.O. Grimm*, ed. Richard Barth (Berlin, 1907) (hereafter *Briefwechsel IV*) 50–3.

with the Mass while I am unclear about this. (Perhaps a string quartet with it?)'[8]

Grimm wrote again on 10 September, and began by excusing himself for having retained the music for so long: 'I could not at all countenance letting the Mass pieces and the Kyrie out of my hands uncopied.'[9] Grimm's copy, which he had by then made, came to light again in 1978 in America, was sold by the firm Stargardt of Marburg in 1981, and at that time was acquired by the Gesellschaft der Musikfreunde in Vienna. This copy contains the Kyrie in G minor for SATB with basso continuo (titled *Kyrie Fuge für Chor*), and Sanctus, Hosanna, Benedictus, Agnus Dei and Dona nobis pacem for SSATB unaccompanied (titled *Missa canonica*). An appendix to the copy contains Grimm's rearrangement of voices for the Sanctus (from Brahms's SSATB to his SSATBB – although there is an increase in the number of voices, this involves only one additional note, at the final cadence) and for the Hosanna (from Brahms's SSAT to his SSAB). His rearrangement does not accord with his detailed ideas of May 1857, but was clearly made for similar reasons.

The Kyrie consists of 99 bars in **C** time, marked Andante; it is fugal throughout and founded on a basso continuo, which does not, however, play continuously. Nevertheless, the Kyrie has Baroque style as its background, and its subjects, with prominent leaps and syncopations, treatments and textures reveal clear resonances of this background. Brahms follows the natural suggestion of the text in making his movement thematically ternary. The opening Kyrie section is based on the subject shown in Example 1a, which is answered by inversion; each part enters with subject or answer, and the section concludes with a further entry of the subject in the soprano, mostly over a subdominant pedal, and leading to a cadence in bar 27. The Christe section has a new subject, being a descending scale with two upward registral shifts involving leaps of a seventh; the cadence to the first Kyrie section and the beginning of the Christe section are shown in Example 1b. In the Christe section the vocal entries are closer and occur on the rising pitch-levels bass G, alto A flat, tenor B flat, soprano C. As another contrast to the first section, the word 'eleison' here is given a separate thematic shape. The Christe section is modulatory, and is overlapped with a return of the Kyrie subject in G minor at bar 41. Joachim particularly liked this passage (see Example 1c), as he noted in his letter of June 1856. In the extended and modulatory

[8] *Briefwechsel* IV, 53–5.
[9] *Briefwechsel* IV, 55.

Example 1. From Brahms's Kyrie:

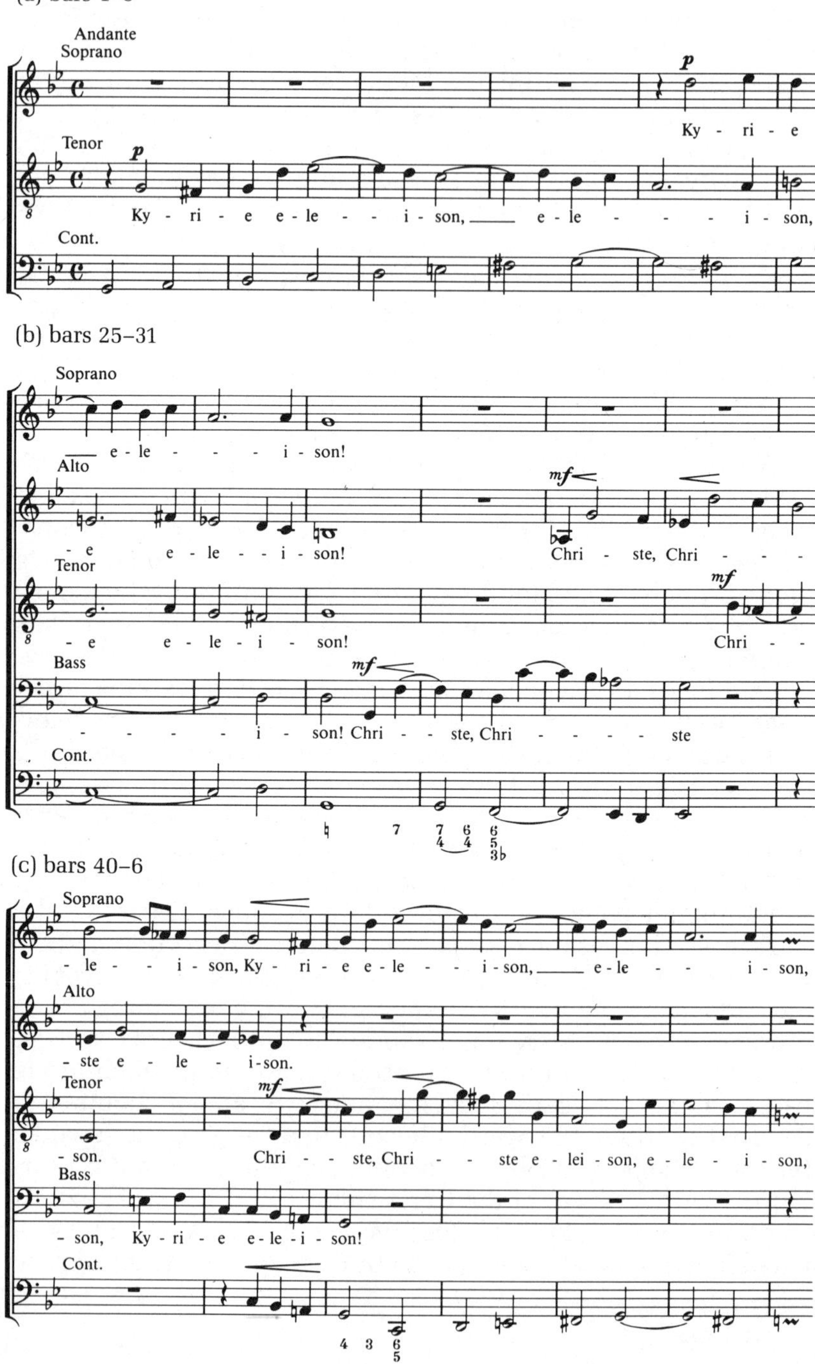

third section thus introduced, the Kyrie and Christe subjects are combined, which now involves the Christe subject in inversion; the Kyrie subject enters both on pitches used in the first section and on others. The movement ends with a twelve and a half bar tonic pedal, over which many A flats reinforce a plagal inflection to the ending.

The movements of the *Missa canonica* are for five voices (reduced to four in some movements and sections) unaccompanied, and have late-Renaissance sacred style as their background. The type of rhythmic flow of the individual lines (except in the nervously-articulated Agnus Dei), their predominantly conjunct motion, alleviated with interspersed leaps, and the canonic and imitative textures all derive from such style. However, the chromatic inflections in the Sanctus, Hosanna and Agnus Dei, some of the melodic leaps in these movements, and the octave doubling in the Sanctus are, rather, nineteenth-century features, and the style of Brahms's movements from his *Missa canonica* must be considered as neo-Renaissance. The Agnus Dei, with its wide-ranging and chromatic themes, its modulatory and progressive tonality, is particularly distant from late-Renaissance sacred style. Brahms was here at his most original in his preserved Mass movements, and it is indeed interesting to note that it was on this section he later founded his recomposition of the Mass movements in his Motet 'Warum'.

The Sanctus opens with a *pp* ₵ Lento section of twelve bars, in two six-bar phrases, each starting with detached chords. The canon is between S_1 (soprano 1) and B at the tenth below at one-bar's distance for the first six bars, and between S_1 (doubled at the octave below by S_2) and A, again at the tenth (and third) below at a half-bar's distance for the second six. The opening phrase is given in Example 2a. The second section of the Sanctus is a $\frac{3}{2}$ Adagio of twenty-five bars, using the unusual textual conflation 'Sanctus Dominus, pleni sunt coeli et terra gloria tua! Sanctus, Sanctus, Sanctus Dominus'. Its predominant descending motion answers the predominant ascending motion of the first section. Here the canon is 3 in 1; S_1 is answered one bar later by T at the eleventh below, and a further one bar later by B at the fourteenth below. This canon is maintained throughout the section, though a subsidiary and briefer pair of canonic entries on the opening theme of the section occurs in A and S_2 about half-way through the section. Example 2b shows the first four bars of this section.

The seven-bar Hosanna in $\frac{3}{1}$ time is for four voices, and

Example 2. From Brahms's *Missa canonica*:

(a) Sanctus, bars 1–6

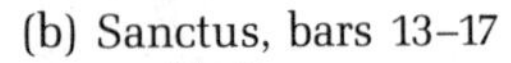
(b) Sanctus, bars 13–17

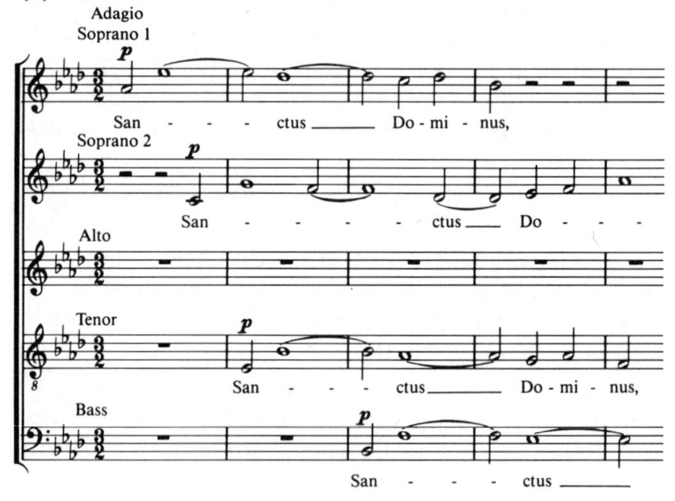

marked 'Noch einmal so langsam' (twice as slowly); the canonic parts are *p*, the non-canonic *pp*. The canon is between S_1 and T at the octave below at one-bar's distance. Although the Sanctus is in A flat, with chromatic inflection, the Hosanna ends on a half-cadence in F minor. The opening of the Hosanna appears as Example 2c.

The Benedictus is of twenty-six bars (including a repeat), all diatonic in F major, for four voices and in $\frac{6}{4}$ time, marked 'Poco

(c) Hosanna bars 1–3

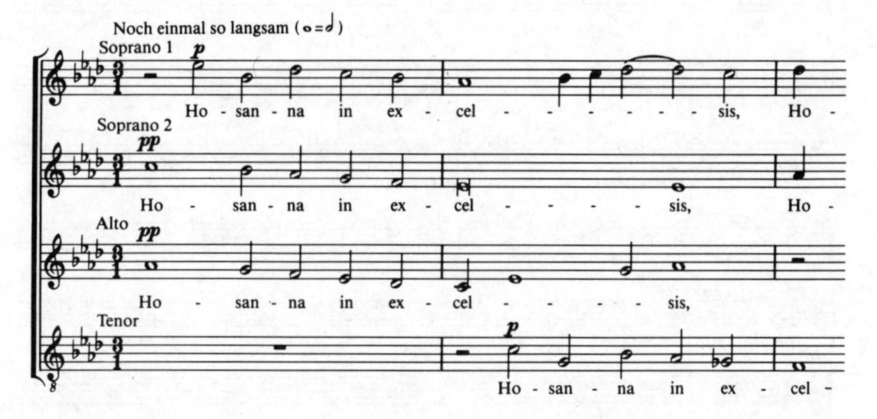

adagio con espressione'. The canon is 4 in 1 at distances of a half-bar at the fourth below, one and a half bars at the fifth below, and two bars at the octave below. There is no separate Hosanna, and a da capo is indicated in Grimm's copies. The opening of the Benedictus is given in Example 2d. Its flowing metrically-dominated lines make a lyrical contrast with the preceding Sanctus and Hosanna.

(d) Benedictus, bars 1–5

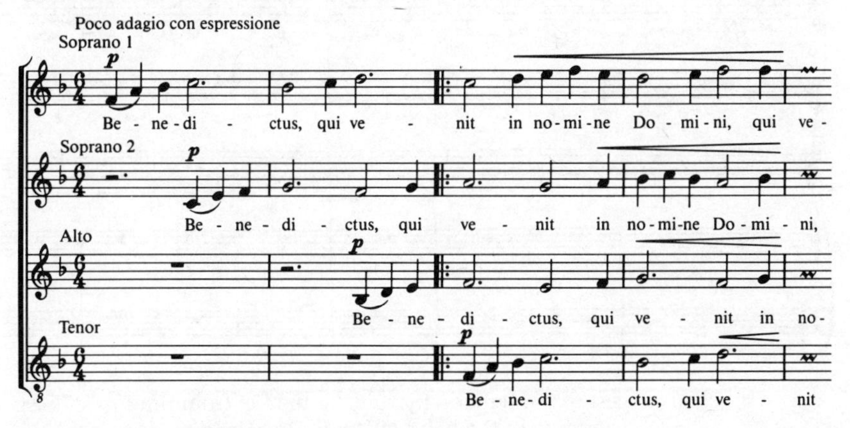

The Agnus Dei divides into two contrasted sections: the Agnus itself and the Dona nobis pacem. The Agnus, of forty-seven bars in ¢ time, marked Adagio, is a canon 5 in 1 on a modulating subject, shown in Example 2e. The entries are at nine-bar intervals and each is a fourth below its predecessor; thus the entries are on F, C, G, D, and A, and the tonality alters accordingly (moving, as Brahms himself wrote, from F minor at

Plate 3 Part of the Benedictus and Agnus Dei from Brahms's *Missa canonica* in the hand of Julius Otto Grimm

(e) Agnus Dei, bars 1–9

the opening to A minor at the end). The Dona nobis pacem is of thirty-three bars (including a repeat) in the same time. Here the canon is between S_1 and A at the fifth below and four-bars' distance. But the five-voice texture is predominantly full throughout, and the non-canonic voices are imitative of the canon, sometimes using inversion and decoration. The section is in C major with a pronounced subdominant inflection, strongly suggesting that transposed Mixolydian mode could be an appropriate analysis; however, as we have seen, Brahms himself wrote of the Mass in tonal terms. The opening of the Dona nobis pacem is given in Example 2f.

The Kyrie and these movements from the *Missa canonica* were first performed in modern times at the Gesellschaft der Musikfreunde in Vienna on 18 October 1983 by the Singverein under Peter Franzmaier. This music was published in 1984 edited by Otto Biba; the edition includes an *ad libitum* continuo to the Mass movements.[10] This printing is the first edition

(f) Dona nobis pacem, bars 1–7

10 *Johannes Brahms Messe*, ed. Otto Biba (Vienna, 1984).

Ex. 2 (*cont.*)

of all the music concerned, save for the Benedictus, which was first published in 1956.[11] The first English performance took place in the Chapel of Keble College, Oxford on 10 November 1984, given by the Oxford Pro Musica under Michael Smedley. The music has been catalogued in McCorkle's *Brahms Werkverzeichnis* as WoO 17 for the Kyrie and WoO 18 for the movements of the *Missa canonica*.[12]

Two further points need to be made here concerning this music. Firstly, it is clear that the surviving Kyrie was never part of the *Missa canonica*, and Joachim and Grimm were well aware of Brahms's intentions in this matter. The differing stylistic backgrounds, tonalities, textural profiles, and compositional techniques between the surviving Kyrie and the surviving movements of the *Missa canonica* make it impossible to regard this Kyrie as part of the work. Secondly, it is also clear that at the time of Grimm's copying of the movements of the *Missa canonica*, this work was not complete, as Joachim and Grimm also knew. A half-finished Credo was still 'resting', and Brahms sent Clara Schumann his completed canonic Credo only in the summer of 1861. She wrote of it in her letter of 29 July that year: 'I have not been able to look through the Credo in this short

[11] ed. E.H. Mueller von Asow (Vienna, 1956).

[12] Margit L. McCorkle, *Johannes Brahms Thematisch-Bibliographisches Werkverzeichnis* (Munich, 1984) 531–5. The *Missa canonica* is there described as in from four to six parts. Brahms himself described it as in five parts (which, according to standard usage for Renaissance works, would include the possibility of reduction to four parts for some sections). His writing in this work is nowhere in six parts, though, as we have seen above, Grimm's arrangement did include six-part writing.

period – to find my way through such a labyrinth of canons I need much time. I wonder only at your expertise in such artful and difficult things, but I shall not appreciate them until I hear them well sung.'[13] Brahms sent the Credo to Joachim at the end of September 1861: 'I enclose the Credo from my canonic Mass, the further [weitere] Sanctus you know. The ending is in counterpoint at the twelfth as is the preceding canon.'[14] The two men met shortly after, and, unfortunately for us, Joachim's comments on the Credo are not recorded in any letter. In 1870, on 12 December, Brahms requested his Mass back from Reinthaler, but there is no further information on its extent at this time.[15] It is particularly noticeable that in all correspondence-references to Brahms's Mass, there is no mention of a canonic Kyrie or Gloria at any time. Thus it remains impossible to say what the full extent of Brahms's Mass was in 1870, the time of its last mention in correspondence; and only the Credo (now lost) is known for certain to have been composed after Grimm's copying of the surviving movements in 1857.

II

Brahms's Motet 'O Heiland, reiss die Himmel auf' Op. 74 No. 2 was composed by 21 February 1870, on which date Brahms mentioned having written it in a letter to Max Bruch.[16] His letter to Reinthaler of December that year, referred to above, shows the Mass still to be a composition in its own right, but Brahms's recall of the work from Reinthaler could betoken the initial consideration of a reworking of the music. Brahms wrote in his manuscript catalogue of his compositions that the Motet 'Warum' Op. 74 No. 1 was composed at Pörtschach in the summer of 1877 (contemporaneously therefore with the composition of the Second Symphony);[17] but his tendency in this catalogue was to record when he finished works, not when he started them.

The generation of the Motet 'Warum' clearly began with the establishment of its text. This text is given in Example 3 together

[13] *Schumann-Brahms Briefe* I, 369–74.
[14] *Briefwechsel* V, 306–7.
[15] *Johannes Brahms Briefwechsel III: Johannes Brahms im Briefwechsel mit Karl Reinthaler, Max Bruch, Hermann Deiters, Friedr. Heimsoeth, Karl Reinecke, Ernst Rudorff, Bernhard und Luise Scholz*, ed. Wilhelm Altmann (Berlin, ^{2}1912) (hereafter *Briefwechsel III*) 31–2.
[16] *Briefwechsel III*, 97–8.
[17] A-Wst. JN 32886 Published by Alfred Orel, 'Ein eigenhändiges Werkverzeichnis von Johannes Brahms', *Die Musik* 29/8 (May 1937) 529–41.

Example 3. The text of Brahms's Motet 'Warum', Op. 74 No. 1

Warum ist das Licht gegeben dem Mühseligen,
und das Leben den betrübten Herzen,
die des Todes warten und kommt nicht,
und grüben ihn wohl aus dem Verborgenen;
die sich fast freuen und sind fröhlich,
dass sie das Grab bekommen.
Und dem Manne, dess Weg verborgen ist,
und Gott vor ihm denselben bedecket?

Lasset uns unser Herz
sammt den Händen aufheben
zu Gott im Himmel.

Siehe, wir preisen selig,
Die erduldet haben.
Die Geduld Hiob habt ihr gehöret,
und das Ende des Herrn habt ihr gesehen;
denn der Herr ist barmherzig,
und ein Erbarmer.

Mit Fried' und Freud' ich fahr' dahin,
in Gottes Willen,
getrost ist mir mein Herz und Sinn,
sanft und stille,
Wie Gott mir verheissen hat:
der Tod ist mir Schlaf worden.

Wherefore hath the light been given to a heart sorrowful,
and the life-blood to the sore afflicted,
who for death are longing, that comes not.
They dig for it more than for great treasure hid,
yea, they are glad, and go rejoicing
when they their grave see open.
Wherefore is light given to men whose ways are hid,
and whom the Lord for ever hath hedg'd in?

Let us lift up our heart,
and with our heart let our hands be uplifted
to God, the Lord of heaven.

Lo, we account them happy
which endure and fail not.
Now of Job's patience ye have had knowledge,
and the end of the Lord, have ye not seen it?
That the Lord, he is gracious,
of tender mercy.

With joy I'll lay me down to die,
when God shall call me.

No evil, when my Lord is nigh,
can befall me.
Thy salvation is my trust,
I'll pass thro' death to waken.

with the English translation published in the first edition of the work. The compilation of quotations from Holy Scripture is Brahms's own, and one of which he was (justly) proud.[18] This compilation is as creatively significant and deep as that he had assembled for *Ein deutsches Requiem*, though here on a more miniature scale. The initial quotation, from Job 3:20–3, in Luther's German, shows the questioning, deserted pessimism of Job's deepest despair. It is answered directly by a quotation from Jeremiah 3:41; the answer is simple, not by argument but by exhortation to turn unconditionally to God. The third quotation is James's extolling of Job's patience, together with the reminder that God's purposes are known and merciful (James 5:11). Finally, Brahms placed verse 1 of Luther's metrical version of the Nunc Dimittis (Luke 2:29–32), Simeon's acceptance of death in joy at having seen Jesus; Simeon departs in accordance with God's will and promise, comforted in heart and mind, gently and peacefully. Death, which Job had sought in despair as release and end to affliction, has now become Simeon's accepted joyous summation. Luther's own gloss on the biblical Nunc Dimittis is God's assurance that death is but sleep. (This gloss is somewhat veiled in Mrs Natalie Macfarren's translation.)

But Brahms chose the metrical rather than strictly biblical version of Simeon's song surely because his musical purpose was to end his Motet with a Lutheran chorale, and indeed the melody of 'Mit Fried' und Freud'' is probably by Luther himself. Such an ending brought Brahms into a strong relationship with Bach's practice of ending cantatas and some motets in just this way. Thus, as Newman found in his consideration of the relationship between Wagner's texts and music, while the establishment of a verbal text is logically and ontologically prior to the composition of the music, musical concerns come vigorously into play in the establishment of the text, and the genesis of the musical part of the work is already in some sense underway.

Broadly considered, Brahms used the Agnus Dei of his *Missa*

[18] *Johannes Brahms Briefwechsel XVI: Teil I Johannes Brahms im Briefwechsel mit Philipp Spitta, Teil II Johannes Brahms im Briefwechsel mit Otto Dessoff*, ed. Carl Krebs (Berlin, 1920 and 1922) 183–4.

canonica, made more taut then greatly expanded by contrast and variation, as movement 1 of his Motet; the Benedictus, with a gloriously transformed ending, as movement 2; the Dona nobis pacem, contracted and with a reworked texture, in movement 3, followed by a new bridge and the shortened return of the music of movement 2. Movement 4 is Brahms's own harmonization, in Bachian style, of the chorale 'Mit Fried' und Freud''. The music of movements 2 and 3 appears at its original pitches in the *Missa canonica*, that of movement 1 has been brought into the orbit of the tonality of the final chorale and transposed into D minor. Brahms owned a copy of *Johann Sebastian Bachs vierstimmige Choralgesänge gesammlet von Carl Philipp Emanuel Bach. Erster Theil* (Berlin and Leipzig, 1765) in which the chorale 'Mit Fried' und Freud'' appears in that key.[19] Thus the music of the *Missa canonica* is not only reworked, but also brought into new thematic and tonal relationships. Brahms found no use in his Motet for his Sanctus and Hosanna, or seemingly any other non-surviving part of his Mass; the new material in movements 1 and 3 could conceivably come thence, but it is non-canonic and stylistically fully mature.

Brahms's choice of a textual–musical ending for his Motet, whether prior to the decision to draw material from his *Missa canonica*, simultaneous with or subsequent to it, enabled him to parallel the movement of meaning of his text-compilation with a large-scale and profoundly significant musical progression. Just as the pessimistic searching for death of the opening biblical quotation is not so much answered as resolved and set aside by Simeon's death in the knowledge of Jesus at the close of the work, so the Agnus Dei-derived music with which the Motet opens is clarified, resolved and purified in the chorale melody with which it ends.

This musical clarification, resolution and purification is present in the relationship of the ending of the Motet to its opening in matters of tonality, melody, rhythm and texture. The heavily chromatic inflections and wide-ranging modulatory scheme of the opening are stripped away in the chorale setting. Thematically considered, both movements are based on a profile opening with an initial octave ascent from d′ to d″ (as can be seen in Examples 4a and 4b). This is articulated similarly in the two themes: ascending leap + descending step + ascending leap. But in the Agnus Dei-derived theme there is a reduplica-

19 Brahms's copy is now at GB-Lbl K. 10. a. 39. See Hancock, 73. C.S. Terry, *The Four-part Chorals of J.S. Bach* (Oxford, 1929) (hereafter Terry) 276, 508.

Example 4. From Brahms's Motet 'Warum':

(a) Movement 1, bars 4–6

(b) Movement 4, bars 1–2

tion of this process, with a further descending step and ascending leap. The Agnus Dei-derived theme has intermediate metrical accents on the non-primary notes $\hat{2}$ and $\hat{6}$, while the chorale relies only on the primary notes $\hat{5}$ and $\hat{4}$. Both themes follow this articulated ascending octave with a scalic descent; in the Agnus Dei-derived theme the scale is interrupted by a sequential remnant (an ascending fourth) and the descent is to sharp-$\hat{4}$; in the chorale the descent is clear, and diatonic in the Dorian mode. Further, there is rhythmic clarification in the chorale first line: the complex three-bar shape of the Agnus Dei-derived theme, with its irregular use of dotted crotchets, becomes in the chorale a two-bar phrase in even crotchets. And the involved texture of the opening of the Motet (from bar 4), strict canon 4 in 1 with complex countersubjects and syncopation, is clarified into the contrapuntally animated homophony of the chorale. While it is clearly most pertinent to attend to the initiations of each of these movements, similarities between their subsequent subsidiary materials, based on falling thirds, and between their scalically descending conclusions, reinforce the cyclic nature of the relationship of movement 4 to movement 1.

This relationship establishes the confines within which Brahms deployed other material from the *Missa canonica* to create an extensive unified design. The Benedictus-derived music as movement 2 and the end of movement 3 surrounds a transformation of the Dona nobis pacem at the beginning of movement 3. This transformation thus becomes the centre of a thematic and tonal arch: movement 1 (D minor), 2 (F major), 3 section i (C major), 3 section ii = 2 modified (F major), 4 = resolution of 1 (D Dorian/minor). This arch is modified in terms of proportion, for its second half is compressed (movement 3 section ii is shorter than movement 2, and movement 4 is distinctly shorter than movement 1). And it is modified in terms of process also, as the relationship between movements 1 and 4 makes clear. The central movement 3 section i is itself a significant part of the motion from movements 1 to 4. It is a chorale-like transformation of the music of the Dona nobis pacem, with elaborately figural underparts; though, because of the melodic profile of its top part, it cannot yet be described as a chorale. But its quaver rhythms recapture the motion of movement 1 part A, after the crotchet rhythms of the Benedictus-derived movement 2. Similarly, movement 4 returns to quaver motion after the Benedictus-derived music at the end of movement 3.

We may now consider the details of Brahms's recomposition of his *Missa canonica* in the Motet, movement by movement. The Agnus Dei becomes the opening movement of the Motet with the following modifications: (1) the addition of a quasi-ritornello, (2) the contraction of the theme itself and its subsequent working out, (3) the reduction of the number of parts from five to four, (4) the large-scale expansion of the form to include contrasted material, followed by a return to the opening transformed. What in the Mass was a unified strict canon becomes a contrasted movement in ternary form, of which the first part only is canonic, framed and articulated by the added quasi-ritornello. The overall form of the Motet movement can be shown as: R (4 bars), overlapped with A (21), R_1 (4), B (22), R_2 (4), overlapped with A_1 (23), R_3 (8).

The quasi-ritornello is a highly original idea, with little precedent. Beethoven's First Symphony opens with chord-pairs, and Beethoven also referred to introductions during main movements. In choral music, a number of Bach movements begin with brief expostulatory chords for voices (for example the Motet 'Komm', Jesu komm' and the vocal entry at the beginning of the *St John Passion*), and Brahms himself had already done so in his setting of the 13th Psalm, Op. 27. Beyond this the brevity and simple recurrences of ritornelli in early Baroque practice offer a distant parallel. In 'Warum' the quasi-ritornello is thematic, and gives the opening of the work a deliberation and weight to its initial generating question which could not have been achieved simply by starting with the Agnus Dei-derived material. The quasi-ritornello consists of two chord-pairs in exact sequence, save that the top part of the first pair is omitted in the second; the registral change this effects, together with a marked alteration of dynamic, is poignantly expressive (see Example 5a). The quasi-ritornello is not strongly key-defining, and V-I in G minor and V-I in D minor are not emphasized by dominant sevenths; but part of the definition of

Example 5. Concerning the relationship between Brahms's Agnus Dei from the *Missa canonica* and the first movement of his Motet 'Warum':

(a) Motet, movement 1, bars 1–4

D minor in this opening is the entry of the Agnus Dei-derived theme over the final chord of the quasi-ritornello (a thematic reinforcement of harmony). This theme opens with a rhythmically diminished inversion of the falling thirds of the quasi-ritornello. The returns of the quasi-ritornello during the course of the movement are always at the original pitches for each part, but R_1 has a decrescendo over its first chord-pair and is not overlapped with following music, R_2 has its final chord sustained and does therefore overlap with the subsequent passage, R_3 is rhythmically elongated (each $\frac{4}{4}$ bar of R becoming two $\frac{3}{4}$ bars), and also has the decrescendo on its first chord-pair.

Example 5b gives the full top part of the Agnus Dei simultaneously with the top part of movement 1 of the Motet from bar 4 to bar 24. Since both Agnus Dei and bars 4–20 from movement 1 of the Motet are in strict canon involving all their constituent parts, this example lays bare the full extent of Brahms's modifications to the Agnus Dei in his recomposition. Bar 4 of the Agnus Dei opening is omitted in the Motet version, as is the articulation into two phrases; other rhythmic changes are applied to duration in bars 1–2 and 6–7 of the Agnus Dei. All these changes in the opening entry of the canonic theme of the Motet are clearly requirements of the new text. As this new contracted version of the canonic theme is replicated in the subsequent canonic entries of the Motet movement, the pitch-levels of which are taken over from the Agnus Dei, so the continuation of the top part (acting as countersubjects) had to be contracted in four subsequent places, as is clearly shown in Example 5b. Brahms also used a parallel contraction in the closing stages of the A section. The contraction applied to bars 12–14 of the Agnus Dei is particularly felicitous, managed by a selective double-diminution of time values, and it engenders a new quaver extension (bars 9–11 of the Motet). The recomposition of the top part continues in similar vein, copying the model in bars 11_3 (bar 11, third beat)–12_2 of the Motet, modifying it in bars 12_3–13_1 and 15_4, supplementing it in bars 14–15_1 and 16–17. Example 5c shows the fourth canonic entry in the Agnus Dei and the Motet, demonstrating the continuation of the top part as countersubjects in a full texture. Bar 18 of the Motet sees a curtailed fifth entry of the canonic theme in the soprano; the curtailment is in bar 20 and the harmony is brought to rest on A major as a very local tonic. The ensuing sequential descent, imitative in paired voices, consolidates A major as dominant of D minor, acts as an elongated substitute version of the end of the previously curtailed fifth entry, rescues a thematic figure from bars 39–41 of the Agnus Dei, and prepares thematic elements of the subsequent B section of this movement.

The B section is perhaps even forced into the tonic by the tonally highly discursive A section; after the D minor opening to this section, decorative keys are C, F, and A majors, before an ending on D major. The texture hovers flexibly between point-imitation (sometimes with paired voices), and rhythmically contrapuntalized homophony. The structure of the section is written into its textual disposition: x (5 bars, 'Die des Todes warten und kommt nicht'), x_1 (6, ditto), y ($3\frac{1}{2}$ 'und grüben ihn wohl aus dem Verborgenen'), z ($7\frac{3}{4}$ 'die sich fast freuen. . . '). The section contains passages particularly reminiscent of material from movement 7 of *Ein deutsches Requiem.*[20] While B remains a thematically progressive section, x and z are both concerned with an initial scalic third descent, which also appears embedded in y.

A_1 presents the theme of A in a $\frac{3}{4}$ transformation, interleaved with textures, cadence-shapes and sequences reminiscent of the close of B; the structure of A_1 can be represented by: a ($4\frac{1}{3}$ bars), z_1 (6), a_1 ($4\frac{1}{3}$), z_2 (8). The *pp* bare octave presentations of a and a_1 are deeply expressive; they eliminate the quaver motion of the A section (which indeed appears nowhere in the A_1 section), and simplify the rhythm and internal structure of the opening theme of the A section; here in A_1 this theme

[20] Compare bars 32–3, 41–2, 43–8 of the Motet, movement 1, with bars 25–6, 29–30, 49–52 of the *Requiem*, movement 7.

(b) Agnus Dei, complete top part, and Motet, movement 1, top part, bars 4–24

(c) Agnus Dei, bars 25–33 and Motet, movement 1, bars 14_3 (b. 14, third beat)–18

(d) Motet, movement 1, bars 54_3–8

becomes two two-bar phrases (see Example 5d). This simplification is not only a progressive means of closure for the first movement of the Motet, but also a stage on the way to the final clarification of the opening of the work in its closing chorale. Further, the simplicity of form in the A_1 section contrasts markedly with the complexity of the canon in section A, as with the progressive thematicism of section B. The final quasi-ritornello is simultaneously a closure, a rounding-off, and also a reopening of the disturbing question which animates the whole Motet.

'Lasset uns', the second movement of the Motet, has the most unaltered retention of material from the *Missa canonica* to be found in the Motet. The Benedictus, with which Brahms had been very pleased when he wrote it (see his letter to Clara Schumann of 26 February 1856, quoted at the beginning of the present study), is kept in all its detail for its first eleven and a half bars. By this stage the initial eight-bar section of the canon has begun its repeat, which Brahms now amplifies and extends by the introduction of two extra bass voices, beginning the point still initially in canon on $\hat{6}$, and paired with alto and soprano respectively in thirds. Structural entries of this point then appear on $\hat{4}$, $\hat{2}$, $\hat{6}$ and $\hat{1}$. This magnificent contrapuntal close is Brahmsian maturity of the very highest order, which nevertheless does not eclipse, but rather glorifies, the young Brahms's opening; it takes place under two slow structural descents of the top part from $\hat{8}$ to $\hat{5}$. The Benedictus music suits the new text well, and by its rising melodic line expresses simply the idea of lifting one's heart and hands to God in heaven; Brahms repeats some words, as he had done in the Benedictus itself, in order to maintain a basically syllabic setting of the words. Motivic connection between this movement and the first is strong. The theme of 'Lasset' ascends through an octave by a fusion of local ascents and descents; after adding a structural auxiliary note to the high octave, it gently but swiftly descends to $\hat{5}$. The repeat eliminates the auxiliary, but greatly expands the descent $\hat{8}$–$\hat{5}$ and reduplicates it. Example 6 shows the new ending.

The third movement, 'Siehe, wir preisen selig', is, on the other hand, much altered from the Dona nobis pacem. Its first three melodic phrases are similar, but Brahms now begins the first on

Example 6. The ending of Brahms's Motet 'Warum', movement 2, bars 12_4–19

the initial strong beat, shortens its last note in favour of a rest, and removes the last two notes of the second phrase of the Dona nobis pacem, thus creating a more positive cadence. The third phrase is intact, with a slightly prolonged final note; he then, sooner than in the Dona nobis pacem, reintroduces the first phrase, now with the syncopated opening as in the Dona. By these means, Brahms fashions from his model a more definitely articulated four-phrase chorale-like melody with an arched profile: phrases 2 and 3 have figures in common, and phrases 1 and 4 are almost identical. This melodic structure sits interestingly *vis-à-vis* the new text, which is in two verbal phrases repeated 1, 2, 1, 2, and thus, Brahms's musical phrases are here not word-specific. The chorale-like melody is based on descending and ascending fourths, and gives prominence to the high F in phrases 2 and 3 (an important link with the Benedictus-derived material which surrounds this section). Brahms thus eliminated bars 11–14 of the Dona nobis pacem, as also its large-scale repeat, and its canon. One is reminded of Brahms's question to Joachim during their contrapuntal studies at the time of the earliest stage of composition of the *Missa canonica* concerning some canonic material: 'Is it, disregarding the art involved, good music?'[21] The old canon could be seen as vestigially present in 'Siehe', shared between the new underparts, but it is fully 'disregarded' and this movement cannot properly be described as canonic. It is rather a heavily figurated chorale-like treatment, with scalic points of imitation in almost continuous quaver motion in the underparts, now increased in number ('Siehe' is for six voices, the Dona nobis pacem was for five); these points are largely independent of the characteristic melody-shapes. The serenity of Dona nobis pacem is not overcome by this transformation, if anything it is somewhat enhanced; the still centre of the Motet is nevertheless mobile. The strong subdominant inflection of C major parallels that of the Mass movement. Example 7 shows the first two and opening of the third phrases of this movement of the Motet; traces of the disregarded canon are marked with crosses. A short antiphonal link of great beauty and progressive thematicism reintroduces the rhythms of 'Lasset', and after seven bars the music of the latter half of movement 2, to a new text, is repeated almost exactly; its initiation is now accompanied by extra lower voices, which makes the junction with the preceding antiphonal passage particularly smooth, and there is a small adjustment of part-writing towards the end.

The six-line Dorian-mode chorale 'Mit Fried' und Freud' ich fahr' dahin', in a Bachian-style four-part setting, concludes the Motet. Bach wrote three such settings of this melody.[22]

21 *Briefwechsel* V, 136–8 (letter of 27 April 1856).

22 Terry, 276–8, 508.

Example 7. The opening of Brahms's Motet 'Warum', movement 3, bars 1–8

Brahms's version of the melody is not cognate with any of Bach's; it is closest to that in Cantata 83, but Brahms replaced the last C sharp with a C natural (as appears in Bach's other two settings). Brahms's harmonization is Bachian in style of harmonic progression, though he uses different progressions from Bach; and he treats the movement of the underparts also in a Bachian way. A small deviation from the prevailing Bachian style is to be found in line 4, where Brahms, perhaps painting the words 'Sanft und stille', keeps a static bass for three beats. Brahms's harmonization is tonal, but in some lines his choice of local keys is clearly influenced by the modality of the melody; the first chromatic inflection in bar 1 points towards G major, and in the last line, where the sequence of local tonics is D minor, A minor, C major, D major, this modally-influenced tonality is particularly apparent. Just this line is marked Adagio by Brahms (see Example 8). This movement responds to the first

Example 8. The ending of Brahms's Motet 'Warum', movement 4, bars 10_4–12

and third movements of the Motet to build a form-determining cyclic structure for the work as a whole in ways discussed above. Part of the clarification, resolution and purification it provides comes from its dwelling on older style. A clearly Bachian movement in a clearly Bachian position lends formality to the artistic expression at this juncture, and the impassioned, original subjectivity of the opening of Brahms's Motet moves to the poise and universality of traditional forms at its close.

The Motets Op. 74 figure prominently in Brahms's correspondence with his publisher Fritz Simrock during the latter half of

1878, and some of Brahms's remarks have important implications for performance practice. On 2 July 1878 Brahms announced his intention to publish the Opus: 'I have in mind to publish two entirely excellent, beautiful Motets for choir. . . They are I think better than others I have written, but also most practical and effective. The one is harder, but as compensation there are many small sections in it, which could most suitably be sung separately in church and concert.'[23] Brahms wanted some parts printed prior to publication so that he could perform the two Motets. On 6 October he asked for about 20 soprano parts, 20 alto, 10 tenor, and 15 bass for the first Motet; and on 11 November he asked for three scores and 10, 10, 6, 8 copies of the parts for the second.[24] This discrepancy could be explained by the fact that the numbers required for the second Motet are about half those initially asked for with regard to the first, and hence the possibility that choir-members were to be asked to share copies. The first performance of the first Motet took place on 8 December 1878 at the Gesellschaft der Musikfreunde in Vienna, Eduard Kremser conducting the Singverein. The two Motets were published that month. The first performance of the second Motet took place in Hamburg on 30 January 1880, Julius Spengel conducting the Cäcilienverein.

The Motet 'Warum' is compared with *Ein deutsches Requiem* by its admirers, and with justice.[25] Albeit on a smaller scale, the Motet is concerned with the necessity to overcome doubt and tribulation with praise and patience before final rest. Its complex multi-movement structure with thematic processes extending across movements, and the depth and originality of its expression all justify its being viewed as the greatest of Brahms's a cappella motets, and a worthy companion for *Ein deutsches Requiem*. Its growth out of the music of the *Missa canonica* offers yet another fascinating glimpse into Brahms's compositional processes, and the evolution of the old into the new is itself original, highly subtle and deeply, powerfully expressive. The study of this evolution is rewarding, for as Heidegger maintained: 'The work's becoming a work is a way in which truth becomes and happens.'[26]

[23] *Johannes Brahms Briefwechsel X: Johannes Brahms Briefe an P.J. Simrock und Fritz Simrock, Zweiter Band* ed. Max Kalbeck (Berlin, 1917) (hereafter *Briefwechsel X*) 79–80.

[24] *Briefwechsel X*, 85–6, 95.

[25] Siegfried Kross, *Die Chorwerke von Johannes Brahms* (Berlin, ^{2}1963) 373. Hancock, 133.

[26] Martin Heidegger, *Poetry, Language, Thought*, trans. Albert Hofstadter (New York, Hagerstown, San Francisco, London, 1971) 60.

MICHAEL MUSGRAVE AND ROBERT PASCALL

The String Quartets Op. 51 No. 1 in C minor and No. 2 in A minor: a preface

[To Theodor Billroth]

Tutzing, July 1873

Dear friend,

I am on the point of publishing string quartets – not the first, but for the first time. It is not merely from the thought of you and your friendship that I now write your name against the first; I also remember you with special pleasure as a violist and sextet player.[1] Would you prefer a volume of really difficult piano variations as more appropriate to your qualities? That is of no use; you must be content with the dedication as a pleasant little afterthought. . .I should not really disclose to you that the quartet in question is in the famed key of C minor; for if, of an evening, you now think of it and then fantasize, you will certainly too easily over-fantasize, and subsequently – find the second one better. . .

With hearty greetings to you and your wife,
Johannes Brahms[2]

We have no reply to this letter. But Billroth vouchsafed his response to his first hearing of the quartets to his friend, the art historian Wilhelm Lübke of Stuttgart:

Vienna, 23 November 1873

. . .The evening before last, Brahms's new quartets were played at my house. They contain much of beauty in concise form; but not only are they enormously difficult technically, neither is the content easy. If they are to be played at Stuttgart, I'd advise you to prepare yourself with the score or the four-hand arrangement. There is too much to be lost otherwise. There is scarcely a concert here now without a work by Brahms. . .[3]

[1] When Billroth, who was an excellent violist, had to play the second viola in the G major Sextet for the first time in the composer's presence, he was so nervous that a deputy had to be found.

[2] Max Kalbeck, *Johannes Brahms* II (Berlin, ^{2}1909) (hereafter Kalbeck II) 442.

[3] T. Billroth, *Briefe von Theodor Billroth*, ed. G. Fischer (Hamburg/Leipzig, ^{7}1906) 166.

Billroth's words to Lübke touch on two of the best-known facts about the background to these quartets. First that, though his first publications in the medium, they only appeared when Brahms's reputation was already well established; second, that they contain some of his most advanced writing. It seems timely to preface two new approaches to the works with a brief review of some aspects of their background, both chronological and critical.

That Brahms destroyed 'over twenty string quartets' (and 'several hundred songs') before releasing Op. 51 is one of the most widely-known indicators of his approach to the medium. This remark was made to his friend Alwin Cranz, though with a qualification which does not perhaps wholly accord with common assumptions about his difficulties with the creative process: 'it is not difficult to compose; but it is incredibly difficult to let the superfluous notes drop under the table'.[4] Just where the present works fit into this pattern of sustained industry and self-criticism is not fully known. Schumann's article 'Neue Bahnen' mentioned 'string quartets' as well as 'single piano pieces and sonatas for violin and piano', every work 'so different from the others that it seemed to stream from its own individual source'.[5] Yet only one of those works can be specified, a quartet in B minor, which Brahms first considered publishing as his Op. 1, though it has never come to light.[6]

Brahms turned again to the string quartet during the glorious flowering of chamber music composition in the early 1860s, working on a C minor quartet in 1865 and completing it by August 1866;[7] in 1867, quartets, in the plural, were mentioned in correspondence with Joachim. Brahms's strong concern with chamber music at this period of his creative life was partly a product of his profound disquiet at the stylistic developments of the New German School, particularly at the symphonic poems of Liszt. While chamber music had a traditional, even conservative, role in the genre-system of these times, it contained within itself an importantly progressive stylistic aspect. That 'thematic density', which formed one of the most significant stylistic continuities from Beethoven through Brahms to Schoenberg, found its most characteristic home in chamber music; and the textural

[4] Kalbeck II, 439.

[5] R. Schumann, *On Music and Musicians*, ed. K. Wolff, trans. P. Rosenfeld (London, 1946) 252.

[6] Kalbeck, I, 11–12.

[7] *Johannes Brahms Briefwechsel VI: Johannes Brahms im Briefwechsel mit Joseph Joachim*, ed. Andreas Moser (Berlin, [2]1912) 40; B. Litzmann, *Clara Schumann: Ein Künstlerleben* (Leipzig, 1909) (hereafter Litzmann) III, 194.

dialogue so fundamental to the genre, gave possibilities of great flexibility and intensity in thematic manipulation which were particularly congenial to Brahms.

In June 1869 Brahms played two quartet movements to Clara Schumann, who wrote in her diary: 'Lately Johannes brought me two wonderful quartet-movements, a first and a last movement, the latter especially successful, highly imaginative and full of verve. The first is not quite to my taste; perhaps he will yet alter it himself, since he does not seem to be entirely pleased with it.'[8] Her lack of reference to music she had heard in 1866 need not betoken anything more than a failure of memory, and we have no way of knowing whether these were new movements or reworked old ones. That same month Brahms wrote to his publisher Fritz Simrock that he wished to 'exert himself strongly' to make 'the one or the other passable. . .if we cannot imitate Mozart and Beethoven in fecundity at least we should try to in purity'.[9] Brahms was also struggling with another supremely Beethovenian genre at this time, that of the symphony. In connection with this other struggle he remarked to Hermann Levi at the beginning of the 1870s: 'You have no idea how it feels to the likes of us constantly to hear such a giant (Beethoven) marching behind one.'[10]

As we know from Brahms's handwritten catalogue of his works, he wrote the two quartets Op. 51 in the summer of 1873 at Tutzing 'for the second time'.[11] Only with several performances by the Walter Quartet that summer – at Levi's house in Munich, as it happens – were the two works completed to Brahms's satisfaction, at which time he wrote the dedication to Billroth. Thus we may with justice assume a long struggle with the genre of the string quartet, and a genesis more specifically for Op. 51 preceding 1873 (probably at least from 1869); but it remains a matter of speculation, on the evidence available, whether either

[8] Litzmann III, 229.

[9] *Johannes Brahms Briefwechsel IX: Johannes Brahms im Briefwechsel mit P.J. and F. Simrock*, ed. M. Kalbeck (Berlin, 1919) 75. It is clear from this letter that Brahms had in mind to hold a rehearsal of quartets of his own with the Florentine Quartet in the summer of 1869. Kalbeck was of the view that this rehearsal took place and concerned Op. 51 (see Kalbeck II, 441 and his footnote to the above letter). (But we need to know the source of Kalbeck's information in order to be able to judge whether it is factual or, as all too frequently with him, merely speculative.) It must also be recalled that 51 is an opus number appropriate to autumn 1869. By November 1873, when these quartets were eventually published, Brahms had already used Op. 55 for the *Triumphlied*. His reservation of Op. 51 as the numbering for the quartets strongly suggests their interim completion in 1869.

[10] 'Du hast keinen Begriff davon, wie es unsereinem zu Mute ist, wenn er immer so einen Riesen (Beethoven) hinter sich marschieren hört.' Noted by Kalbeck as directly communicated to him by Levi. See Kalbeck I, 165 and footnote.

[11] A-Wst, JN 32886.

or both of these quartets were originally written in the mid 1860s. The identity of key between the 1865–6 quartet and Op. 51 No. 1 is suggestive but clearly not conclusive. What does remain obvious however, is that the terse concision of the Op. 51 quartets reflects a movement away from the quasi-symphonic extension and gestural grandeur of the completed chamber works of the early 1860s; and the C minor Quartet, Op. 51 No. 1, together with his First Symphony, are the most Beethovenian of Brahms's mature masterpieces.

In placing critical reception of the two quartets in some perspective, the 'advanced' qualities – especially thematic ones – on which Schoenberg focused his examination of 'Brahms the Progressive' offer a familiar point of reference. Yet Schoenberg's focus is itself placed in important perspective by earlier responses, beginning with that of Eduard Hanslick, who shared with Billroth the closest friendship with Brahms in Vienna, and whose aesthetic principles may well be seen as fulfilled in aspects of the analytical approaches touched on here.

Hanslick's first published review is reproduced in the collected reviews of 1874,[12] the works having been published the preceding November and first performed on 11 December and 18 October respectively. Its very brief coverage devotes most attention to the C minor work, especially to the treatment of the 'magnificently passionate theme' of its first movement. He finds preference for the works to be divided: 'The passionate allegro and droll scherzo' of the C minor Quartet 'overtop the analogous movements of the A minor work', though the latter 'still eclipses its predecessor in the deep and peaceful melancholy of its Adagio and rhythmic drive of its finale'. As with the more familiar review of the First Symphony, Hanslick's point of reference is late Beethoven, recalled for him in the A flat Adagio of the C minor work. A more lengthy response a decade later was occasioned by a performance of the A minor work by the Heckmann Quartet, whose reading Hanslick regarded as the most

[12] E. Hanslick, *Concerte, Componisten und Virtuosen, 1870–1885* (Berlin, ^{2}1886) 116. The title of these reviews is strange: 'Three Quartets Op. 51'. This must have been a publisher's error, since Hanslick would have known as well as any that the first two works had been published and first performed late in 1873 as Op. 51. However, reference to the later, B flat work in the review indicates that the whole must have postdated 1874, since this work was only published in November 1876. Brahms wrote this Quartet in the summer of 1875 in Ziegelhausen near Heidelberg (see his handwritten catalogue of compositions), where he stayed from 20 May until the beginning of September. But the first acknowledgement of completion and impending performance appears to be by Billroth, who requested the accustomed first performance in his house in a letter to Brahms of 4 April 1876 (*Briefe von Theodor Billroth*, 196), a month earlier than previously noted in the literature.

perceptive thus far. The review finds its context in relation to Schumann and Beethoven, both represented in the programme (by the A major Quartet Op. 41 No. 3 and C major Quartet Op. 59 No. 3 respectively), with Brahms seen as absorbing the influences of both composers 'the first more in the early works, the second in the latter, but both so fully that one cannot mistake him anywhere'. But it is again Beethoven who provides the persistent theme of reference, and again likewise in the slow movement of the A minor Quartet: 'an Adagio of such sweet, long-breathed melody has not been written since Beethoven'. Writing only four years later in 1888, the author of the first important study of Brahms, his friend Hermann Deiters, expressed himself very similarly on this theme. Deiters sees Brahms as striving to follow Beethoven's lead, not only in his 'rare skill in form and modulation', but in his wealth of melody: 'the melodious Adagio overflows with hope and resignation and breathes a tone of earnest meditation'.[13] Such poetic response bespeaks a different generation from that of the most influential twentieth-century analysts of Brahms – Heinrich Schenker and Arnold Schoenberg – vividly so in Schoenberg's famed analysis of this very theme. Yet it was not only Schoenberg who was preoccupied with Brahms's themes. Schenker's obituary article in the progressive Berlin journal *Die Zukunft* also places an emphasis on melody, as well as offering other important perspectives in relation to both Deiters and Schoenberg.[14] For Schenker now sees Brahms not only as heir of Beethoven, but of a much longer tradition. Moreover, he is seen not as antithesis of the great 'progressive' of the period – Wagner – but as complement; Brahms and Wagner represent the two sides of a musical world which embraces both absolute and theatrical musical values, just as 'Bach and Handel' and 'Mozart and Beethoven'. Yet it is not Brahms's largest works which are seen as providing the focus for his achievement, the symphonies standing 'somewhat in the background'. And in this descent, the most prominent characteristic is melody: 'to the master Brahms was given a great characteristic melodic energy' ('eine grosse eigenthümliche Melodiekraft'), making him, further, 'a Mozart of our day'. The greatest feature of this melody is its freedom, permeative in the classics, yet, alone in the modern world, uniquely restored by Brahms. In the conflict between music depicted by Schenker as 'Neues' and 'Epigonenhaft' in this cru-

13 Hermann Deiters, *Johannes Brahms: A Biographical Sketch*, trans. with additions by Rosa Newmarch, ed. with preface J.A. Fuller-Maitland (London, 1888) 50.

14 *Die Zukunft*, ed. M. Harden, 19 (Berlin, 23 April 1897) 261.

cial period of transition, it is Brahms's freedom which is truly modern, much more so than that of 'those with whose names a new era of musical art is supposed to have begun' (chiefly Richard Strauss, as other comments confirm).

If this style of thought all seems extremely familiar from Schoenberg, it should serve to remind us that the tendency only to contrast Schoenberg and Schenker is mistaken; that rather – and uniquely so in their generation in the depth of their understanding – they shared basic values in their apprehension of a great tradition, both saw in Brahms the embodiment of purely musical values which transcended passing fashion: values that, since timeless, could not be new or old. This attitude led Schenker to dedicate his Beethoven study of 1912 to 'Brahms, the last master of German music'[15] and Schoenberg to adopt, as Stuckenschmidt so aptly put it 'a creed in Brahms'.[16] And if the absolute melodic ideal for Schenker was Mozart, he was no less so for Schoenberg, clearly the implicit point of reference for the modern subtleties of 'Brahms the Progressive'.[17]

Yet if the values were shared, their mature expressions were certainly very different. The kind of motivic logic Schoenberg demanded in his writings was steadily dismissed by Schenker, who finally stated in *Free Composition*[18] that 'music finds no coherence in a "motive" in the usual sense'; one can only imagine the kind of invective Schenker would have reserved for Schoenberg's exclusively motivic reading of the theme of the slow movement of the A minor Quartet. But Schenker's attitude had not always been thus. The remarks of 1897 contain no music examples and give no indication of what he meant by 'coherence and freedom'; (in striking contrast to the devalued master to whom Schoenberg directed his audience, Schenker's audience of 1897 needed no such prompts). Yet the presentation of his thought in the first major work, *Harmonielehre*,[19] published nearly a decade later in 1906, shows how strong was his traditional view of 'motive' even then, though a wider context of reference is implicit at various points; repetition is the basis of form, mirrored in nature, and its artistic realization is the motive, 'the only way of associating ideas in music'. In the one

[15] Heinrich Schenker, *Beethovens Neunte Sinfonie* (Vienna, 1912).

[16] H.H. Stuckenschmidt, *Arnold Schoenberg*, tr. H. Searle (London, 1977) 355.

[17] Arnold Schoenberg, *Style and Idea*, ed. L. Stein with trans. by L. Black (London, 1975) 414–15.

[18] Heinrich Schenker, *Free Composition* (*New Musical Theories and Fantasies*, III) trans. and ed. Ernst Oster (New York and London, 1979).

[19] Heinrich Schenker, *Harmony*, ed. and annot. O. Jonas, tr. E.M. Borgese (Cambridge, Mass. and London, 1954).

example of Brahmsian thematicism in the book, the composer is admired for having 'elegantly fulfilled the requirements of form without violating in any way the principle of repetition' by his subtle connection of ideas at bars 80–4 of the Finale of the Horn Trio; this device, later to be designated by Schenker as 'Knüpftechnik' ('linkage technique'), is also characteristic of Schoenberg's example, though his analysis reveals it by implication rather than by statement.

Which of the traditions of thought handed down by these two writers sheds most light on Brahms's processes is for the individual to decide. But, in the context of the present essay, it seems not inappropriate to conclude with a passing observation on this same familiar A major theme by a musician and writer of the same generation who, though sharing an intimate connection to the Brahms tradition, worked within a different cultural orbit – Donald Francis Tovey (1875–1940). He observed that 'the ruminative. . .theme is of a kind that many Brahmins [sic] have eagerly imitated under the mistaken impression that such things can be achieved by "logical development"'.[20] Whether approached as a model for imitation or as a demonstration of the composer's art at its highest, its aesthetic qualities were clearly recognized by writers as vindicating Brahms's faith in the long-standing values of the tradition he had inherited – a faith which has since been reflected in the steady growth of understanding of so many aspects of two quartets once regarded as 'advanced'. By the same token, they continue to offer a challenge to the modern analyst of music, whose task it is to seek some rational account of what lies behind these familiar experiences.

[20] D.F. Tovey, 'Brahms's Chamber Music' in *Cobbett's Cyclopedic Survey of Chamber Music* I (London, [2]1963) 174.

ARNOLD WHITTALL

Two of a kind? Brahms's Op. 51 finales

I

No music analyst will deny that one of his tasks is to relate parts to wholes. But one of the reasons why analysis is not always seen at its best in relatively short essays or conference contributions is that – unless the scope of material is very severely restricted – the exercise of relating parts to wholes can be undertaken only in part. To deal with the finales of the Op. 51 Quartets is to compound the hazard – to be not only selective, but also comparative as well. Even so, there is no attempt to exclude all reference to the position of these finales in the works from which they are taken or to their possible function in relation to the other movements. This is not an essay about the general issue of the character and function of finales, a subject well worth pursuing. But whether or not all the important features evident in these movements can be explained as part of their function as finales is a fascinating and complex question, which it might be possible to approach a little more confidently after the preliminaries with which I am concerned here.

These quartets are often written about comparatively, as the opus numbering seems to invite: and there is even an article called 'Brahms' opus 51 – a Diptych', which claims to demonstrate not only that 'the principal ideas, the basic motives, of the two quartets are. . .almost identical' but also that 'the quartets are individually and independently cyclic'.[1] A less positive reason for discussing the quartets as a pair is to deal more manageably with doubts and misgivings – not about unity but about quality. Many authorities, even when they acknowledge the expected subtleties of form, find the composer rather ill at ease with the medium (despite those twenty or so earlier and destroyed efforts); and – in respect of the C minor Quartet, at any rate – they talk of thematic material which lacks something in personality and potential. Even the normally loquacious

[1] William G. Hill, 'Brahms' opus 51 – a Diptych', *Music Review*, 13 (1952) 110–24.

Tovey grows rather tersely defensive about the C minor finale, and can muster only one distinctly gnomic sentence about the A minor, in which moral tone predominates over analytical substance: 'The finale', Tovey writes, 'is a lively rondo, not tragic, but master of its fate and in high spirits of a kind which exhilarate the listeners without suggesting that their temper is to be trifled with.'[2]

The less convinced the analyst is of the quality of musical ideas in specific cases, the more tempted he may be by the possibility of extending comparisons to other regions, and to a wider sample. Certainly, it often seems that for specialist commentators the two Op. 51 finales are most interesting when they can be brought alongside the other members of that richly rewarding collection, the examples of Brahmsian sonata form. It is not my intention to survey that material here. But we should note at once that Tovey's throwaway statement – calling the A minor finale 'a lively rondo' rather in passing, as if hoping that the reader will not feel it necessary to ask for further clarification – has not invariably been accepted as a sufficient explanation of the movement's subtleties of form. After all, Tovey himself wrote elsewhere, with equally disarming directness, that no two of Brahms's forms are alike;[3] and analysts today are unlikely to regard as too extreme a generalization Charles Rosen's remark that 'more than any other composer, Brahms exploited the possibilities of overlapping sections, the ambiguities of the boundaries of sonata form'.[4] Robert Pascall has rehearsed the ramifications of that version of sonata, evident in the C minor finale, in which development and recapitulation do not merely overlap but are in some sense conflated, thereby not only strengthening awareness of the binary background of the form, but also creating what he calls a 'bias' in the direction of rondo characteristics. And, in the case of the A minor finale, Tovey's rondo is, to Pascall, a sonata form 'where the development section begins with a statement of the first subject in the tonic'.[5]

The study of the ambiguous boundaries of Brahms's forms may often be more attractive to the analyst than the detailed tracing of still more elaborate thematic processes; but it is

[2] D.F. Tovey, 'Brahms's Chamber Music', *Essays and Lectures on Music*, ed. H.J. Foss (London, 1949) 253.

[3] Tovey, *Musical articles from the Encyclopaedia Britannica*, ed. H.J. Foss (London, 1944) 231.

[4] Charles Rosen, *Sonata Forms* (New York and London, 1980) 322.

[5] Robert Pascall, 'Some special uses of sonata form by Brahms', *Soundings*, 4 (1974) 61–2.

undeniable that in recent years the study of the forms has been greatly enriched by the analysis of such processes – for example, that 'developing variation' of which we hear so much, and rightly, since the term at once suggests a technique of composition impatient of that pure classical emphasis which seeks to confine working-out primarily if not exclusively to the central phase of the sonata movement. Those toiling in this vineyard – including Carl Dahlhaus and Walter Frisch[6] – have naturally had to decide how much use they feel able to make of Schoenberg's seminal yet sketchy demonstrations, as well as of Brahms's own apparent belief that 'the sonata form must of necessity result from the idea': 'it must grow logically from a theme'.[7] In developing this notion, it is all too easy to imply that Brahms was rejecting such features of harmonic integration and unity as Schenkerian analysis is intended to demonstrate – or was he simply taking such features for granted, as prior and inescapable conditions of viable musical structures of any kind?

At this stage, it might seem that motivic analysis and harmonic analysis are confronting each other – although, as Allen Forte, for one, demonstrates elsewhere in this volume, confrontation becomes unnecessary if a Schenkerian view of both motivic and harmonic coherence is adopted. But even if we, like Dahlhaus, persist in taking Schoenberg's name as synonymous with the search for motivic coherence, and Schenker's with the search for tonal coherence, there is perhaps no necessary and irreconcilable conflict between Schoenbergian and Schenkerian approaches to harmony. For Schenker, Brahms was 'the last master of German music', a composer whose 'masterful capacity for synthesis' was expressed through his 'special mode of diminution'.[8] For Schoenberg, who discusses an extract from the first movement of the C minor Quartet alongside passages from *Tristan* and *Salome* in his *Structural Functions of Harmony* under the heading of 'extended tonality', Brahms was 'a profound thinker and a great virtuoso in the treatment of harmonic problems'.[9] It is one of my contentions

[6] Walter Frisch, 'Brahms, developing variation, and the Schoenberg critical tradition', *19th-Century Music*, 5 (1981–2) 215–32; Carl Dahlhaus, 'Issues in composition', *Between Romanticism and Modernism*, tr. Mary Whittall (Berkeley and London 1980) 40–78.

[7] According to his pupil Gustav Jenner, quoted by Walter Frisch, *19th-Century Music*, 5, 232.

[8] Heinrich Schenker, *Free Composition*, tr. and ed. Ernst Oster (New York and London, 1979) 94, 106.

[9] Arnold Schoenberg, *Structural Functions of Harmony*, rev. edn, ed. Leonard Stein (London, 1969) 78.

that Brahms's virtuosity was not adversely affected by the presence of what some critics claim to be substandard thematic material: and that is very definitely an analytical rather than a critical contention. I am not claiming that these works are neglected masterpieces, and that all we need to do in order to recognize their true quality is to ignore their thematic content. Brahms was not only a virtuoso in the post-classical art of manipulating and merging traditionally separate formal elements to achieve a highly personal degree of ambiguity or multiplicity: he was an even more remarkable master of the art of recognizing and solving the harmonic problems posed by such formal stratagems. And there are few more fascinating harmonic problems than this: how stable and secure is the minor mode as the basis for sonata composition? In *Structural Functions of Harmony* (under the heading 'Interchangeability of Major and Minor') Schoenberg could declare in blasé fashion that 'in classical music, major and minor are often exchanged without much ado'[10] – which appears to square with Schenker's observations about mixture in the middleground: 'Less form-indicating, less form-generating than division or interruption'.[11] These two finales seem to suggest, however, that – at least when minor is exchanged for major – the late classical master Brahms could create a powerful sense of much ado about a great deal! Brahms is able to offer two approaches, two answers to the question about the stability of the minor mode, answers which hinge on such factors as the interaction between diatonic and chromatic elements, between tonal affirmations and tonal evasions, between symmetrical and hierarchic tendencies.

II

The finales of the Op. 51 Quartets reveal an intriguing balance of differences and similarities, only some of which I can deal with in the space available. As initially experienced in listening, the most fundamental differences between the finales might be in the types of continuity between the ends of third movements and the beginnings of finales: in the C minor, continuity of emphasis on the subdominant, very brief but very significant; in the A minor, a continuity of emphasis on the tonic. As Tovey writes of the C minor: 'From the F minor key of the scherzo the opening figure of the short finale arises in wrath. . .[Brahms]

[10] Schoenberg, *Structural Functions of Harmony*, 52.
[11] Schenker, *Free Composition*, 41.

here for the first time contrives to make a short finale gain in weight by its effect as a kind of epilogue to the previous movement and to the whole work. . .This impression of finality is reinforced in the C minor quartet by the fact that the opening figure of the finale is a compound of those of the Romanze and the first movement.'[12] Tovey does not spell out the fact that the third movement actually ends on a chord of F major, not minor, but in any case his prime concern with thematic features is clear. And the problem many people have with the themes of this finale is precisely that the initial figure – an example of Brahmsian 'Tristanizing' perhaps – is so striking, so allusive, and yet so patently introductory, that it cannot convincingly dominate the movement to the extent that a principal theme should. There is a clear contrast with the A minor finale in this respect: and although Tovey twice describes the C minor finale as short, someone whose hearing of the movement is dominated by thematic factors may well feel that it takes Brahms rather too long to get round to working intensively with the principal motive – seventy bars, in fact.[13]

From a more harmonic perspective, it might be thought that Brahms's strategy, and his reason for launching the movement from the note F rather than C, would be to spend a large part of the movement in a dramatic search for the work's 'true' tonic. But the composer's purpose at the highest level in this finale seems not so much to keep the identity of the tonic note in doubt – whatever such a concept may mean to those who know the actual music well. Most important is an interaction between tonic major and minor modes – an interaction which comes perilously close to fusion in places, thereby opening the door to those highly charged notions of 'chromatic tonality' so attractive to aspiring analysts of music drama. But there are other kinds of interaction too: between a tendency to direct the music towards tonics and a tendency to direct it towards dominants, whether of the tonic region itself, or of other regions. And with those other regions in mind, it is not in the least surprising to find that Brahms does not parallel his exploitation of tonic major and minor with an exploitation of the tonicized dominant in all its familiar, minor mode ambiguity. Instead we get a

[12] Tovey, *Essays and Lectures on Music*, 252.

[13] A case for regarding the movement as *necessarily* short, on the grounds that it continues to develop material already explored in the three previous movements, is presented in Rainer Wilke, *Brahms, Reger, Schönberg Streichquartette: Motivisch-thematische Processe und formale Gestalt* (Hamburg, 1980) 79–80, 82–4. (See the discussion in Walter Frisch, *Brahms and the Principle of Developing Variation*, (Berkeley and London, 1984) 110.)

masterly demonstration of what can be done with third relations. The chain of events centres on a relatively unstable E flat major succeeding a relatively stable C minor; then a relatively stable A minor precedes a relatively unstable C major, and this leads finally to the return to a relatively stable C minor. Such a highly schematic statement seems to suggest that the formal conflation which is fundamental to the character of the C minor finale is complemented by a tendency to stress the symmetrical balance of regions a minor third on either side of the tonic: but 'balance' is hardly the right term when vastly different degrees of tonicization are involved, and when minor is offset by major around a tonic which is itself transforming its modality from minor to major and back again. The essence of the C minor finale is that it is modally mobile as well as formally compressed.

The A minor Finale is more expansive in form, and if anything more explicit in harmony. But whereas the C minor finale gives considerable attention to the relative minor of C major, the A minor finale goes out of its way to avoid tonicizing F sharp minor. While the C minor finale is extremely reluctant to tonicize its mediant major (E flat), the A minor finale gives C major great emphasis. But this is the point at which to explore such rudimentary comparisons in a little more detail, without excluding the occasional critical observation.

III

Taken as a whole, Brahms's 93-bar exposition in the C minor finale might actually seem a model of harmonic orthodoxy, firmly establishing its tonic after the first 20 bars, and then moving to the relative major after bar 40 for the principal contrasting material. Though far from purely diatonic, these first 40 or so bars certainly do not constitute an exposition with very spectacular chromatic excursions; and there is a neat consistency in the way the initial 20 bars of progress towards the C minor tonic are balanced by another 20 bars of development and transition which focus on that tonic with clarity and persistence – at least until bar 38. It is at this point that Brahms opens the door on the mediant, relative major region of E flat: and, from bar 39 to bar 93 (note the mirror symmetry!) openness is the key word. I do not claim that the root position tonic chord of E flat major or minor never occurs, but it is not prominent enough to create a sense of closure comparable to that achieved by the C minor tonic in the movement's second 20 bars. The first

29 bars of this E flat section – bar 41 to bar 69 – are notable for the contrapuntal fluency with which they work out material which is perhaps not related to the basic shape quite clearly enough to satisfy those who search Brahms for anticipations of Schoenbergian – even Webernian – monothematicism. But it could be argued that Brahms more than compensates for any thematic featurelessness in the music between bar 41 and bar 69 by technical and textural subtlety: principally through his handling of sequence, so that it is just as capable of enriching and destabilizing as it is of strengthening the sense of forward motion – such techniques are clearly at work between bar 46 and bar 53. And even before this, destabilization is promoted by the 'odd' bar which breaks down the duple successions at bar 41 (Example 1).

Example 1. Op. 51 No. 1, fourth movement, bars 39–53

Ex. 1 (*cont.*)

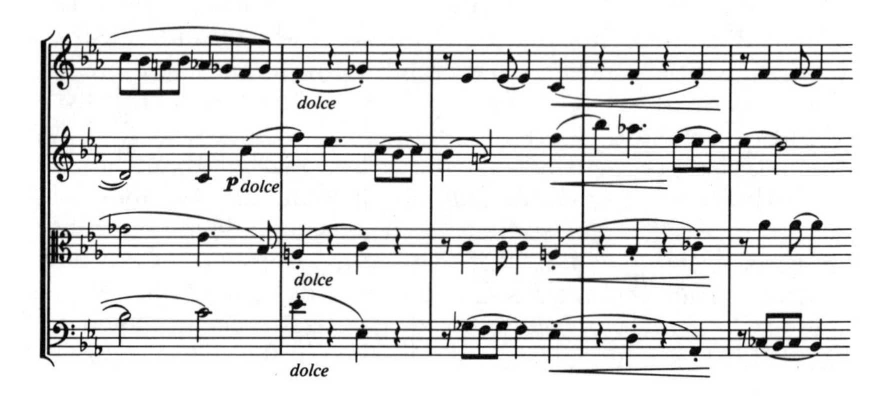

The harmonic drift in this section from bar 41 to bar 59 is to direct the play of dominants back towards C minor, and the recall of the movement's main motive at bars 68–9 would serve to initiate a repeat of the exposition, if the contrapuntal material from bar 41 onwards had been felt to provide an adequate 'second group'. Brahms's view seems to be that the process of exposition, involving as it should the establishment of an alternative harmonic area, is still incomplete at bar 69, for he directs the harmony back onto the dominant of E flat and composes a lyric expansion of the main motive – which, even in the context of this essay, it would be foolish to detach from its partial function as a reminiscence of second-movement material. It is the passage from bar 71 to bar 81 which confirms and clarifies Brahms's preference for representing the relative major – so far his main subsidiary region – through emphasis on its dominant. And this lyric expansion generates such a determined, intensifying sequential development, from bar 81, that the movement's fourth statement of its initial motive, at bar 94, cannot possibly herald anything other than further development – except, that is, recapitulation (Example 2).

The 93-bar exposition is followed by 98 bars of development recapitulation – and this statistic encourages the argument that the conflated development recapitulation is, in its concentration, as much a formal complement to the expansive exposition as it is a harmonic complement. For one unmistakable fact about Brahms's conflated development and recapitulation in this finale is that C minor does not decisively reappear until those final stages which conflate recapitulation and coda.

Example 2. Bars 70–95

Ex. 2 (*cont.*)

Instead, A minor and C major – with emphasis on the dominant – are preferred. Given the developmental associations in the first movement, A minor here in the finale provides a powerful focus for the tensions which conflation of development and recapitulation create. A minor is established by a full close at bar 110 after only 14 bars of development involving an enharmonic shift around the briefly tonicized D flat/C sharp at bar 102 (Example 3).

Devotees of *Terzverwandschaft* and axis-systems will naturally pay tribute to the fact that this is the only point in either finale where the tonicized dominant appears, in the guise of its tritonal counterpole. But what matters is that the A minor

Example 3. Bars 102–11

Ex. 3 (*cont.*)

established at bar 110 is a good deal closer to home than what immediately precedes it, and also a good deal more stable. After the A minor full close at bar 110, the next 14 bars grow closer and closer to exposition material, until, from bar 124, we have a recapitulation in A minor of what was exposed in C minor at bar 33. And what was, in the exposition, one of Brahms's least artful sequences, employed to hoist the music from C minor to E flat minor (bars 37–40), is now, in bars 128–31, the means of establishing the dominant of C major (Example 4).

Example 4.

(a) Bars 37–40

Ex. 4 (*cont.*)

(b) 128–31

The recapitulation then proceeds in orderly fashion until the lyric expansion of the introductory motive, whose enrichment of the C major dominant is further elaborated between bars 162 and 192: this elaboration involves increasing interaction between tonic major and tonic minor tendencies, and it is the intensity of the harmonic confrontation here which motivates the coda. This is still developmentally recapitulatory, as far as its thematic material goes. But harmonically its decisive event is at bar 231, where the repeat of the exposition's last C minor full close (from bar 33) is no longer an incitement to vagrancy but a point of closure to be reinforced (Example 5).

Example 5.

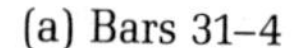
(a) Bars 31–4

Ex. 5 (*cont.*)
(b) Bars 229–33

And so the primary function of C minor in this structure can scarcely be denied when the movement is taken as a whole. It is a C minor in which the tonic chord is clearly more vitally in evidence than the dominant: whereas in the exposition the enrichment of the dominant of E flat major draws attention to the relative instability of the mediant region, the enrichment in development and recapitulation of the dominant of C major has the wider perspectives and more fundamental structural significance of direct subordination to the tonic, C minor chord. There is barely more than a hint of that dominant itself being tonicized: and the skill with which Brahms delays the two principal assertions of the C minor tonic – at bar 21, and at bar 231 in the coda – serves to dramatize its own overriding structural power. It may be something of an absentee landlord, but it is an effective one, preventing the emergence of genuine alternative authorities. (Maybe it is only through such metaphors that we can do justice to the vital force of Brahms's conservatism!)

IV

As is well known, it is not difficult to relate the main theme of the A minor finale to earlier material in the work, most obviously the theme of the third movement. And anyone who wishes to discuss the finale in terms of special features is more likely to talk about syncopation and three-bar phrases than about a tonal scheme which cannot by any stretch of imagination or intellect be held to keep the identity of the principal tonic note in doubt: the principal mode, of course, is another matter. As I have already suggested, in harmonic terms we can find something comparable to the C minor finale: but may it not also be something complementary? A movement, perhaps, whose main process is to undermine a tonic all too plainly displayed at the outset? But just as it will not do to describe the C minor finale as a *Parsifal*-like quest for the ultimate enlightenment of its principal tonality, so too the A minor finale cannot be said to submit its tonic to a series of dramatic ordeals. Once again, it is more a matter of types of extension, of regional and modal exploration: not so much of doubts about identity as of distinctions of function. And, on the highest level, it does seem that the greater expansiveness of the A minor finale brings with it a lessening of the sense of tritonal opposition, so basic to the C minor, between the relative major of the tonic and the relative minor of the tonic major. There is absolutely no lessening of the primary tension between tonic major and minor in this second finale.

In terms of numbers of bars, the conflated development and recapitulation of the C minor finale was very little longer than the exposition: 98 bars after 93. The A minor offers more orthodox tripartite proportions, in keeping with the fact that both its development and recapitulation, if we can call them that, begin with tonic (minor) statements of the main theme: the totals are 115 bars of exposition, 82 of development (116–97), and 136 of recapitulation (198–333), with a 26-bar coda, *più vivace*. Without getting embroiled in the sonata-versus-rondo debate, it is clearly possible to divide the 115-bar exposition into two, and in at least two different ways: first, we can make the principal division at bar 41, regarding the entire section after that point, which tonicizes C major, as a second-subject group; second, we can make a division between a two-theme exposition which extends to bar 55, and an episode of contrasting but less characterful thematic content from bar 55 onwards. Harmonically, such a choice is neither necessary nor helpful: for if we take the 115-bar section as a whole we can observe that, after the relatively straightforward tonic emphasis of the first-theme area (bars 1–37), Brahms presents his lyric second theme as a prolongation of the relative major's dominant; a most interesting parallel with his procedures in the C minor exposition, though in the A minor that emphasis on the relative major's dominant occurs at a much earlier stage (Example 6).

Example 6. Op. 51 No. 2, fourth movement, bars 43–55

But the passage from bar 56 to bar 100 is remarkable chiefly for the fact that, far from regarding this chaste opening as a licence for excursions to remote and exotic harmonic regions, it concerns itself principally with establishing and defining the tonic chord of the mediant, C major. There are no fewer than three full closes (at bars 71, 79 and 100) and despite such a passage as the play around the dominant (and the overall tonic) that occurs between bars 91 and 99 – not to mention the presence earlier of invertible counterpoint – this treatment of the mediant region is clearly quite different from that in the C minor finale (Example 7).

Example 7. Bars 91–9

The development section of the movement (bars 116–97) offers a compressed variation of the events of the exposition. Here, differences from the C minor finale are most evident. The A minor development steers a remarkable course from initial expansion (three-bar phrases grow to four) to a crisis of compression. The A minor material is adjusted to prepare the dominant of the submediant, F major, which the second theme duly prolongs (bars 143–54). But instead of an extended episode establishing the tonic of F major, we have 25 bars which seem bent on reasserting that symmetric ploy of the C minor's finale, whereby the early stages of development establish the relative minor of the tonic major. There is a sense in which the A minor's dominant preparation of F sharp minor (bars 174–7) – but failure to tonicize that F sharp minor – is a failure to match the symmetry of the C minor. But in the A minor's own context it may also serve to delay the crucial appearance of the tonic major (Example 8).

Example 8. Bars 172–87

Brahms resolves the developmental crisis onto the dominant of A minor at bar 186. And once this is achieved, he projects some particularly concentrated development of the main motive against it to prepare for the recapitulation at bar 198: this actually extends the treatment of the first theme, though without weakening the essential diatonicism of the harmony. Indeed, one of the purposes of the lengthening which takes place here is to direct the harmony towards A minor's dominant for the third and final statement of the movement's main contrasting theme (Example 9).

Example 9. Bars 238–48

Although it is once again a dominant chord which is prolonged, from bar 238 to bar 248, there is a clear sense of the tonic key having switched mode from minor to major, a mixture which the rest of the movement explores in depth: and this time, in contrast to the C minor finale, the tonicization of the tonic major is fully realized. In the C minor finale, the tonic chord of the tonic major was far less in evidence than it is in the A minor finale. So, in the C minor, Brahms did not actually need to transform tonic major into tonic minor: instead he used his teasing protraction of the dominant to prepare the tonic minor through a transformation of the context in which that dominant occurs. In the A minor finale the atmosphere is rather more relaxed. Brahms does not rudely contradict major with minor, but composes a 41-bar development between bar 293 and bar 333, which tries out a major-key version of the main theme, before providing transformation of major harmony back into minor. If I may be forgiven a further, final foray into anthropomorphism: it is a transformation the coda is so pleased with that it almost forgets the need to provide a proper root-position statement of the tonic chord itself until the last two bars.

V

As far as it has been taken, then, the answer to the question, 'Two of a kind?', has to be 'yes and no – but mainly yes'. In both finales, the tonic minor survives the challenge of more stable major harmony, whether of tonic major or relative major: and while, in the case of the C minor, A minor might be felt to function very much as a transposed tonic – an axis relative – the A minor finale, making a climax from its failure to reproduce a comparable device, thereby also fails to tonicize a second minor-mode region. The main difference is the fact that A minor recurs twice during the course of that finale, while in the C minor the tonic key appears twice only, near the beginning and at the end. That may justify a claim that the C minor finale is really in C minor/major/minor; alternatively, it is possible to see its relative instability as providing an appropriate C minor conclusion to the whole quartet, even if the harmonic identity of the Finale remains ambiguous when taken in isolation. But such issues simply reinforce the obvious fact that this essay, even in its final sentence, will not provide the last word on the subject. The delights of full, technical probing of fundamental structural elements have been happily sacrificed for the more narrative style of a comprehensive overview in which passing reference has been made to just some of the salient issues and some of the significant structural techniques. I regard the result as an intersection between my own historical consciousness, and what I see and hear as Brahms's historical consciousness. The consensus today is that Brahms's willingness to enrich the 'sonata principle' from within was a strength, not a weakness, and we can accept that, without necessarily making Brahms more palatably progressive in the way the Schoenberg–Dahlhaus tradition attempts to do: and also, of course, without applying the rigorous Schenkerian tests designed to demonstrate the presence or absence of sonata form. We can accept that Brahms did not remain indifferent to those processes of harmonic enrichment which moved more fully into the foreground – and perhaps into the middleground as well – during the later nineteenth century: and we may occasionally choose to compare those passages in his work where a dominant harmony is more fully realized than a tonic to similar instances in Wagner and other text-obsessed composers. We may even sense in the techniques of enrichment which seem to involve the suppression rather than the full expression of fundamental tonal entities an adumbration of that harmonic primitivism which – from one perspective at least – might be felt to have run riot in music of the last seventy years or so. To do this, however, is to run the risk of seriously underestimating what Schoenberg seized on when, in his *Fundamentals of Musical Composition*, quoting extracts from several of Brahms's chamber works, he remarked that 'they differ from the classic examples in a more prolific exploitation of the multiple meaning of harmonies'.[14] The vital thing about Brahms is that, even when his generative ideas themselves are less exciting, and less pervasive, than when he is at his most progressive, his formal procedures and harmonic techniques remain positive and purposeful. It is probably true to say that in these finales the idea of multiple meaning is more directly applicable to form than to harmony. After all, it might well be that a finale can fulfil its function with respect to the harmonic structure of the work as a whole only if it is tonally definite and singular, rather than ambiguous and multiple. But even when the singular is the order of the day, the subtlety with which basic models are transformed offers the analyst as clear a demonstration of mastery as he could wish. In these finales, Brahms's enrichments add to meaning, undermining nothing and subtracting nothing. Among all the late nineteenth-century composers, Brahms's mastery is the most self-evident, the most susceptible to clear and unambiguous definition. But the analytical presentation of the evidence for that mastery is still, I would suggest, an eminently worthwhile musical activity.

[14] Schoenberg, *Fundamentals of Musical Composition*, ed. Gerald Strang and Leonard Stein (London, 1967) 30.

ALLEN FORTE

Motivic design and structural levels in the first movement of Brahms's String Quartet in C minor[1]

With the exception of a few recent studies, little analytical work of any depth has been published on the music of Brahms. Even Heinrich Schenker, whose admiration for the composer is well known, did not publish extensively on his music. It is not difficult to ascertain the reason for this: Brahms's music, even when ostensibly simple, is full of complications and projects unusual structures which have no counterparts in the music of the Classical masters generally regarded as his model repertory.

Although this study is founded upon Schenkerian principles, demonstrating a belief in the sanctity of the tonic triad and a reverence for the transcendental reality of the *Urlinie*, it often departs from Schenkerian paradigms in order to cope with the special features of Brahms's music. In particular, it emphasizes the primal importance of the motive – to be construed in a sense somewhat broader than traditionally conceived – as a determinant of musical gestures at levels beyond the scale of the foreground.

After a brief review of the form of the movement, with some attention to other features of interest, I will proceed to a discussion of motives in the foreground, beginning with a general statement concerning the concept of motive in Brahms's music, as exemplified in the subject work.

I shall then discuss instances of motivic penetration of the middleground, a strong feature of this work and probably a structural aspect of widespread significance in all music of the later nineteenth century.

[1] This essay is part of a set of three studies of late nineteenth-century works by the present author. The others are: 'Motive and Rhythmic Contour in Brahms's Alto Rhapsody', *Journal of Music Theory*, 22/2 (Fall, 1983) and 'Middleground Motives in the Adagietto of Mahler's Fifth Symphony', *19th-Century Music*, 8/2 (Fall, 1984), 153–63. It was first published in *The Musical Quarterly*, 69/4 (Fall, 1983) and is reproduced here by kind permission of G. Schirmer Inc.

I shall also touch upon certain traditional features of the music, for example, the use of imitation and double counterpoint as well as extensions of these as they relate to the motivic design. In this connection, I emphasize that certain pitches – both single pitches and dyads – as well as a particular triad (not the tonic triad) are of special importance and may be regarded as having a catalytic role.

Form and Some General Features

The overall formal plan of the movement is that of the Classical sonata – with, of course, many departures from any stereotype of that pattern. However, as can be seen in the Overview of Form, Brahms maintains in the reprise a precise correspondence of the parts of the exposition, with few exceptions – and those always in details.

The Overview of Form also reflects the complicated segmentation of the traditional parts of sonata form. The second subject area is especially elaborate, with at least five identifiable parts. Of these, the developmental episode, which begins in bar 45 of the exposition, is perhaps most unusual, since it apparently interrupts the established continuity of the music and has the effect of an interpolation. The structural meaning of this passage will be discussed in connection with Example 10, which presents the episode as it occurs in the reprise. (The reader may wish to keep the Overview of Form at hand as the discussion moves forward.)

A word about the unusual key relations is in order before I proceed to a consideration of motivic detail. In particular, the second subject is in E flat minor, instead of the traditional key of the mediant, E flat major. This unusual key provides a hint of the identity of the work to which Brahms refers elsewhere in the movement: the Piano Sonata in C minor, Op. 13 (*Pathétique*), by Beethoven.[2] The A major/A minor cast of the development, as well as of the developmental episode mentioned earlier, also has a special meaning, to which I will return later.

[2] This key relation was pointed out by Roger Graybill in his dissertation, *Brahms's Three-Key Expositions* (Yale, 1983). The key of E flat minor had a special significance for Brahms, as in the slow movement of the Horn Trio, a dirge for his mother. So did C minor, of course, because of its special role in music of the Classical period. However, it is the *Pathétique* Sonata and not other famous pieces in C minor – for example, Beethoven's Op. 18 No. 4 – to which he refers in his C minor String Quartet. The resemblance between the two works extends to other features as well. The second theme of the Beethoven work also incorporates motive alpha (described below) and the second movements of both are in A flat, with motive beta bar prime prominently represented in the first theme of the *Pathétique*.

OVERVIEW OF FORM
Exposition
  First Subject (c)
    Part 1: bars 1–8
    Part 2: 9–22
    Part 1 modified: 23–7
    Transition: 27–34
  Second Subject (e♭)
    Part 1: 35–40
    Part 2, extension in double counterpoint in the 15th: 41–4
    Part 3, developmental episode: 45–52
    Part 4, resumption of V from b. 41: 53–66
    Part 5, cadenza: bars 67–70
  Closing Subject
    Part 1: 71–5
    Part 2: 75–82
  [Repetition of Exposition]
Development (a/A)
  Transition/Introduction: 80b–91
  Part 1, first subject: 92–5
  Part 2, second subject: 96–107
  Part 3, first and second subjects: 108–17
  Part 4, 118–29
  Transition: 129–32
Reprise
  First Subject (c)
    Part 1: 133–50
    Part 2: 151–63
    Part 1 modified (f); 164–75 (cf. first subject of finale)
  Second Subject (c)
    Part 1: 176–82
    Part 2, extension in double counterpoint in the 15th: 182–5
    Part 3, developmental episode: 186–93
    Part 4, resumption of V from b. 182: 194–207
    Part 5, cadenza: 208–11
  Closing Subject (c)
    Part 1: 212–15
    Part 2: 216–23
  Coda
    Part 1: 224–32
    Part 2: 232–9
    Part 3: 240–60

Finally, I wish to draw attention to the existence of many short traditional canons as well as the extension of the canon idea to the sphere of rhythm. In both cases, the canons are intimately bound up with the motivic design which is the primary focus of this presentation.

Before considering the motivic constituents of the movement as they appear in the foreground level, I wish to set out four general analytical guidelines related to the notion of motive in Brahms's music:

1. The motive is primarily an intervallic event, distinct from any particular pitch manifestation.
2. The original pitch or pitch-class representation of a motive is of singular importance, however, and we call this referential function of a particular form *pitch-specific* which means that the motive designated consists of the same pitches as the original form of the motive; and the term *pitch-class specific* means that the motive is recurring, but at some level of octave transposition with respect to the original form.
3. The boundary interval of the motive is its most salient feature. The internal structure is variable or may even be absent in some representation of the motive. The boundary interval may undergo octave inversion, or – more appropriate to Brahms's usage – expansion by octave displacement, as major third and minor sixth.
4. A motive may be transformed without losing its basic identity. The transformations which Brahms uses are retrograde, inversion, and retrograde inversion. He also uses a transformation which I will call *minor to major* or *major to minor*, depending upon the circumstances.

In the examples that accompany this essay, Greek letters designate motives, while two symbols attached to the letters designate transformations: the prime superscript signifies that the motive is in its retrograde form, while the bar above the letter signifies inversion. Thus, alpha bar prime is the retrograde of the inversion of alpha. No special symbol is used for the minor-to-major transformation.

It should be observed that the transformations will alter the internal intervallic organization of the motive, but – with the exception of the major-to-minor transform – preserve the boundary interval which is the distinguishing feature of the motive.

And it is essential to bear in mind that these atomic constituents, however commonplace they may seem out of their musical contexts, are not in the least trivial. Nor are they floating about in some random musical space, but are attached to other elements in the composition at a specific structural level or levels, so that each motivic particle, however minuscule, relates to the whole through the organizational hierarchy.

The Table of Motives offers a convenient summary of the main motives in the movement. We will consider these from top to bottom, beginning on the left side, then proceeding from top to bottom on the right side.

Motive alpha (1) is without question the most prominent motive in the movement. As every musician will recognize, it consists of the first three notes of the *Pathétique* Sonata, identical even with respect to register and with the further association through the dotted rhythm. Moreover, Beethoven accompanies his motive with its retrograde, a procedure upon which Brahms elaborates in the string quartet movement. The three transformations of alpha are given in the table, in somewhat arbitrary pitch forms, since they occur in many ways in the work: first, alpha bar, the contour inversion of alpha, then the reverse of alpha, alpha prime, and finally, the most complicated transformation of alpha, alpha bar prime.

While alpha is first presented as the first three notes in the melodic first subject (b. 1), beta, the triadic formation shown in the Table of Motives, is presented as the next three pitches. Beta bar then becomes a major triad, in the first inversion, while beta bar prime presents the ascending form of beta bar, a motive of singular significance to this music, especially in the pitch-class form shown in the table (A flat major triad).

Motive gamma (2) is introduced as the descending skip of a diminished seventh in the subject at the beginning of bar 2. Gamma bar is shown in the table, but no further transforms, since obviously they would not be distinct from gamma and gamma bar with respect to contour. Although gamma has the notational boundary interval of a diminished seventh in its initial manifestation, it also occurs frequently with the boundary interval of a major sixth.

Motive lambda (3) is, like the previous motives, a component of the melodic first subject. Its pitch-specific form f sharp-g^1 has a special meaning throughout the work, as will be shown. Lambda bar, the inverse of lambda, is the final dyad of the first part of the first subject, the dramatic conclusion of the long opening phrase (b. 7).

In motive theta (4) we have a constituent which might not even be accorded motivic status in a more conventional reading. This is the octave motive which occupies an entire bar alone (b. 8), and, if only for that reason, deserves special attention. In bar 24, as first violin accompaniment to the subject in the cello, it assumes a prominent role in the foreground and has two shapes, designated theta and theta bar in the Table of Motives.

The next motive is delta (5), with the boundary interval of a perfect fourth. This motive first occurs in the middleground, beginning with g^1 in bar 2. Subsequently it becomes prominent in the foreground as well – the reverse of the usual chronology. Motive delta incorporates gamma as its first dyad, an observation that suggests further connections among the basic motives of the movement. Delta bar and delta bar prime are given in the table for the sake of theoretical fastidiousness, but they are not represented in any significant way in the music.

Table of Motives

Motive sigma (6), the diminished triad, is the secret emblem of the work, as will be explained at an appropriate time. The bracketed form of sigma reminds us that the diminished triad delimits the opening gesture of the first subject. Notice also that c^1-e $flat^2$ is nothing more nor less than an expansion of the boundary interval of alpha.

Motive phi (7), the minor triad, shown at the top of the right side of the Table of Motives, is also outlined by the opening of the first subject, as c^1-e $flat^2$-g^1.

Motive chi, which first occurs as a melodic leap in the first subject, is included in the table, but is not an especially significant or prominent motive.

Motive omega (8), the descending fifth, is reserved for closure and also reflects the basic melodic background in the Schenkerian sense. That is, the background melodic space in the upper voice is defined by the fifth from the primary tone G to the tonic C.

While the motive (9), which first appears as the melodic figure in bar 39, might be regarded as a new structure in the music, it is viewed here as a composite of three previously stated motives. Its boundary interval, the major seventh, is a registral expansion of lambda, and the internal components are explained as interlocking forms of phi and phi bar.

And last is the motive epsilon and its inverse (10), with the boundary interval of a major third. So closely is this associated with motive alpha that one might almost regard them as equivalent. However, they have been given separate names here. At an appropriate time we will invoke the minor-to-major transformation to explain the relation between the two.

It is hoped that this somewhat detailed coverage of the basic motives will have served a useful purpose when we proceed to examine portions of the music at hand. As an adjunct to this survey of the pitch motives, the table headed Some Prominent Rhythmic Motives (see p. 172) affords a concise overview of seven patterns which are multiply represented in the composition.

Certainly the opening rhythmic figure, item 1, dotted crotchet-quaver-crotchet, is the rhythmic hallmark of the piece. The table shows a few of its associations with the pitch motives. Notice, in particular, that it articulates both alpha and (in b. 133) beta bar prime, the A $flat^6$ formation, shown at the end of the top line in the table.

The rhythm originally associated with motive gamma, the descending diminished seventh, also relates gamma to its

Some Prominent Rhythmic Motives

inverse, a flat^2-g^2, as shown in item 2 of the table. In doubled form as semibreve-minim, it relates gamma to the registrally expanded form of the boundary interval of epsilon (b. 35) and to lambda (b. 45).

Item 3 consists of the three semibreves motive, a characteristic hemiola pattern which appears in several unexpected ways in the work. One of these is shown in the table, the melody at bar 39. As is evident, the semibreve components of the pattern result from compounding of the dotted crotchet-quaver figure.

The symmetrical rhythm quaver-dotted crotchet-quaver, item 4, distinguishes motive beta, and the same pattern is also an element of the semibreve pattern in item 3 where it is associated initially with beta bar. (The dotted rhythm of beta bar at the opening of the Romanze of this quartet is surely not happenstance.)

The semibreve-dotted semibreve originally associated with theta has other connective functions, most notable of which are the setting of gamma in bar 29, about which more will be said when we come to Example 7, and the consequent phrase of Part 1 of the Second Subject (b. 37), as illustrated in connection with item 5. Here the breve is detached from the complete figure and followed by its halved replicas, representative of a rhythmic generative process which seems to be common in Brahms's music.

Although a detailed study of rhythmic relations is not within the scope of this essay, it is perhaps not inappropriate to remark that the semibreve-dotted semibreve motive is exactly proportional in duration to the quaver-dotted crotchet-quaver motive in item 4: it is exactly four times as long; that is, the minim serves as multiplier.

The figure quaver rest-four quavers displayed as item 6 clearly derives from the dotted crotchet-quaver pattern of item 1, as indicated by the notation above the staff of item 6. This upbeat figure is then carried throughout the movement as the primary rhythmic contour of the first part of the second subject, beginning in bar 35, as shown. In the rhapsodic passage that begins at bar 65 the quaver rest is replaced by a tied quaver, yet the association remains unmistakable. Out of this grows the constant quaver pattern of the cadenza from bar 67, completing a chain of rhythmic development that began in the opening bar.

Finally, item 7 shows the four-quaver motive initially associated with motive theta in bar 24 and subsequently manifested by the arpeggiation of bar 53, a form of beta bar prime. This motive has many other associations throughout the movement, as does its offshoot, the crotchet rest-crotchet figure shown at the end of the example.

As a way of organizing the discussion of motivic design while keeping complexity reasonably under control, I will take up each motive in turn as it appears in various passages throughout the movement. The numbered examples that follow consist for the most part of fragments of the score that have been annotated analytically by the addition of stems, beams, brackets, and the Greek letter designations for motives which are by now familiar.

Motive alpha, originally the head motive of the first subject, proves to be the source of the head motive of the second, as alpha bar prime (Example 1). The melodic figure here consists of two parts, first alpha, then lambda bar, g flat^2-f^2, the latter a pitch-class specific form of lambda bar as it occurred in bar 9. Lambda is also present, as indicated by the beamed minims in Example 1, albeit not as a contiguously formed dyad. As if to conceal the foreground pattern here, Brahms introduces a voice exchange at the end of bar 36 (Example 1), as indicated by the crossed lines connecting first and second violin parts. As a result, the first two notes of the descending major third motive, epsilon, are brought into the upper voice and, indeed, complete epsilon by descending to g flat^2 in the next bar (see score). However, epsilon, in its inverse transform, epsilon bar, has already contributed to the counterpoint of the passage: the cello presents its boundary interval in the form of the minor sixth b flat^1-d, the second time including the passing tone c^1. The cello then continues in the next bar with a series of three gammas as descending major sixths (see Example 24, the corresponding passage in the reprise), an instance of the minor-to-major transformation, which thus links the two motives, epsilon and gamma.

In Example 1, we see that motive theta is also a participant in the second subject as the octave figure in the viola. This is effectively an inner-voice B flat (dominant) pedal. In fact, the pivotal role of B flat in the passage is underscored by the relation between epsilon bar and epsilon here: epsilon is an inversion of epsilon bar about B flat as axis pitch class.

In Example 2, from the developmental episode (Overview of Form), alpha is set out against its reverse transform, alpha prime. While this may be regarded as a voice exchange, and, indeed, is so marked on the example, surely the interaction of the two forms of the motive is the most basic musical occurrence here. Associated with alpha prime in the first violin is

Example 1. Bars 35–6

Example 2. Bars 45–6

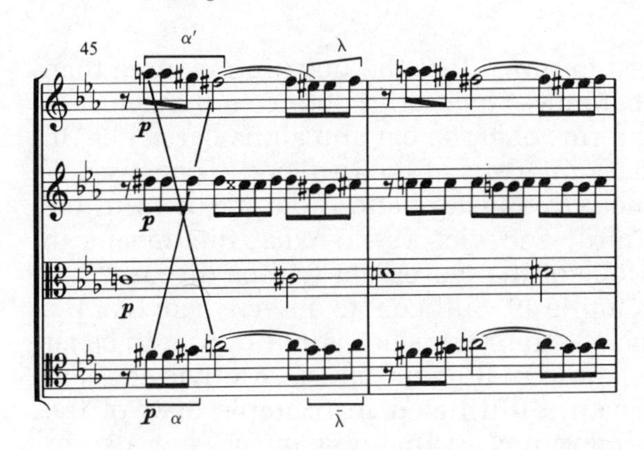

lambda, pitch-class specific with respect to bar 9, just as was lambda in Example 1. Lambda bar in the cello is also a significant pitch-class form of the motive, for it refers directly to the climactic motion in the upper voice of bar 129 (Example 21). It seems gratuitous to say that Brahms was always attentive to particular pitch classes, and I only do so to point up the importance of pitch class with respect to motive, the primary focus of this essay.

Example 3 illustrates two general aspects of Brahms's music: (1) the development of associations between initially distinct motives; and (2) motivic counterpoint. Here epsilon bar in the first violin unfolds in quasi-imitation against alpha bar and alpha bar prime in the second violin and the cello. Only a slight

Example 3. Bars 70–3

reduction is required to reveal that the imitation is more than 'quasi,' for epsilon bar moves in a series of three minims just as do the interlocking forms of alpha bar and alpha bar prime. In this way the boundary intervals of the two motives are associated. In terms of motivic transformation, the major third becomes the minor third, and vice versa. What this means in terms of other portions of the movement will be discussed in connection with Example 19. Suffice it to observe here that the minor-major and major-minor transformations appear to be far from trivial manipulations in Brahms's music. Motivic counterpoint, the second feature illustrated in Example 3, is of the utmost significance, not only in Brahms's music, but also in much of later nineteenth-century music altogether: the components of contrapuntal passages are often motivic in nature and not arbitrary collections of notes.

Example 4, from the beginning of the reprise, offers a particularly striking instance of motivic association. Whereas beta originally succeeded alpha in the first subject (b. 1), here, in its manifestation as beta bar prime, it precedes alpha. Again, the basis of association is rhythmic, specifically through the dotted crotchet-quaver figure. The association continues into bars 137–8, where both motives receive the three semibreve pattern, again in rhythmic canon. A further association becomes evident when one considers the boundary intervals of beta and epsilon, minor sixth and major third, respectively. The boundary intervals of epsilon and alpha have already been linked, as shown in connection with Example 3; now beta is associated with alpha (and epsilon).

Perhaps the strongest initial presentation of motive beta occurs at the end of the first phrase of the first subject (Example 5). Here again is a rhythmic canon involving the succession of three semibreves. The upper component of the canon is an arpeggiation of an A flat triad, while the lower component, beamed in Example 5, is beta bar prime, in exactly the pitch-class form in which it appears at the beginning of the reprise (Example 4). Moreover, this form of beta bar prime is pitch-class specific to the bass figure at the beginning of the Romanze of this quartet. Why Brahms chose to repeat beta bar prime there will be explained at the end of this essay.

Against beta bar prime in the upper part, beta bar unfolds in the bass, in breve (i.e., full-bar) values. Here the motivic counterpoint involves a single motive, beta.

Example 4. Bars 133–7

Example 5. Bars 5–6

Example 6 shows beta bar prime again, with its tail note in the first violin, b flat[2] reinstating that important middleground pitch from the beginning of bar 53. (In the reprise b flat[2] is replaced by g[2], the primary melodic tone of the movement.) Equally important at this point in the music is the bass motion A flat-G, motive lambda in pitch-class specific form with respect to its climactic occurrence at the end of the first part of the first subject (Example 9).

Example 6. Bars 53–4

The fact that I have given only examples of beta bar and not beta in the music does not imply that the former is of greater importance than the latter – since beta appears with every statement of the first subject – it is only intended to emphasize the notion that transformations of motives are as viable as original forms.

In general, gamma is reserved for special moments in the music, notably in the first subject, where it originally occurred. It is also strongly linked to two pitch-class representations: E flat-F sharp (G flat) and A flat-B. Example 7 shows what is perhaps its most striking appearance in the movement, in the cello, bars 29–30. It is at this point that the key of the second subject, E flat minor, is prepared. Since gamma plays such a crucial role and, in particular, since F sharp of the original statement in bar 2 has now become G flat, it is not difficult to conclude that the original gamma foreshadowed, in a very specific way, the large-scale tonal reorientation effected when the E flat minor of the second subject arrives. This general idea – which is, of course, Schenkerian in its theoretical origin – that foreground events can influence events of larger scale is amply

Example 7. Bars 29–31

demonstrated in other sections of the music, as will be shown.

In Example 7 the close relation between gamma (in the cello) and lambda bar (in the first violin) is strongly suggested, but in Example 8, where gamma occurs in its A flat-B form, the relation is unequivocal, since the upward motion of gamma bar from b^2 to a flat^3 through successive forms of alpha culminates on lambda bar, here pitch specific with respect to its first occurrence (Example 9).

Example 8. Bars 229–32

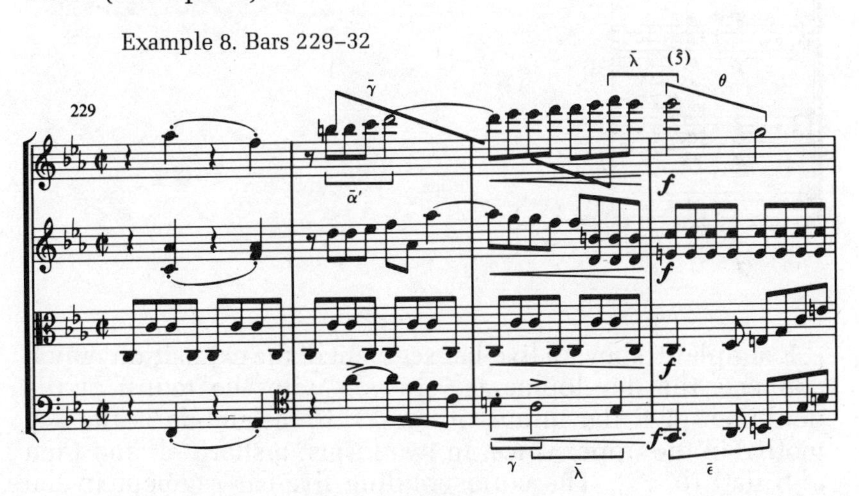

Instances of Motive Lambda

The role of lambda and lambda bar in the second subject has already been discussed in connection with Example 2. Its position at the end of the first phrase of the first subject was also mentioned, but Example 9 offers a closer look. Two additional factors are of importance. First, the register in which lambda occurs is significant throughout as the register of structural climax – in particular, bars 125–9 in the development section, where lambda and lambda bar combine on the pitches g sharp^3-a^3 finally to define the apex pitch a^3, an event of very special significance in the music. In bar 7 (Example 9) lambda is the motive which introduces the *Kopfton* of the movement, g^3, and thus the motive is directly connected to the fundamental structure of the work. The second factor of importance in Example 9 is the relation between lambda and theta at this crucial moment: the onset of theta in the viola coincides exactly with the termination of lambda bar. Moreover, theta then initiates a large-scale linear progression (not shown in any of the examples) which incorporates the second part of the first subject, descending through delta prime, ultimately reaching c^1 in bar 23 (Example 23), just as the first subject returns in the bass.

Example 9. Bar 7

Example 10 shows a five-bar segment of the exposition which connects the developmental episode with the return of the dominant of E flat minor in bar 53. Here lambda is the key motive in the upper voice, in two forms: g sharp^2-a^2 and then a^2-b flat^2 (b. 53). The corresponding five-bar segment in the reprise is also shown in Example 10, aligned with its counterpart in the exposition. Now lambda is first e sharp^2-f sharp^2, then f sharp^2-g^2. In this latter, culminative position it is once again directly attached to the *Kopfton* of the movement. Moreover, its inverse, F sharp-F, forms the bass progression which leads to the $^4_2$ that supports the *Kopfton* g^2, a telling instance of motivic counterpoint involving a single motive. And again Brahms enhances the return to the dominant by reintroducing motive beta bar prime in bars 53 and 194, as indicated in the example.

Example 10. Bars 49–53 and 190–4

Ex. 10 (*cont.*)

As a final instance of motive lambda, Example 11 shows the return of the first subject, now in E flat minor, at the beginning of the last part of the closing section of the exposition. Here lambda bar is in counterpoint with alpha and the two motives join on the octave G flat, to form theta. This beautiful confluence of motives dramatizes the motivic origin of the E flat minor key, which was mentioned earlier. It also heightens the central role of alpha. What was apparent in the first subject in its C-minor form is even more strongly presented here, namely, motive alpha in expanded form as it moves from the low E flat to g flat at the top of the ascending motion (b. 76). At that point another motive comes into play, sigma. Again, I postpone discussion of that motive until an appropriate moment.

Example 11. Bars 75–6

In Example 12 we see motive theta in the first violin, theta and theta bar to be precise. It enters exactly within sigma, the vertical designated by the up arrow on the example, and remains fixed while gamma, lambda, and beta enter below as part of the first subject in the bass. Not shown in Example 12 is the structure of larger scale that theta builds, beginning from bar 24, that is, a descending linear progression that spans a fourth: a large-scale replica of delta prime.

Theta in the viola part of Example 13 is reversed with respect to its appearance in Example 12: the upward contour precedes the downward. Brahms distinguishes between the two patterns throughout, with the upward-downward pattern always signalling the approach of the second subject, as here in part 2 of the development.

Example 12. Bar 24

Example 13. Bars 96–8

In bar 143 of the reprise, shown in Example 14, theta reappears in its basic guise as a simultaneously stated octave. Here, however, the reprise differs from the exposition: the line that departs from g[1] in the viola continues downward until it reaches g in bar 151. At that point the second part of the first subject commences, and motive lambda enters in the inner voice. Thus, motive theta has been prolonged by the octave line, 'composed out', in Schenkerian terms. Also of interest is the fact that motive theta is succeeded by lambda in the inner parts, an event which occurs elsewhere (e. g., in Example 13) and which suggests a kind of motivic progression.

In bar 176, the beginning of the second subject in the reprise (Example 15), theta comprises g and g[1], thus pitch specific with respect to its first appearance in bar 8. This is also exactly the octave that was composed out in bars 143–51 (Example 14).

Example 14. Bars 143–51

Example 15. Bars 176–7

At the beginning of the coda (Example 16) theta has completed its many peregrinations and ended up in the lowest octave of the quartet, the cello's great C to c. Above this ostinato figure is a motivic panoply of some complexity. The new figure in the viola, bars 226–7, comprises beta prime (a rather rare occurrence of that form of beta), followed by gamma bar and lambda bar. In this configuration, Brahms places accents on a flat^1 and a flat, highlighting that pitch within beta prime and lambda bar, a clear reference to the important thematic function of that pitch class at the end of the first subject in the exposition (Example 9) and elsewhere throughout the movement (Examples 4, 5, 8).

Example 16. Bars 224–7

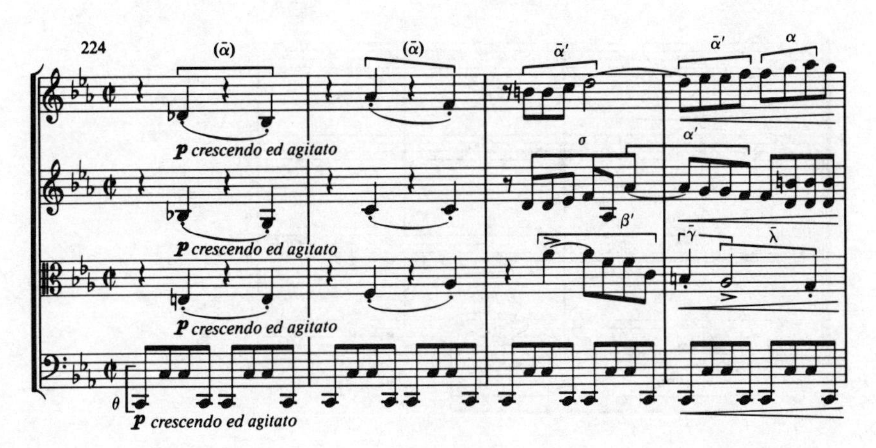

As mentioned earlier, delta is a motive that originates in the middleground of the first subject. Indeed, its main occurrences are in the middleground, often in the reverse transform, delta prime. These will be displayed later on as part of the analysis of middleground representations of motives.

Example 17 shows delta in its major foreground appearance as the melody of the second part of the first subject in the exposition. The boundary interval of a perfect fourth is preserved, but the internal structure, as given in the Table of Motives, is altered. Specifically, a passing tone is omitted, which reveals the second dyad to be lambda bar, as indicated in the example: a flat^1-g, a pitch-class specific form with respect to lambda bar in bar 7 (Example 9). Moreover, delta prime in this setting is pitch specific with respect to its middleground progenitor in bars 2–5, the boundary interval of which is formed by g^1 and c^2.

Example 17. Bars 15–21

Other motivic features of the second part of the first subject are shown in Example 17. In particular I draw attention to the arpeggiations in the second violin, bars 16 and 18. In both cases the interval of the major sixth expresses gamma, while the arpeggiation suggests beta and sigma, as indicated by the Greek letters in parentheses. In bars 19–21 lambda is set out in expanded form in the bass, incorporating epsilon bar. In counterpoint to this is delta, now with boundary pitches b^1-f $sharp^1$. The pitch class F sharp is of singular importance to the movement, as suggested earlier, since it foreshadows the E flat minor tonality of the second subject in the exposition. Here it appears just before the return of the first subject in the bass (b. 23).

Motive epsilon is the first motion in the bass, from c to A flat (Example 18). In this capacity it carries the progression from tonic to submediant, the A flat harmony which is to assume so many important functions in the music.

Example 18. Bars 4–5

Perhaps the most remarkable event involving epsilon is the metamorphosis which it undergoes at the beginning of the closing subject in the reprise (Example 19). There, counterpointed by alpha bar and alpha bar prime, it appears, prolonged, in its inverse form in the first violin. The change is unmistakable: c^3-d^3-e^3 is exactly analogous to alpha's C-D-E flat. That is, epsilon has become the minor-to-major transformation of motive alpha, and the presence of alpha as counterpoint in this passage only enhances the relation between the two motives, both now represented by their inverse forms.

The significance of motive sigma will be revealed during the forthcoming discussion. However, a particularly beautiful example in the foreground cannot be overlooked, namely bars 107 and 109 in the development (Example 20). There sigma is

Example 19. Bars 212–15

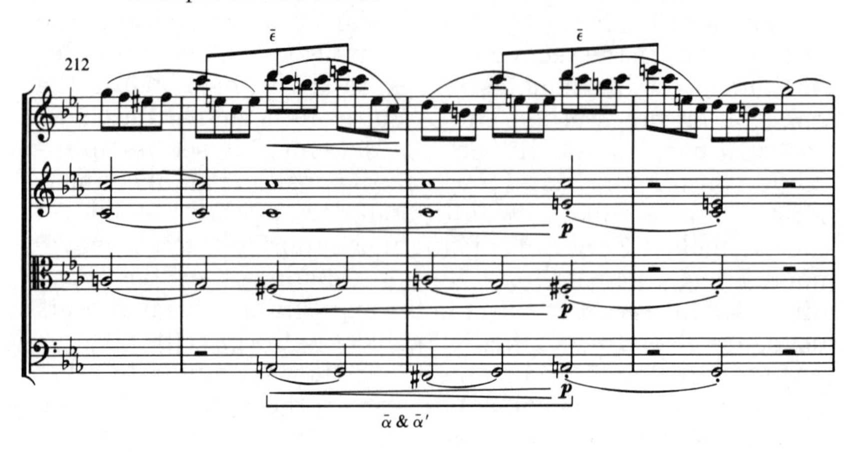

Example 20. Bars 107–10

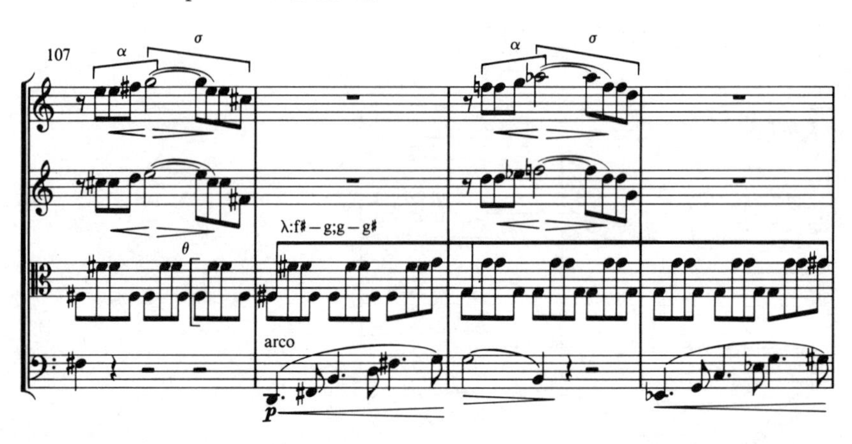

attached to the motive of the second subject – in this instance expressed as alpha, since the motives of the first and second subjects are completely interchangeable in the development. Sigma thus replaces lambda bar as the consequent motive of the second subject (Example 1). Motive lambda, however, unfolds in the same context, as indicated in Example 20. Motive theta is carried by the viola here, but theta is in the service of lambda: f sharp-g and g-g sharp, a chromatic motion that finally culminates on a^3, the climax of the development in bar 129. It is important to recognize that the chromatic motion is motivic, not arbitrary chromatic motion.

Perhaps the most remarkable aspect of the motivic design of this music is the occurrence of several motives as middleground (prolonged) structures. Of these, alpha is the most interesting and immediately apparent. The interval of alpha, specifically the minor third from c^3 to a^2 (alpha bar or alpha prime), dominates the music from bar 84 to bar 92, after the beginning of the development. Alpha prime is also lucidly presented in the upper voice of bars 151–7, part 2 of the first subject in the reprise.

Example 21 shows two long-range forms of alpha, first in the bass beginning in bar 118 and then in the upper voice beginning in bar 122. The double counterpoint in the octave which relates these two passages thus assumes a special motivic significance, as do voice exchanges, and is not merely an academic contrapuntal device. I would like to remark here that its F sharp minor cast, within the framework of A major, was foreshadowed by the developmental episode that began in the reprise at bar 45.

Example 21. (Bars 92–129)

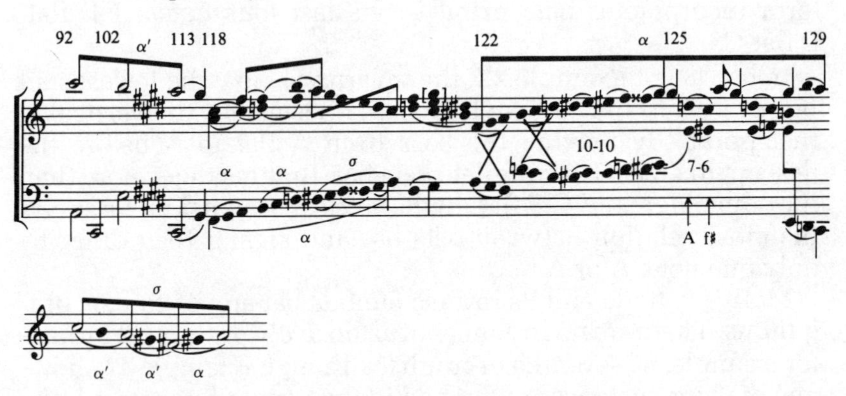

The first alpha in Example 21, in the bass, unfolds in a perfectly straightforward way, traversing the tenth from F sharp to a, exactly the way in which alpha occurs in expanded form in the first subject. However, it is prolonged by stepwise detail, two forms of alpha in the small followed by more than a hint of sigma.

The second alpha in Example 21 is presented in a far more elaborate fashion. The counterpoint is modified, so that the lower voice now exchanges with the upper, just as it did in the developmental episode at bar 45. More important, the upper voice now arrives on the middleground passing note g $sharp^2$ in bar 125 and this is sustained while the harmonies below it change its meaning from scale degree 7 in A to scale degree 2 in F sharp minor until E is taken up by the bass just before bar 129 and descends through D to C sharp, at which point the upper voice completes alpha, arriving on the climactic note A in the final music of the development.

The small illustration below Example 21 is a schematic to show how concatenation of forms of alpha during the development sets out a concealed form of motive sigma, a motivic relationship which is exemplified elsewhere in the movement and which has a special significance, as suggested earlier.

Motive beta is prominent in the foreground of the reprise (Example 22). It also occurs in prolonged form as beta bar in the bass, extending from bar 137 to bar 141, when the entire motive is repeated in contracted form from a flat down to great C, a motion which is temporally coextensive with beta in the first violin's self-contained canon. Not only does beta occur in this intensive way in the passage, but also its relation to delta is made manifest. As shown by the bracket beginning on the last bass note of bar 139 (Example 22) beta bar in this composed-out form incorporates beta prime as its last four notes: F-E flat-D flat-C.

In bar 138 of Example 22, the up arrow below the lowest staff points to A in the cello, while sigma designates the vertical at that point. By moving the bass from A flat to A before the descent to great C to complete beta bar, Brahms does more than introduce sigma, A-C-E flat, in the vertical dimension: he shows the close relation between beta bar and sigma; they differ by only one note, A or A flat.

Motive lambda and its inverse lambda bar are, of course, ubiquitous. There are no instances of extensively prolonged forms – for example, as sevenths or ninths, although Example 17 shows one of many instances of lambda in the deeper foreground (the cello). However, there are telling instances of half-step voice-leading which surely refer to this motive in a nontrivial way. For example, in bars 112–17 of the development section, the dyad A-G sharp foreshadows lambda bar in the upper voice as it leads to the climax of the development beginning in bar 125 (Example 21).

Theta has already been shown as it is composed out through an octave descent (Example 14). In bars 178–85 another octave descent occurs, this time in the upper voice. However, its structural integrity is broken by background functions – in particular, by the occurrence in the middle of the line of the primary melodic tone g^2, as shown in Example 24.

Motive delta comprises perhaps the most important middle-ground motion in the work and occurs many times, sometimes

Example 22. Bars 133–43

without the internal structure of the motive as shown in the Table of Motives. The beamed stems in the first violin part in Example 23 mark the progress of delta prime as it descends from e flat³ in bar 24 to its completion on b flat² in bar 30. Here the terminal note of the progression is the head note of the second subject, and, in the corresponding passage in the reprise, it is the primary melodic tone, G.

Motive delta, pitch-class specific with respect to its initial occurrence, also unfolds in the bass of Example 23, beginning on G in bar 24 and ascending to C in bar 27, the latter pitch a participant in motive beta bar prime.

Example 24 shows how delta prime organizes the foreground of the consequent phrase of the second subject in the reprise, which incorporates alpha prime and epsilon. Perhaps even

Example 23. Bars 22–31

more interesting is the motivic relation between gamma and delta which this passage reveals. Beginning in the bass of bar 178 three sequential statements of gamma, associated with the three semibreves rhythmic motive, are followed by a stepwise form of gamma bar, from F to D (Example 24). Within this latter motion occurs delta, pitch-class specific with respect to its initial form.

Example 25 presents two successive unfoldings of the almost-delta motive, that is, forms of delta which in internal organization do not correspond to the original statement of the motive. Both are marked '4-prg.' in Schenkerian fashion in the example. The second delta, beginning in bar 198, is embedded in a linear intervallic pattern of the 10–7 variety, and the music becomes very exuberant by virtue of the pitch-rhythmic canon involving the three semibreves pattern. The passage ends with the melodic dyad C-D, which, as indicated, is the first dyad of alpha. There follows a section of considerable complexity, the motivic constituents of which will be very evident to the reader who has followed the analytical argument this far.

Finally, the appropriate moment to elucidate motive sigma has arrived. Sigma, the musical emblem of the first movement of the first string quartet, which Brahms certainly regarded as a signal achievement, is, in its primal form, composed of the pitches A-C-E flat – that is, C and A as in Clara, and Es as in Schumann.

This symbolic structure is expressed in many nontrivial ways in the music, perhaps most strikingly in the key relations C minor, as first subject, E flat minor as second subject, and A major/minor as the main tonality of the development. The A-minor tonality is also interjected with great urgency and with a corresponding break in the continuity of the music to form the developmental episode to which I have referred several times.

Foreground examples of sigma can be found everywhere in the movement, although not all have motivic significance. Those labelled in the examples previously discussed will serve to illustrate the point, and I refer the reader to Examples 3, 11, 12, 13, 20, 21, and 23 for further consideration of musical factors attending the appearance of this emblem.

Not only sigma as an entity but also its pitch-class components have striking roles in the music.[3] The highest note

3. There are, of course, other references to letter names associated with friends of Brahms which appear in his music. In the first movement of the G major Sextet Op. 36, bars 162–8, occurs the sequence A-G-A-H-E, a reference to Agathe von Siebold. And at the beginning of the A minor String Quartet Op. 51 No. 2, the first subject presents A-F-A-E, a reference to Joachim's motto, 'frei aber einsam'.

Example 24. Bars 178–86

Example 25. Bars 194–204

before the reprise, for instance, is b^3 in bar 129, which leads to the climactic a^3, the goal of the middleground progression shown in Example 21. Moreover, the sigma structure explains, in a motivic way, certain of the otherwise enigmatic tonalities. In particular, the strong references to F sharp minor at several points – notably in the passage shown in Example 21 – with corresponding melodic motions involving F sharp and A appear to reflect the extension of the C-E flat-A structure to include F sharp, forming the diminished seventh chord with its four forms of sigma.

Corresponding to the pitch motive sigma, in the programmatic sense, is the rhythmic motive composed of three semibreves. This motive is associated with beta bar prime, initially in bars 5–6 and most importantly in the reprise at bars 137–8 (Examples 4, 22). Now, beta bar prime is almost like sigma, as noted earlier. This is why Brahms brings back the programmatic beta bar prime at the beginning of the reprise: it refers to sigma. Similarly, this is why beta bar prime occurs at the beginning of the second movement. The Romanze, however Brahms may have interpreted this programmatic title, begins with a concealed reference to Clara.

This essay has attempted to show that motivic design and structural levels are intimately related in the music of Brahms. In particular, a motive is not restricted to a foreground role, but may extend into the middleground level of a composition.

Motives have multiple meanings and associations, depending upon context. When they interact, motives may exhibit resemblances to other motives. As a particularly striking case, one motive may contain another.

Pitch and pitch class are of special importance to the study of motivic design. In the work which is the subject of this analysis specific pitch classes and dyads serve throughout to initiate motions, to terminate them, and to refer to musical events already completed or forthcoming. Although this feature is by no means restricted to the music of Brahms, the elegance and subtlety with which Brahms negotiates motivic relations leave him without peer.

CHRISTOPHER WINTLE

The 'Sceptred Pall': Brahms's progressive harmony

I

My title[1] brings together the words of two musicians who have made seminal contributions to Brahms studies. 'Gorgeous tragedy in sceptred pall' was the epithet applied by Sir Donald Francis Tovey to one of the pieces I shall be discussing in this essay, the Sonata in E minor Op. 38 for Piano and Violoncello.[2] Of course, the term 'tragedy' used in this context would have had a special appeal to Tovey's puritanical temperament, which enjoyed imputing to passages of Brahms's chamber music a greater dramatic intensity than anything it could find in Wagner. But the darkness and high seriousness of 'sceptred pall' had some parallel in the nature of the dramatic texts kept in the theatre-lover Brahms's personal library: Michael Musgrave[3] lists Sophocles, Shakespeare, Goethe and Schiller, F.M. Klinger, A.W. Schlegel and Ibsen. Schoenberg, too, was conscious of the dramatic nature of Brahms's music. In singling out harmony as the dimension most appropriate to frame a discussion of the 'progressive' aspects of Brahms's musical language, he attributed to it nothing less than the capacity to revitalize music-drama (and this from Schoenberg in 1947).[4]

I am not proposing to open up yet again this traditional issue of Wagner *versus* Brahms: in any case, recent attempts to draw parallels where previously only oppositions had been found – and one thinks principally of the writings of Carl Dahlhaus[5] –

1 I am especially indebted to Paul Banks, William Drabkin, Jonathan Dunsby, H. Diack Johnstone and Siegfried Kross, for suggesting improvements that have been incorporated in the text.

2 D.F. Tovey, 'Brahms's Chamber Music', *Essays and Lectures in Music* (London, 1949) 246.

3 See 'The cultural world of Brahms' in *Brahms: Biographical, Documentary and Analytical Studies*, ed. Robert Pascall (Cambridge, 1983) 7.

4 Arnold Schoenberg, 'Brahms the Progressive', in *Style and Idea: Selected Writings*, ed. Leonard Stein, with tr. by Leo Black (London, 1975) 439–41.

5 As for example in: C. Dahlhaus, *Between Romanticism and Modernism: Four Studies in the Music of the Later Nineteenth Century*, tr. Mary Whittall (Berkeley and London, 1980). For further commentary on this see: C. Wintle, 'Issues in Dahlhaus', *Music Analysis*, 1/3 (1982).

have offered the more stimulating line of approach. Yet Schoenberg's concerns, which, like Tovey's, are not necessarily opposed to more modern ones, are too thought-provoking to be left as relatively unexplored as they still are, not least because they pose interesting problems. Michael Musgrave,[6] for example, is surely right to query some of Schoenberg's analyses (and not only of Brahms), just as Jonathan Dunsby[7] is also right to ask how Brahms's harmony may be thought 'progressive', when each example is related so conscientiously to classical precedent; here, Schoenberg the analyst seems to be projecting onto Brahms's music the anxieties that Schoenberg the composer felt about his own. Then, as far as Tovey is concerned, James Webster[8] has demonstrated how secure a foundation his writings can provide for more detailed investigation, while leaving his central claim that 'thematic organization can no more build Wagnerian music-drama or Brahmsian symphonies than tracery, mouldings, and stained glass can build cathedrals'[9] with still more to be said about the nature of the main edifice.

As is well known, Webster's articles amplify Tovey's observation that 'upon Brahms the influence of Schubert is far greater than the combined influences of Bach and Beethoven'[10] and I shall pursue this point in due course. For the moment, let us turn back to Schoenberg.

In *Style and Idea* two approaches are offered to Brahms's 'immensely advanced harmony'. The first[11] takes as its starting point the opening of the last movement of Beethoven's Quartet in E minor Op. 59 No. 2. Schoenberg comments not only upon the tonality here, which fluctuates between C major and E minor, but notes the meaningful contradiction between the destabilizing effect of the harmony, and the stabilizing demands of form at this point. 'I could cite many such instances in Beethoven, Brahms, and other masters', he writes, 'where, in an extremely fine and ingenious manner, the ambiguity, that is, the indefiniteness of a key, is made apparent.' To discuss this issue has become a commonplace of Brahms criticism, and in what is to follow, the theme of ambiguity *per se* is only secon-

[6] M. Musgrave, 'Schoenberg and Brahms: A study of Schoenberg's response to Brahms's music as revealed in his didactic writings and selected early compositions', unpublished PhD dissertation, University of London, 1980.

[7] J. Dunsby, *Structural Ambiguity in Brahms* (Ann Arbor, 1981) 88.

[8] J. Webster, 'Schubert's sonata form and Brahms's first maturity', *19th-Century Music*, 2/1 (1978–9) 18–35 and 3/1 (1979–80) 52–71.

[9] Tovey, 'Brahms's Chamber Music', 240.

[10] 'Tonality in Schubert' in D.F. Tovey, *Essays and Lectures in Music* (London, 1949) 151.

[11] 'Problems of Harmony' in A. Schoenberg, *Style and Idea*, 275.

dary to the other theme,[12] which deals with tonal and harmonic events related by a semitone. This is the concern of the essay 'Brahms the Progressive'. Schoenberg draws his examples from J.S. Bach (*St Matthew Passion*). Beethoven again (the openings of the String Quartets Op. 59 No. 2 in E minor and Op. 95 in F minor), Schubert (a B minor harmony leading to a B flat major one in the song 'In der Ferne') and Wagner (two examples, both including Neapolitan moves, from *Tristan*). These he relates, first, to an example of passing chromatic harmony, and second to a modulation by a semitone, in two extracts from Brahms's C minor String Quartet Op. 51 No.1. That these are unsatisfactory examples should not blind us to the fact that the principles they are intended to demonstrate are indeed representative, or that the example he cites in *Structural Functions of Harmony*[13] is an important one:

In the 'Cello Sonata in F major, Op. 99, one is surprised to find the second movement in F+major, only to discover later that F major and f minor are contrastingly connected with F+(G♭) major and f+minor in all four movements. What makes these Brahms examples so striking is that most of them do not occur in *Durchführungen* but in places where 'establishing' conditions exist – in regions, that is.

Here, Schoenberg integrates all four movements of the work through harmonic moves that involve not only Neapolitan relations, but also the duality offered by the tonic major/minor alternation. And the tendency of the rest of 'Brahms the Progressive' is to integrate the discussion of harmony with that of other dimensions – especially form, theme, phrase, motive, questions of 'basic shape', and even, where appropriate, word-setting. Yet this is not a tendency peculiar to this essay; in a discussion of Schoenberg's treatment of Brahms's symphonies, Michael Musgrave remarks interestingly:

The case for 'thematic key relationships', to borrow Réti's term, becomes much stronger if one can observe significant key relationships as emanating from themes which exploit particular intervals or are characterized by one individual interval, significantly placed. A case can be made in (the Fourth Symphony) op. 98 for a relationship between the falling third, the role of which has been shown in the first

12 Ambiguity, of this and other kinds, is discussed in most of the sources cited in this article (including Tovey). Other interesting discussions take place in: David Epstein, *Beyond Orpheus: Studies in Musical Structure* (Cambridge, Mass., and London, 1979) and also in: Jean-Jacques Nattiez, *Fondemonts d'une sémiologie de la musique*, 10/8 (Paris, 1975).

13 Arnold Schoenberg, *Structural Functions of Harmony*, rev. edn., ed. Leonard Stein (London, 1969) 73.

subjects of the first and second movements, and the tonal scheme of the work, whose limitation is itself striking: E minor – E major – C major – E minor, with a particular exploitation of the pattern at the end of the slow movement.[14]

Example 1 recalls not only the Phrygian opening of the movement, but brings together the two approaches to Brahms's harmony that have been observed in *Style and Idea*: on the one hand, the E/C relationship and on the other, the colouring of E by F major and minor.

Example 1. Fourth Symphony Op. 98, end of slow movement

It is tempting at this point to review those other, no less important, features of Brahms's harmony mentioned by Musgrave: the roving harmony, the archaizing modes, the mixed modality, the play between incidental and structural chromaticism, the 'prolific exploitation of multiple meanings of harmonies'[15] (augmented triads and diminished sevenths especially), and so forth. But I shall resist this, and turn instead to Tovey and Webster.

In fact, there is a great deal in Webster's writings that parallels that of Schoenberg, most strikingly when the large-scale tonal events of an entire work are related to a motive prominent at its beginning: the discussion of the role of the relationship D flat-C established in the first movement of the F minor Piano Quintet is just such a case.[16] But the Tovey-inspired investigation of the influence of Schubert (balancing Schoenberg's of Beethoven) opens up new vistas. Here is how Webster sums up what he considers Brahms learned from Schubert in the handling of sonata forms: 'juxtaposition of major and minor, the impulse towards lyrical breadth and closed forms, the double second group, the structural use of remote keys, and the transformation of these

[14] Musgrave, *Schoenberg and Brahms. . .*, 203–4.

[15] A. Schoenberg, *Fundamentals of Musical Composition*, ed. G. Strang and L. Stein (London, 1967) 30.

[16] The examples in this paragraph are all taken from Webster, 'Schubert's Sonata Forms. . .'.

elements in the recapitulation'; and Schubert, no less than Brahms, 'uses the first significant tonal event in a movement to generate key relationships – and hence form – on the largest scale'. Without denying the terms of this influence, it is important to remember, if we are to accept Webster's conclusion (which follows Mitschka's) that Brahms integrated these Schubertian features 'into a coherent large-scale sonata-form exposition in a manner that more nearly recalls Beethoven', that all these features may be found together in Beethoven, too. In the first movement of the D major Piano Sonata Op. 28, for example, there is an extraordinary lyric breadth to the themes; there is a double second group, comprising an F sharp minor and an A major tonality (cf. Brahms's Second Symphony); the first tonal event (the dominant seventh of IV, D-F sharp-A-C natural, at bar 2) not only links first and second groups by being reinterpreted as an augmented sixth leading to an F sharp minor six-four chord, an ambivalence exploited again (under transposition) in the development, but also colours the other movements as well; at the close of the development, the retransition (such as it is) is initiated by a striking change from a B major to a B minor chord; and so forth. Evidently, there are other, equally important things that Brahms must have learned from Schubert. And, indeed, some of these Webster airs.

That Schubert's lyricism, and his incorporation of closed forms (such as ABA) into sonata structures, created, as Webster describes it, a 'disassociation' between the 'passive' demands of song and the dynamic, dramatic demands of classical form, and that Schubert was only partially successful in resolving the problems raised by this disassociation, is a familiar theme, but one that, for present purposes, may be focused into a single question: if the germinal idea of a sonata movement (and other movements too) that effects the drama by including pregnant and even disruptive elements is incompatible with lyric material, how (if at all) can it make its presence known? Schubert's answer was: in the subsidiary sections, which assume a new importance; in transitions, extensions, introductions, and codas. The opening of the B flat major piano sonata of 1828 offers a well-known example of this, and turns disassociation to powerful expressive effect. The opening lyrical eight bars are extended to a ninth to permit the addition of the F/trilled G flat in the bass; and this G flat, as has often been pointed out, forms the catalyst for the central part of the ABA structure that comprises the first group, and for much else besides. In another well-known example, 'Der Lindenbaum' from *Die Winterreise*, the catalyst for the ferment of the central section, which contrasts the turbulent, unstable present, coloured by F minor elements, with the repose of an E major past, is an accented, reiterated passing B sharp (alias C natural, the dominant of F minor) in the piano introduction.

These instances, one involving relations by a third, the other implying one of a semitone, bring us back to Schoenberg's two approaches. But before drawing consequences from all these preliminaries, I shall pursue one of these issues, that of Neapolitan relations, a stage further, though still remaining with Webster and Tovey.

First, a formal matter. In describing how Neapolitan relations 'play an essential' role in Schubert's sonata forms, Webster writes:

> When the first part of the second group appears in ♭VI or ♭vi, the subsequent move to the dominant mimics a move from the Neapolitan (♭II) to a major tonic.

The point is easily reinforced by comparing the exposition and recapitulation of the Octet, where on repetition the double second group is restated at a fifth below, transferring the Neapolitan relation from the dominant to the tonic:

Exp: F — D flat — C
Recap: F — G flat — F
(Np — I)

(Schoenberg makes a comparable point with regard to the first movement of Brahms's F minor Piano Quintet.)[17]

Then there is Tovey's discussion of Neapolitan relations in the article 'Tonality in Schubert'. Both Schoenberg, in his Chart of the Regions,[18] and Tovey, in his Table of Key Relationships,[19] accord these relations a special place in the scheme of things. Schoenberg describes the ♭II degree as 'Indirect and Remote', but places it between the minor subdominant and the flat submediant major (in C, between F minor and A flat major), in both major and minor modes. This is refined in Tovey, who includes both Neapolitan major (in C, D flat) and minor (D flat), and complements these with an inverse Neapolitan relationship, based on the major and minor tonalities raised over the leading-note

[17] A. Schoenberg, *Structural Functions of Harmony*, 73: 'In the recapitulation, the first subordinate theme (ms. 201), which in the first division stood on *sm* (c+), ms. 35, should have been transposed to tonic minor (f). Instead it is transposed to Msm (f+).'
[18] Schoenberg, *Structural Functions of Harmony*, 20.
[19] This is laid out most clearly in 'Harmony', from the *Encyclopaedia Britannica* articles.

(VII and vii: in C major, B major and B minor). This inverse relationship, however, is both problematic and puzzling, although undeniably thought-provoking, and need concern us no further here.

Example 2. Schubert: String Quintet in C, end of second movement

More important for this discussion is the passage Tovey quotes from the coda of the slow movement of the String Quintet in C, which is reproduced as Example 2. These four bars do not merely summarize the course of the movement, but constitute its 'germ cell', or 'basic idea', stated for the first time: the formulation of the movement's 'theme' – in effect a succession of harmonies – is its goal, and not its beginning; the context in which it is presented is the coda, and not the exposition. And its substance is strikingly similar to that of Example 1, from the Brahms symphony – only here the movement from one harmony to the next involves a higher degree of ellipsis: between E major and C major is an implicit E minor; between C major and F minor (in this context) an implicit F major; and the harmony following the F minor one plays on the familiar ambiguity between dominant seventh and augmented sixth. (To return to the Schubert example from 'Brahms the Progressive': in the F minor Piano Duet, Schubert spells out the common-tone relationship between the two adjacent triads E major and F minor, pivoting on the enharmonically-related G sharp/A flat, at bars 90–1).

The idea that a complex of harmonies may form the substance of a movement is not, of course, a new one in nineteenth- and twentieth-century studies – or indeed, in eighteenth-century studies either: but not enough attention has been paid to the way Brahms adapted to various contexts, what will be described (for want of a better term) as the Neapolitan complex. This essay will begin to make good the omission. Brahms's manipulation of Neapolitan relations is extensive, and for this reason two restrictions will be imposed on the discussion, which will relate Brahms's treatment to Schubert's. First, the argument will continue the pattern of many of the examples quoted so far, and deal only with those movements in E major or minor, which invoke Neapolitan relations in F major or minor. This not merely makes comparison easy, but highlights a special attitude adopted to these tonalities by many composers in the nineteenth century (it is, of course, not the only way that Brahms approached either of these tonalities). It also recalls the traditional role of the notes E and F in the Phrygian mode. Secondly, the examples show the same dramatic extremes associated with these tonalities – between passivity and turbulence – as were found in Schubert. Of course, not all shifts from E major to F major progress to F minor, and in these cases, in Brahms as much as in Schubert (and, indeed, in many other composers besides), the F major tends to enhance, rather than to contradict, the serenity of the E major. This is the case, for example, with the slow movement of Schubert's Piano Sonata in A minor Op. 164. But the Neapolitan complex as such is concerned with the extremes invoked by E major and F minor, and from this point of view Brahms's treatment confirms Tovey's suggestion that it was the late works of Schubert that were especially influential. This influence, however, needs to be put in perspective, and the later part of this essay will suggest that both Schubert and Brahms drew upon a broader repertoire still in their handling of Neapolitan relations.

II

Both Tovey and Webster remark upon the expressive extremes of the first movement of Brahms's E minor sonata Op. 38. Tovey contrasts the 'indignant "second subject"' with the 'quiet major end' of the exposition, which is 'expanded into a pathetic coda in which the movement expires in peace'; comparably, Webster refers to the 'agitated' and 'ethereal' aspects of the music. If this recalls Schubert, then so too does Webster's observation that the exposition 'could even be considered [to contain] a triple second group if the independent transitional theme in C were counted'. And Tovey probably had in mind the expansive lyricism of the generally low-lying cello part in saying that 'the development is very broad, and is remarkable in form for using very large unbroken passages of exposition, instead of following the orthodox habit of breaking the material up'. Schoenberg,[20] on the other hand, drew attention to the concentrated

[20] Schoenberg, *Fundamentals of Musical Composition*, 79–81.

motivic working of the two principal themes, thereby indicating some of the triumphs of transformation that inform the piece as a whole.

Drama, lyricism, formal anomalies, motivic evolution: all these disparate observations may be brought together under the aegis of the Neapolitan complex. Although the significance of

Example 3. Neapolitan complex

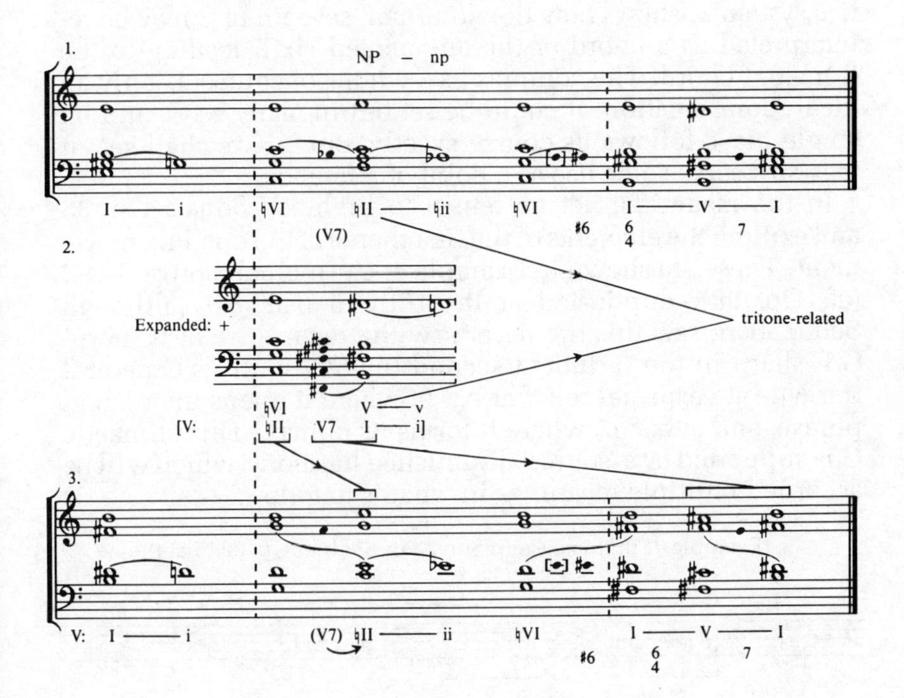

the elements of this complex will only become apparent during the course of this essay, it is useful at this stage to survey them briefly. The three parts of system 1 show: the E major/minor alternation; the ambiguous use of the C major harmony to lead, on the one hand, to F major/minor, and on the other to a return to E major, with the earlier seventh (B flat) reinterpreted as an augmented sixth A sharp; the return to E, leading to a full close (it is written here in the major although it could, of course, include minor elements, as did the first part of the system). The expansion of the complex in system 2 shows how, for example, in sonata movements, the C major harmony may itself act as Neapolitan to the dominant. This dominant (B) is a tritone away from the original Neapolitan (F) to which C led in the first system. System 3, which takes as its model system 1, and amplifies system 2, shows how the dominant seventh of C may be reinterpreted as a chord of the augmented sixth leading to the B major $^6_4$ chord. The complex as a whole, of course, is only an ideal representation: it could be set out in many ways, and no single piece follows its course exactly. But, as we shall see, it may still serve some use as a point of reference.

In the meantime, let us return to Brahms's Sonata Op. 38 and explore the elements of the first theme of the opening movement. These are shown in Example 4: a principal motive B-C-B (cf. Op. 98), duplicated at the fifth in bars 6–7 (although Schoenberg saw this, he never saw the recurrence of F sharp-G-F sharp in the turbulent second theme), with its C natural thrown into especial relief at bar 9, where it opens the second phrase, and at bar 17, where it forms its climax. This climactic C is supported by a 'source' diminished harmony, which will be accorded multiple meanings in what is to follow.

Example 4. Brahms: Cello Sonata in E minor Op. 38, first theme

Now, although the notes C and B have a Phrygian (and Neapolitan) potential, the first theme has embodied no Neapolitan elements *per se*. These, characteristically, are introduced into the traditionally subordinate counterstatement, which, reciprocally, surrenders its conventional quality of tonal instability, and becomes broadly stable within E minor. This is shown in Example 5 (this bass graph is, of course, highly selective), which also reveals that, so far, only a limited number of elements of the Neapolitan complex have been exposed: E minor, a tonicized C, and a tonicized F major. The dramatic oppositions of F minor and E major have yet to come. We have seen, from Example 3, system 2, that, in larger forms, the Neapolitan complex has to absorb, and accommodate itself to, the traditional form-defining opposition of tonic and dominant. In the transition and second group of Example 5, this absorption is shown in three ways. First, as has already been noticed, the second group projects the conflict between agitation and serenity through the transformation from B minor to B major. In the recapitulation, shown in Example 5 in the system beneath the exposition, this conflict is meaningfully duplicated in the tonic, introducing the all-important E major for the first time. Second, the relation of the C major of the transition to the B of the second group mimics, to use Webster's word, a Neapolitan approach. As with the example from Schubert's Octet, what is implicit in the exposition becomes explicit in the recapitulation, where, as the bottom stave of the system reveals, the larger Neapolitan relation of the three tonalities outlines the contour of the principal motive. Third, to return to the transition of the exposition, there is a nice example of developing variation that reveals the dual function of the C tonality: on one hand, as we have already seen, C leads to V-I in B; on the other hand, it is approached and quitted in much the same way as occurred in the counterstatement: initially it is tonicized by the two-bar extension to the counterstatement in bars 32–3, before moving on towards F in bar 42 through a B flat that is shortly reinterpreted as an A sharp (there are other fascinating enharmonic changes in this passage too).

This still leaves the F minor of the Neapolitan complex unaccounted for, and, almost inevitably, this emerges as the goal, from every point of view, of the development section. Its arrival, at bar 126, unleashes an awesome rhetorical power, as the canonic second group establishes unequivocally a tonality foreshadowed in the previous twelve bars by the heavy chromatic inflections of the underlying F major (notice the derivation of the semitonal figures from the principal motive, especially D flat-C, which stands a semitone higher from C-B). The very broad scheme of the development raises an issue that will be explored later, namely the tritone relations invoked by moving from the dominant (B) to the Neapolitan (F) and back onto the dominant for the re-transition. Brahms, in effect, derives this most anti-functional of relations from a projection on the large-

Example 5. Op. 38, first movement

EXPOSITION

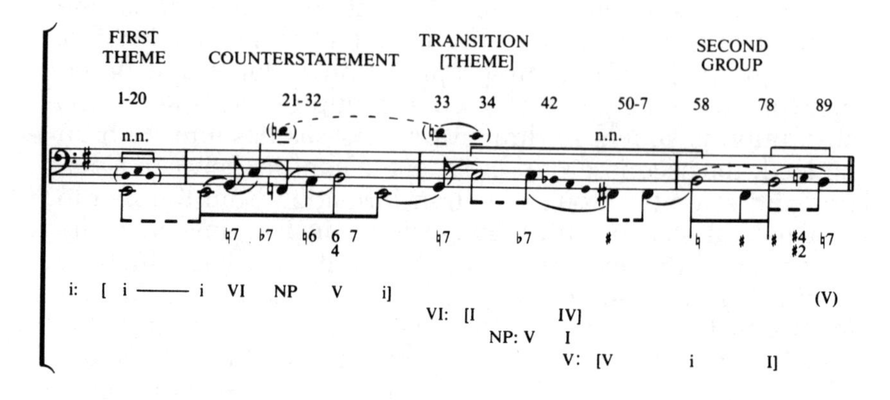

RECAPITULATION

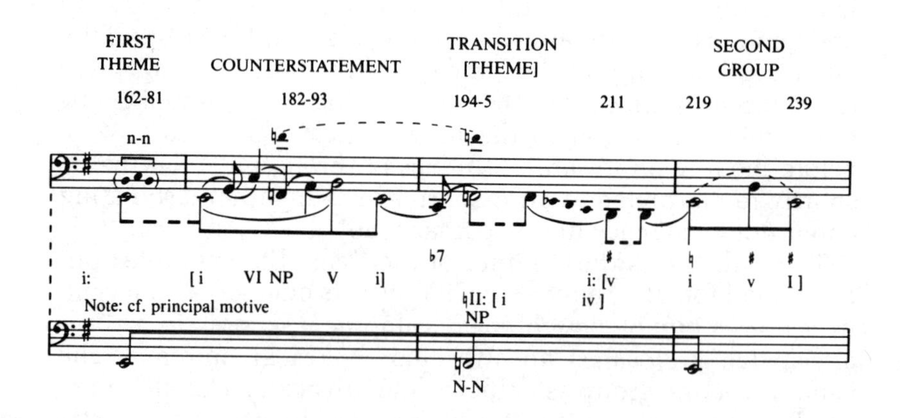

DEVELOPMENT

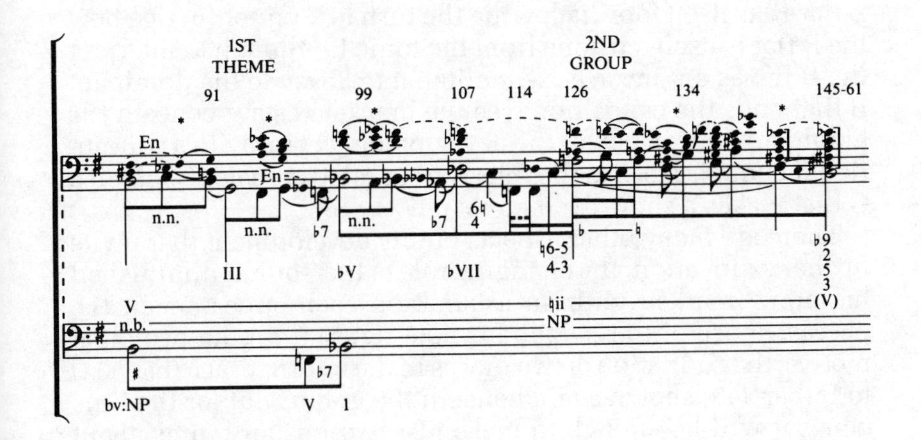

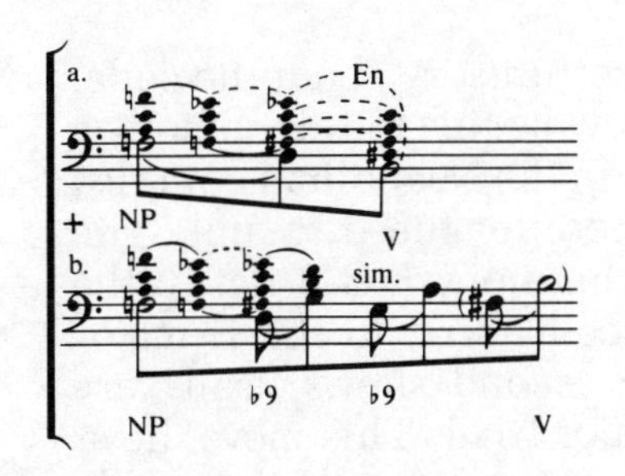

CODA

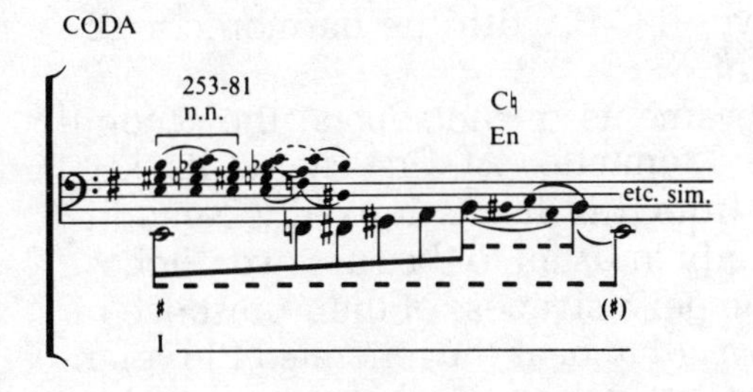

scale of the root-progression implicit in the conventional cadence involving the (linear) Phrygian second, and the (harmonic) Neapolitan sixth: ♮II-V-I. Furthermore, it would not be fanciful to see the bass arpeggiation from bars 99–126, B flat-D flat-F, as itself foreshadowing the turn to F minor (notice how the B flat is itself a tritone from the tonic E), though to interpret the B flat as an 'inverse' Neapolitan *à la Tovey* to the dominant B that ends the exposition (see the bracketed stave beneath the graph) might well be: for the development begins with a conventional enough move to the intervening relative major G, albeit a G that makes a short-lived appearance.

There are many other aspects of this development that invite further explication: the changing role of the 'source' diminished harmony (marked with an asterisk on each appearance), the pervasive use of the neighbour-note figure from the principal motive, the conflation of two moves in the return from F (bar 134) to B (bar 145) shown again beneath the graph. But for the time being it will be enough to make just two further points about this sonata.

As in Schubert, there is nothing perfunctory about the coda. On the contrary, Example 5 shows how its first moves embody a number of issues. The only element in the Neapolitan complex not included so far is introduced here for the first time. The graph shows two functions for the harmony E-G-B flat-C: the first resolves back by stepwise voice-leading to the E major triad from where it emanated; the second shows itself very locally as the dominant of the F major triad. This move, however, not only encapsulates the harmonic drama of the whole into a single aphorism – purged, one might say, of the torment of F minor – but reveals plainly and impressively the connection of the principal motive, B-C-B, with the harmonic argument of the entire movement.

There are only three movements in the sonata, the second being an Allegretto quasi Menuetto. At first sight, its key, A minor, may seem remote from this discussion of the Neapolitan complex. But one has only to listen to the first two pitches, F and E, to acknowledge the pervasiveness of their presence in the following bars, and above all to hear the reiterated Phrygian cadences, with the F-E now in the bass, to recognize how important it would be for a complete reading of this piece to follow the advice of Schoenberg and Musgrave, and search for a larger unity that embraces the entire work.

Example 6.

(a) Op. 38, second movement, bars 1–14

(b) Motivic derivation

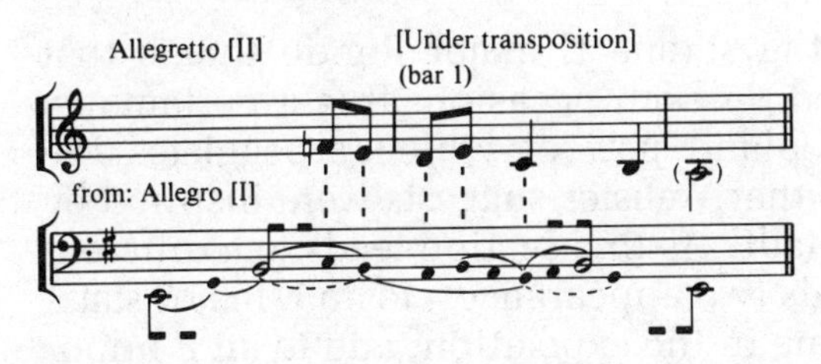

III

An essay comparing Wagner's music – drama with Brahms's 'dramatic' instrumental music might well choose the first movement of the E minor Sonata Op. 38 to illustrate Brahms's 'art of slow transition' from one expressive extreme to another. It would probably ignore the slow movement of the A major Piano Quartet Op. 26. Indeed, its elemental, sectionalized structure led Tovey into comparisons with Bruckner. But, he said, 'the difference between such masonry as of these [two piano] quartets (Op. 25 and Op. 26) and that of the proverbially *lapidarisch* Bruckner is that Brahms takes his risk in forms of lyric melody, whereas Bruckner's materials are huge Nibelungen-Ring processes'. He might also have made a further point: that the sectional structure is a rationalization of the sharply opposed states of such pieces as the slow movement of Schubert's C major String Quintet, and that the risks Brahms takes with lyricism are comparably mitigated by a dependence upon the cohesive power of the Neapolitan complex.

Let us look at this movement's clearly delineated form, which Tovey described as a 'fully developed rondo', but which may be better described as a sonata form without development and hence may be divided broadly into exposition and recapitulation:

Brahms: A Major Piano Quartet Op. 26, slow movement

Exposition					
	A	B	A	C(i)	(ii)
	1–14	15–23	24–41	42–57	58–85
	E	e	E	b	B
		unstable		unstable	
Recapitulation					
	A	B	C(i)	A	Coda
	86–99	100–8	109–26	127–40	141–55
	E	e	f	E	E
		unstable	unstable		

In this scheme, A is the serene E major Rondo theme that returns texturally varied on each occasion, B is a portentous, unstable episode, the piano part of which arpeggiates the diminished harmonies that Webster suggests were inspired by Schubert's song, 'Die Stadt'. As this section leads to a different conclusion on each of its two appearances, to an E major statement of the Rondo theme in the exposition, and to an F minor reprise of the second theme C(i) in the recapitulation, it might well have been important to Brahms that its two statements were identical. The C(i) section is, of course, the turbulent, imprecatory second theme, opening in the dominant minor, but unstable thereafter; c(ii) is a transition (and melodically a retransition) to the recapitulation that restores to the dominant the major modality necessary to effect an easy return to the Rondo theme.

Even from the formal scheme, all the tonal elements of the Neapolitan complex encountered in the E minor sonata may be seen again here: the presence, in the exposition, of E major and E minor, as well as of B major and B minor; the broad outlining of a Neapolitan relationship E-F-E in the recapitulation; and the association of the turbulent second theme with the tritonally-related poles, F minor and B minor. But there are refinements to be noticed here, which emerge by attempting to answer two questions that Tovey and Schoenberg might well have asked of this scheme: why, in the recapitulation, is the reprise of the C(i) section interpolated *within* the previously closed ABA form; and what, if any, internal logic could account for the repetition of this section in the Neapolitan, rather than in the tonic minor? These questions may be answered with reference to Example 7, again a highly selective representation of just those elements relevant to this discussion.

In the exposition, we may see at once that the stability established by the E major of the A section is undermined in the B section. Three things are important here: first, the descent through the minor tetrachord E to B in the bass, ending with the Phrygian second C-B; second, the local harmonic colouring of this Phrygian second by an F minor six-four chord resolving to its dominant C major (notice the momentary E minor six-four that links this chord with the restored E major at the return of the Rondo (A) theme); and third, a 'source' diminished harmony, marked with an asterisk. As has been seen before in this essay, it is a subordinate episode that exposes the dramatic conditions of the movement.

Two of the three features just described return in the next subordinate section, the extension to the A section at bars 38–41. This changes the modality in preparation for the B minor of the next section, C(i). In doing so, it reintroduces, first, the C-B semitone (in the upper voice of the example), and second, the descending tetrachord E to B in the bass, now with a C sharp in place of the earlier C natural.

With the C(i) section, we come to the most important part of this analysis. From bar 42 to bar 54, the bass ascends through an octave, which it divides at the tritone at bar 50. In other words,

Example 7. Piano Quartet in A major Op. 26

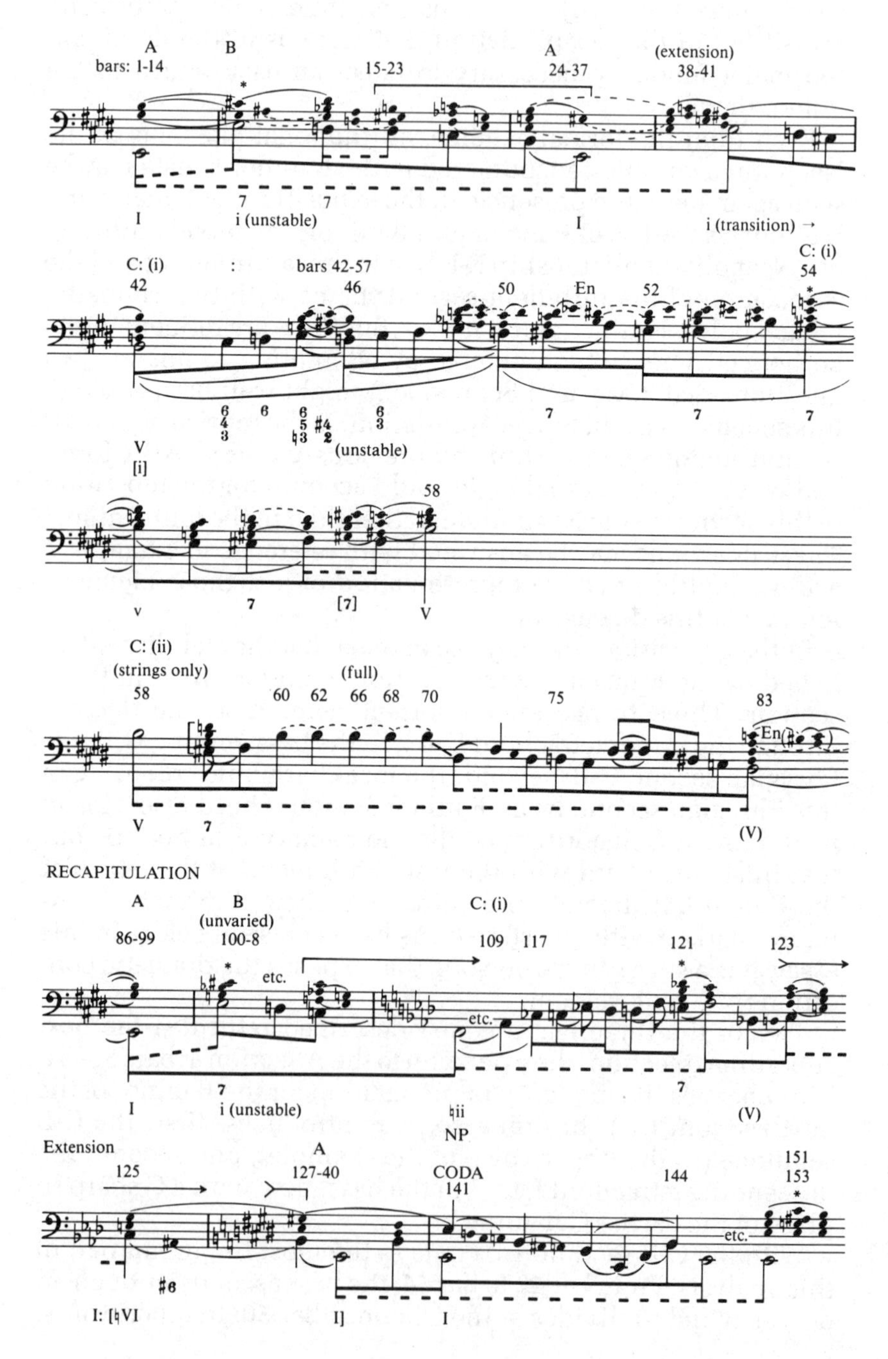

the pitches B-F assume a structural significance. At the corresponding point in the recapitulation, from bar 109 to 117, this significance becomes apparent: the bass divides the octave progression F to F at the tritone C flat, alias B. The B-F tritone relationship, at first so startling, established *between* the two C(i) sections, is in fact projected *within* each of its statements: and, as observed earlier, this tritone is an integral feature of Brahms's expanded notion of the Neapolitan complex.

At this point, it is worth remarking on the various reinterpretations of the 'source' diminished seventh, E-G-A sharp-C sharp. When it is introduced at bar 15, it leads away from the preceding E major. At bar 54, the melodic climax of the C(i) section, it leads to B minor. At the comparable point in the recapitulation, bar 121, it leads to F minor. When therefore it returns in the coda, at bars 151 and 153, it represents more than the remembrance of turbulent things past: it forms a résumé of the salient tonal events of the piece.

This discussion of the tritone and diminished elements in the music answers the second of the two questions – the tonal one – raised about the scheme of the movement. What of the other question, concerning the formal arrangement in the recapitulation? Let us approach this by taking another of the features exposed in the B section of the exposition, the Phrygian C-B, and observe its treatment in the recapitulation.

First, at the approach to the recapitulation in the C(ii) section from bar 75 to 86, the bass graph shows how Brahms mixes minor elements into the prevalent B major (he will do this again in the E major coda), most notably the C natural. This C natural is picked up again, according to expectations, in bar 108, at the end of the restated B section. If, however, we compare bar 108 and the extension to the surprisingly interpolated C(i) section, at bar 125, we may see Brahms exploiting the two functions of the C major harmony offered by the Neapolitan complex: leading, on one hand to the F minor of bar 109, and on the other, through an augmented sixth to the return of E major at bar 127. In the recapitulation, therefore, this turbulent second theme is shown as the direct outcome of what was merely episodic in the exposition. Indeed, put as dramatically as the case demands, this section is a prolongation of the bass Phrygian cadence, C-B, realizing the implication of the F minor six-four harmony first heard at the end of the B section. Form, tonality, the relation of incidental to structural chromaticism, and the Neapolitan complex, are all locked into one at this point.

As with the E minor Sonata, there are many other features

that invite further consideration. The way, for example, in the transitional C(ii) section, the diminished harmony, with E sharp in the bass, tames, so to speak, the anarchic, tritonal elements in the previous section, condensing the B-D-F-A flat of the bass line into a single diminished harmony, where the F becomes a mere tonicizing leading-note to the dominant's dominant. And the way, in C(i), the bass diminutions take up the span of a fourth from the B section, an interval that is made into the principal span of the melody. These and many other features only confirm what will be clear from the preceding analysis: that however Brucknerian in its formal appearance the movement may seem, its lyricism is placed in a context where the working out of the dramatic implications of some of the elements suggests a complexity that might even bear comparison with anything to be found in the *Ring*.

IV

Tovey made one further observation about the slow movement of the A major Piano Quartet, which followed on from his remark that 'the first theme may be usefully quoted as an example of the kind of phrase that can occur to no composer who is not constantly in the practice of setting words to music'. He wrote:

> We must learn to understand Brahms's mastery of absolute musical form in the light of the fact that fully two-thirds of his work, from first to last, was vocal, and that this prince of absolute musicians was the most circumstantial of verbal illustrators where words were involved. That is why there is no composer with whom it is more futile to impute unauthorized 'programmes' to his instrumental works.

There is, perhaps, an implicit invitation here to look for manifestations of the use of the Neapolitan complex in the vocal music, and to see whether it is associated with any particular set of poetic images. But the results of such a search are of limited interest only. From a preliminary point of view, one might cite 'Der Frühling', Op. 6 No. 2 (1852) (J.B. Rousseau), 'An die Nachtigall', Op. 46 No. 4 and 'An ein Veilchen', Op. 49 No. 2 (both 1868, and both with texts by Hölty), and even the more mature 'Heimweh II', Op. 63 No. 8 (1874) (Groth). Yet despite the fact that all these are in E major, none pursue the Neapolitan associations with the same vigour as may be found in the instrumental music. Before 1871, Brahms wrote many songs in E major or minor; after that date, very few. And although, as

Arnold Whittall[21] has demonstrated, there is a sophisticated mixture of E minor and major elements in the third of the *Vier ernste Gesänge* Op. 121 (1896), in the famous 'O Tod, O Tod', the Neapolitan dimension is quite simply absent.

Rather, it is only the beautiful 'Unbewegte laue Luft', Op. 57 No. 8 (Daumer), composed and published in the year 1871, that seems to extend the range of manipulations belonging to the Neapolitan complex. The languid opening depiction of the 'tiefe Ruhe der Natur' (Example 8a) foreshadows, through its voice-leading 'french sixth', the pulsating music associated with the 'heissere Begierde' in the second section (Example 8b). Here, in (b), the tonic E major acts as dominant to the chord of its subdominant minor (A minor). This in turn transforms by stepwise movement of its outer voices directly into the F minor harmony, in effect bypassing an intermediate F major one. Furthermore, not only are both major and minor versions of the dominant present beneath the words 'Begierde mir', but the dominant's dominant is approached by the harmony G-B-D-F (=E sharp), which reproduces under transposition by a fifth, the augmented sixth element of the complex (in Example 3, C-E-G-A sharp). The later parts of the song dwell at a certain length upon the Neapolitan F major, although Brahms also draws a parallel (found elsewhere too) between the C natural of the complex, and the B sharp which is the leading-note to the relative minor of E major, C sharp minor.

This song, then, gives concrete meaning to the opposition between E major and F minor, and the relation of F major to both. And it is tempting, in the light of the discussion of the parallel treatments found in Schubert and Brahms, to search for comparably concrete meanings in Schubert's stage works. Yet the fact that Schubert does not significantly oppose these tonalities in these dramatic contexts must at least suggest reservations about proposing Schubert too strongly as Brahms's source for his Neapolitan manipulations. Indeed, in Schubert's stage works E major is associated with fast, boisterous music. Both *Die Zauberharfe* (1820) and *Alfonso und Estrella* (1822) even end in this key. And when, in Act II of *Fierabras* (1823), two consecutive numbers are set in E major (No. 11) and F minor (No. 12), separated only by *Singspiel* dialogue, the E major number (Allegro moderato) is still not the serene piece that such an opposition would presuppose. Of course, elements of the Neapolitan complex may be found in several numbers from

[21] A. Whittall, 'The *Vier ernste Gesänge* Op. 121: enrichment and uniformity' in *Brahms*, ed. R. Pascall, 194 ff.

Example 8. (a) 'Unbewegte laue Luft', Op. 57 No. 8, bars 1–4

(b) bars 25–30

these and other stage works (above all, though, in *Alfonso*) as they may also be in the sacred music (see especially the sublime setting of 'Quoniam tu solus sanctus' from the E major Gloria of the Mass in A flat major). But in no single case is it critically necessary to invoke the idea of the complex *per se*.

On the other hand, the broader field of eighteenth-century opera offers more readily demonstrable precedents for Brahms's (and Schubert's) instrumental use of Neapolitan relations. Generally speaking, there is a tendency to associate E major with a sublime love, as in, for example, the Trio for L'Amour, Euridice and Orphée from the Paris version of Gluck's *Orpheus* ('Quels transports et quel délire, ô tendre Amour', they sing, 'ta faveur nous inspire'), and F minor with the expression of anxiety and even the diabolical, as in the 'Choeur des Dieux Infernaux' from Gluck's *Alceste*. For the most part, these associations are preserved in Mozart, whose E major is further characterized by a poignant idealism: this is the case with Sarastro's 'In diesem heil'gen Hallen' from *Die Zauberflöte*, Fiordiligi's celebration of a triumphant, tested fidelity from *Così fan tutte* (No. 25), and the prayer, from the same opera, of Fiordiligi, Dorabella and Don Alfonso for the lovers' safe passage (No. 10). (Not surprisingly, for so unrelentingly ironic a work, this characterizaton of E major is satirized when Despina appears as the lawyer.) The opposition of E major and F minor is most strikingly projected, however, in *Idomeneo*, once again at a moment of sea-borne departure. The chorus's halcyon 'Placido e il mar, andiamo' in E major is followed by the touching farewell Terzetto 'Pria di partir oh Dio' for Idamante, Elettra and Idomeneo in F major (the same tonality used for the farewell quintet (No. 9) in *Così*). But this Terzetto fails to close in F major: and the turbulent F minor that emerges in its place is explained by the stage instructions 'mentre vanno ad imbararsi sorge improvvisa tempesta'.

More locally, there may well be other influences upon Brahms's Neapolitan practice. For instance, as far as the Op. 38 Sonata for Piano and Cello is concerned, Wilhelm Klenz's[22] proposal that it was 'necessary for Romberg to have written his Sonata in E minor before Brahms could have composed his E minor Cello Sonata' seems even less startling than it might do at first sight, when the Neapolitan parallels are acknowledged (Klenz's argument, apart from commenting upon the shared opus number (38) and tempo indication (Allegro non troppo), is confined to thematic comparisons). Example 9a shows the opening four bars of Romberg's first theme, which spans eight bars in all; (b) reveals how, during his counterstatement, the process of destabilization begins with a move to the Neapolitan area, in a manner similar to Brahms; (c) quotes the end of

[22] Wilhelm Klenz, 'Brahms, Op. 38: Piracy, Pillage, Plagiarism or Parody?', *Music Review*, 34/1 (1973) 39–50. The Sonata for Cello and Piano, Op. 38/1, by Bernhard Romberg (1767–1841) is published by the International Music Company, edited by F.G. Jansen.

Example 9.

(a) Bernhard Romberg: Cello Sonata in E minor, bars 1–4

(b) Bars 9–14

(c) Bars 45–50

Romberg's exposition, here in the relative major rather than in (Brahms's) dominant major, and the arresting adoption of F at the very opening of the development (rather than at its climax, as in Brahms). On the other hand, the F is heard here very much as a Phrygian degree (notice the B natural); F minor *per se* occurs in no part of the sonata; and the textural oppositions central to Brahms's exploitation of the Neapolitan complex are not invoked by Romberg. The work, therefore, could hardly have taught Brahms about the complex as such, although it might well have provided an incentive for its use in this context.

Robert Pascall concluded the introduction to his own Brahms symposium with the following words:

> A special type of intertextuality is the relationship between a piece and its remote successors, and our view of Brahms's influence on subsequent composers has surely undergone radical revision in recent years. The importance Brahms had for the evolution of Schoenberg's musical styles and techniques, especially in the area of thematic material and its treatment, now makes it clear that Brahms does not only represent a stylistic culmination, in the grand sweep of musical history, but, in a very powerful sense, also a beginning.[23]

One might add, that Brahms contributed in the area of harmonic material and its treatment no less importantly. For while it is possible to find in Brahms ample precedent for the handling of the D tonalities used so extensively at the turn of the century, notably by composers of the Second Viennese School, the same kind of comparison might also be made with respect to the E tonalities. Indeed, in an unpublished paper, Derrick Puffett has spoken of the 'dual obsession' of the Schoenberg school with D minor and E major.[24] In Schoenberg's early song, 'Traumleben', Op. 6 No. 1, for example, a lover's rapture is projected through a tonality that fluctuates between E major and F major, using most of the procedures of the Neapolitan complex, even if it does not establish the counterpole of a turbulent F minor. To pursue this line, however, would require us to reconstitute Schoenberg's influences in a way that, at the very least, would include Wagner. In the second scene, for example, of *Lohengrin*, Elsa turns the rapture of her E major marriage into the irreversible E minor of its destruction, through the disruptive agency of an F natural. And, ironically, the Neapolitan F was precisely the element that characterized the exaltation of Lohengrin's 'Du süsse, reine Braut'. It is impossible to say, of course, whether Schoenberg would have taken note of this network of relations. Yet, even from this example, it is clear that Brahms's Neapolitan treatment was not unique in the middle and later parts of the nineteenth century.

When all the historical comparisons have been made, however, it becomes clear that from a compositional point of view the Neapolitan complex could only ever have a restricted usefulness: its characteristics are perhaps rather too powerful, its extremes eventually limiting. There are examples by Brahms, of

23 *Brahms*, ed. R. Pascall, viii.

24 Derrick Puffett. 'D minor and E major in Schoenberg: A dual obsession' (unpublished, 1980).

course, that have not been discussed here, and indeed one of them, the Variation movement from the G major Sextet Op. 36 (1864–5), deserves a complete monograph to unravel its intricacies. On the other hand, the general moral to be drawn from this essay might well have a wider application: namely, that the modern study of harmony may no longer confine itself to the cataloguing and describing of local phenomena, but must expand to integrate formal, thematic, textural and expressive issues within its terms of reference. And this, in turn, argues for a very substantial new programme of study.

LOUISE LITTERICK

Brahms the indecisive: notes on the first movement of the Fourth Symphony[1]

I

The autograph score of Brahms's Fourth Symphony contains evidence that the composer had planned an alternative opening for the work. At the end of the first movement, after the double barline, appear four bars of music that were to be inserted at the very beginning of the symphony, as a note in his hand at the bottom of the first page indicates: 'NB: die ersten 4 Takte stehen Seite 51 bei ⊠' (See Plate 4). These additional bars convert the opening from the form in which it has always been known to the form represented in Example 1.

The position alone of the extra bars in the manuscript makes it clear that their addition – and subsequent deletion – took place at a very late stage of composition, postdating at least the completion of the first movement in all but its very final details.[2] Last-minute as this change may have been,[3] however, it did not represent Brahms's ultimate opinion on the matter, for the work still opens as first written in the autograph. Some time before the publication of the symphony in October 1886 – possibly even after the first performance on 25 October 1885, but certainly before Joachim conducted the work on 1 February the following year – Brahms changed his mind yet again and

1 Earlier versions of this article were read at Mount Holyoke College (February 1980) and the University of California at Santa Barbara (January 1981). I wish to thank Christoph Wolff, Harvard University, for encouraging me to follow through with this topic, and Joshua Rifkin, Wissenschafts-Kolleg, Berlin, for reading the article in its various permutations and offering useful suggestions at each stage.

2 Whether the bars were added to the manuscript immediately upon the movement's completion or at a later date is difficult to determine, though the fact that Brahms wrote the sign in thick blue pencil – a writing implement he typically reserved for proofreading and editorial revision – suggests that he did not enter the alternative opening until he was going through at least that movement for a last proofreading and the addition of rehearsal letters, dynamic markings, and so on.

3 It is also possible that the alternative opening represents an idea that had initially occurred to Brahms at an earlier stage of work now untraceable.

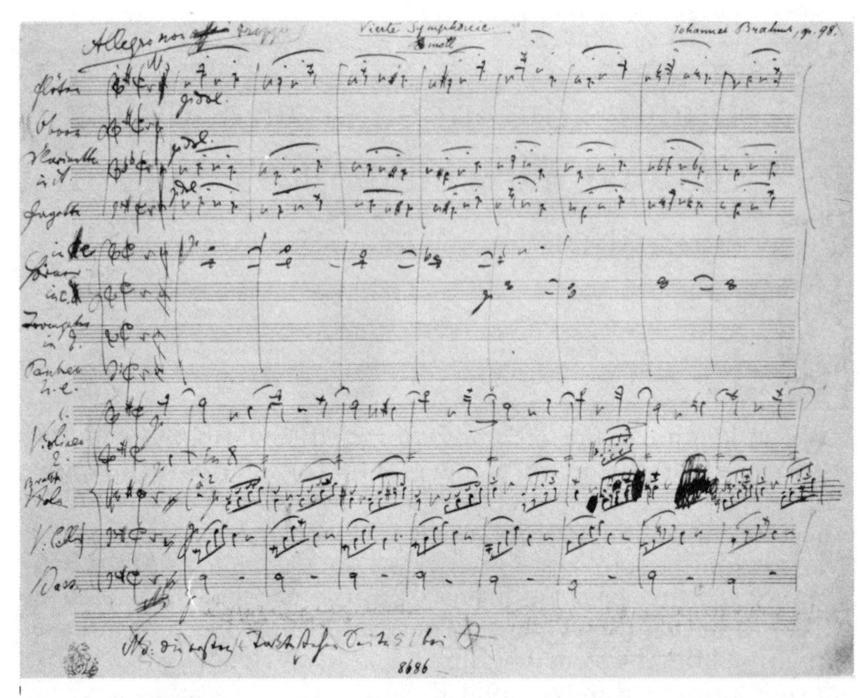

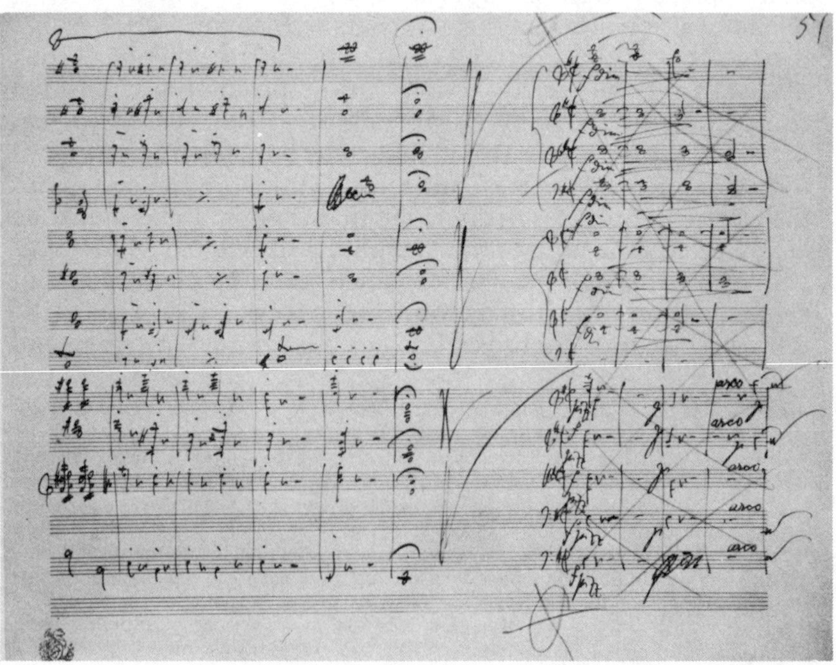

Plate 4 Brahms: Fourth Symphony in E minor Op. 98. Autograph full score of the first and last pages, movement 1

Example 1. Fourth Symphony Op. 98, first movement, alternative opening

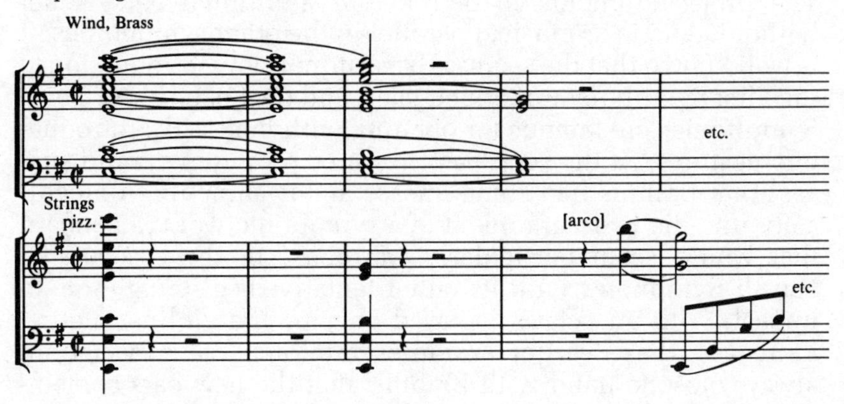

crossed out the inserted bars as well as the instruction for their inclusion.[4]

Since the publication of a facsimile edition of the manuscript,[5] the evidence of the contemplated change has been readily available. While this revision has been noted in passing – it is even mentioned by Günter Birkner in the extremely short introduction to that edition – it has not been given much attention, perhaps because so few bars of rather unprofiled music, that were furthermore ultimately rejected, may seem of little interest. Yet given the extraordinarily high degree of structural integration in Brahms's compositions, any changes – retained or unretained – that go beyond the most trivial matters of detail can be expected to have a bearing on issues dealt with throughout the composition; and while such emendations may not, strictly speaking, reveal secrets not also deducible through close examination of the finished work, their very conspicuousness in all but clean copies can draw our attention to aspects of the composition otherwise potentially overlooked. Indeed, the very existence of such late revisions in music whose essential nature would seem to preclude them is provocative and raises new questions about that nature. In such instances, fundamentally unpromising material paradoxically becomes a prime means of achieving further insight into the composition itself.

[4] See the letter from Joachim on the day of his first performance of the work, in which he writes to Brahms: "dass Du die einleitenden Takte weggestrichen, möchte ich fast bedauern'. *Johannes Brahms Briefwechsel VI: Johannes Brahms im Briefwechsel mit Joseph Joachim*, ed. Andreas Moser (Berlin, 1912) 221.

[5] Published in 1974 by Eulenburg GmbH, Adliswil-Zürich; the autograph itself, the property of the Allgemeine Musikgesellschaft Zürich, currently resides in the Zentralbibliothek of Zürich under the call number AMG 309a.

II

The projected inclusion of the four additional bars is not without genetic or musical parallel in the other symphonies. It is well known that the seemingly germinal slow introduction to the First Symphony was added later; and the Second and Third Symphonies are famous for opening with motto-like introductory gestures. At the very least, all three precedents could suggest that Brahms had some unease about launching immediately into the main argument of a symphonic work, a concern that would seem particularly warranted in the case of the Fourth Symphony, with its rather tentative beginning – on an upbeat, with an octave B played only by the violins, *piano*.[6] Moreover, these earlier examples reinforce the expectation, always close to hand with Brahms, that the new bars contemplated for the Fourth will, even if by implication, set at least one of the principal terms of the argument to follow. The slow introduction to the First Symphony, after all, sets out systematically all the essential thematic material of the movement, and the significance for their respective works of the d-c sharp-d motto heard in the first bar of the Second or the f′-a flat′-f″ motto enunciated at the start of the Third is too well known to require further comment.[7] Particularly measured against these precedents, however, the Fourth Symphony appears wanting. The prefatory material consists in essence of nothing more than a harmonic progression – two bars of IV^6_4 followed by two bars of resolution, each chord articulated by pizzicato crotchets in the strings and sustained by woodwind and brass – with no obvious motivic component and, for that matter, virtually no linear motion at all apart from the progressions C-B and A-G with which the $^6_4$ resolves.[8] In this instance, however, appearances deceive. A more careful investigation – prompted by the very anomalous nature of these bars – reveals that they in fact form part of a densely knit web of associations, possibly one of the richest and subtlest even in Brahms.

[6] Joachim felt sufficiently uneasy about the bare opening of the final version to suggest to Brahms that at least some, if even more minimal, prefatory gesture was requisite (see the letter referred to in n. 4 above).

[7] I have in mind solely the musical function of the f′-a flat′-flat″ motive. On its supposedly literary connections, see Michael Musgrave, '*Frei aber froh*: a Reconsideration', *19th-Century Music*, 3/3 (1980) 251–8.

[8] The descending third, B-G, in the middle register in bars 3 and 4 (clarinets, bassoons, and horns 3 and 4) can certainly be viewed as an anticipation of the first notes of the primary subject and of the pervasive use of third relationships at all levels throughout the movement; but the omission of this descent in the upper register (flutes, oboes) as well as the absence of a firm rhythmic profile to the gesture make such an interpretation seem tenuous.

The most obvious of these associations is also the very last one: the movement closes with a series of cadentially alternating I and V chords, followed, as a final confirmation of the tonic, by a bar of IV^6_4 (underscored by four timpani strokes) that resolves to the concluding chord (Example 2).[9]

Example 2. Bars 432–40

This close is like the rejected opening, not only in harmony, but also in scoring (except for the inclusion of timpani in bar 439) and texture (sharply cut off, staccato strings, sustained woodwind and brass).[10] The most prominent elements in the final pair of chords (other than the timpani strokes) are, as in the prefatory bars, the linear resolutions C-B and A-G (Example 2). As both elementary contrapuntal logic and the immediate context make clear, these lines, and the entire IV^6_4-I progression, are nothing more than part of a double neighbour-note elaboration of the third and fifth degrees of the tonic triad (Example 3); and it is the prolongation of the fifth degree con-

Example 3.

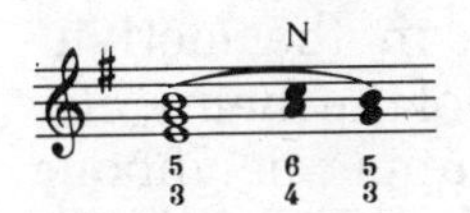

tained within this elaboration that forms the binding element in the larger network of associations to which the ending and, by extension, the rejected introduction both belong. Indeed, it seems fair to say that the $\hat{5}$–$\hat{6}$–$\hat{5}$ neighbour-note progression plays as vital a role in the integration of this movement as the famous chain of thirds emphasized in so many discussions of the symphony.[11] To be sure, the neighbour-note progression has

[9] It is even possible that the reading of these bars as he revised the manuscript prompted Brahms to conceive – or realize – the idea of the prefatory music, however fleetingly.

[10] It may be worth noting that both gestures seem to relate to the IV^6 opening of the last movement; and, indeed, the pervasive harmonization of the passacaglia theme retains the subdominant beginning.

[11] This latter property of the opening theme has been frequently remarked upon since at least as long ago as 1914, when Walther Vetter's long and informative analysis of the symphony appeared (Walther Vetter, 'Der erste Satz von Brahms' e-moll-Symphonie: ein Beitrag zur Erkenntnis moderner Symphonik', *Die Musik*, 13/3 (1913–14) 3–15, 83–92, and 131–45).

also not gone entirely without comment, most notably in the more recent literature;[12] but several significant manifestations of it – manifestations particularly relevant to the questions raised in this article – have remained unremarked.

Right at the start of the principal subject, the first of the chains of thirds from which the theme is fashioned is so disposed registrally and rhythmically as to put into prominence the $\hat{5}$–$\hat{6}$–$\hat{5}$ neighbour b″-c‴-b″ (Examples 4a and 4b).

Example 4.

Moreover, the termination of the second chain, which coincides with the first significant departure in the motivic-rhythmic pattern established at the beginning of the theme, also coincides with another melodic move to the upper neighbour, here sustained for four bars (bars 9–12; Example 4b). Finally, the resolution of this longer-spanned C neighbour to the B of the theme's conclusion (bars 17–18), which is followed by a cadential descent to the tonic, has superimposed above it a final instance of the neighbour: while the b′ is still sustained in the first violins, the first oboe, echoing at the half bar, duplicates it, pulls it up yet another octave, and then pushes it to a c‴ that is the ninth of the dominant chord formed simultaneously below it. This dramatic final neighbour is left hanging and resolves only with the entry of the second violins on the b″ with which the restatement of the theme begins. Thus the entire theme itself assumes the aspect of a large neighbour-note motion with two smaller neighbour-note progressions nested at the beginning and end (Example 5). Furthermore, the final instance of the

[12] See in particular Jonathan Dunsby's perceptive study of this movement in *Structural Ambiguity in Brahms: Analytical Approaches to Four Works* (Studies in British Musicology, Ann Arbor, Michigan, 1981) 41–83.

Example 5. Bars 1–19

neighbour is doubly significant in its own right: it verticalizes the neighbour-note relationship – a point to which we shall return – and, as we shall also see, it generates the very close of the movement.

The neighbour motion underlying the principal theme is made explicit at the recapitulation as part of a large expansion in time achieved through an abstraction of the two subphrases that make up the subject's first four bars. The first three notes of each subphrase are treated similarly: played by woodwind only, in octaves, they move in even semibreves after a minim upbeat. The concluding pitches of each subphrase, however – respectively the c‴ neighbour and its resolution, b″ – are sustained for three and a quarter bars each (249–52 and 255–8) and are given full triadic support: the C with its own root (VI in root position instead of the IV^6_4 of the exposition) and the B with an incomplete III (instead of the tonic) (Example 6). The prepara-

Example 6. Bars 246–58

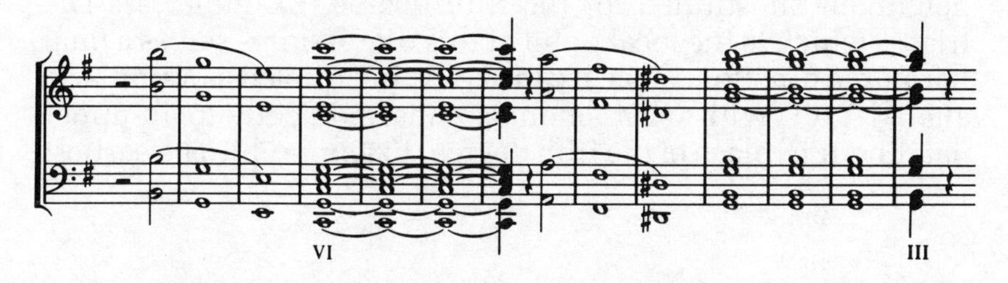

tion for this striking restatement of the theme, moreover, takes the form not of a simple B major triad but of an implied dominant ninth, with C as the uppermost dissonant pitch (bar 246) – another notable instance of the combining of linear and vertical already present at the end of the first theme; the only resolution comes, as before, with the b″ of the theme's beginning.

The specific harmonic reinforcement given to the neighbour-note motion at the recapitulation forms part of a sub-network of relationships, in which the neighbour progression is transferred to the bass and becomes a harmonic generator. The emphasis on VI and on III – the latter most likely to be understood less as III than as VI/V – is connected with a pervasive harmonic tendency at structurally important points throughout the movement: the 'deceptive' progression of cadential dominants to the submediant rather than to the expected tonic.

To take an especially noticeable example first, the section of the development starting with the statement of the main theme in triple counterpoint (bar 169) settles into B minor (bar 181) and appears to confirm that arrival with a large suspension cadence on V/V (bar 183), which, however, suddenly veers off to VI/V on the downbeat of the next bar. (This VI/V, or G major, leads at the next important point of articulation to C minor and thus mirrors the succession that opens the recapitulation.)

Other, less emphatic, instances of the V-VI motion occur: at the approach to the transition in the exposition (bars 43–5) and within the transition itself (72–5 and 76–9) as well as at the corresponding bars of the recapitulation (287–9, 316–19 and 320–3); and at the passage heard in the development at bars 209–10 and correspondingly in the coda (376–7). These examples all share a distinct variant of the progression that merits a brief digression.

The particularly tentative quality of these interrupted cadences derives not only from their less strongly articulated surface texture but also from their utilization of a special form of dominant preceding VI: instead of the expected major triad on V (or V/V), Brahms writes an augmented triad, with the upper neighbour substituted for the fifth degree (Example 7a). The triad – which is the focal point of this digression – serves a dual harmonic function, since it can also be interpreted as a similarly altered V/VI, with what amounts enharmonically to an upper neighbour in place of the fifth degree (Example 7b). The earliest

Example 7.

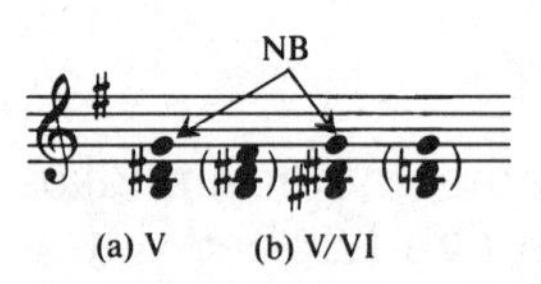

instance of this special formulation – the twice stated cadence at bars 43–5 (Example 8) – seems at pains to clarify the relationship between the normal V-VI progression and the augmented form, and at the same time to make explicit the connection between the bass motion from V/V to VI/V and the underlying neighbour progressions. Brahms first approaches VI/V, then restates the cadence using the augmented form of the dominant with D in the bass to yield the quasi-dominant V/VI function.

Example 8. Bars 43–5

After a following sub-thematic articulation on C (bar 49) – yet another reflection of the fifth relationship proceeding from the sixth degree already noted at the recapitulation and in the development (see above) – this bridge section arrives on V/V at the start of the transition section proper (bar 53), thus completing a long-range $\hat{5}$–$\hat{6}$–$\hat{5}$ bass neighbour-note motion on the dominant.

The true significance of the augmented cadential preparation, however, lies not so much in its relationship to the 'ordinary' form of the dominant as in a remarkable internal property: as Example 9 makes clear, the deceptive cadence with

Example 9.

augmented dominant is nothing more than a verticalization of a segment of the chain of thirds that underlies so much of the movement. This connection is made explicit both in the passage just discussed and elsewhere. At bars 208–10, for example, the first violins state a complete seven-pitch, eight-member chain of thirds spanning e‴ to e″, with the augmented dominant of bar 209 represented linearly by the last three pitches in that bar; the bass states a segment of the same chain at that point, and further segments appear in the second violins and in the violas (Example 10). Since the augmented dominant involves neighbour-note substitution (see Example 7 above), this characteristic cadential formulation provides another instance where Brahms confirms the ties between the neighbour-note principle and the chain of thirds. It might also be noted, moreover, that the cadential ramifications of the chain of thirds extend even further than the augmented dominants. As Example

Example 10. Bars 208–10

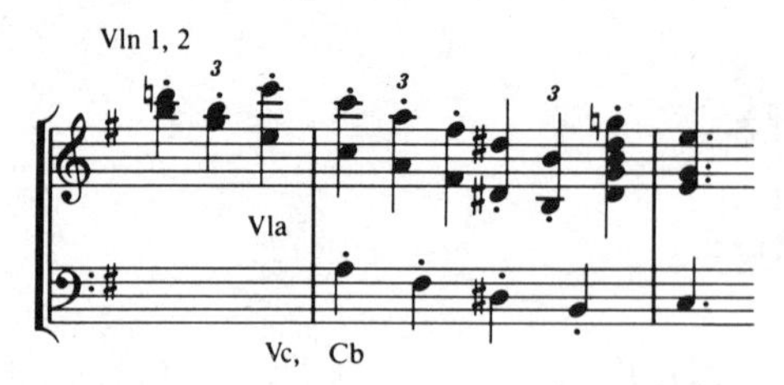

9 shows, read literally, the first chain includes a ii^7 at its beginning, a V – and a V^7, V^9 or the augmented V – in the middle, as well as the implicit possibility of a further extension to VI. It is not difficult to see the connection between the specific pitch content of the thematic chain, with its underlying harmonic implications, and the preparation of the recapitulation (Example 6), the final cadence of the movement (Example 2) and other places as well.

Let us turn back from the chain of thirds to the neighbour-note progression with which we have been chiefly concerned. The incomplete neighbour $\hat{5}$–$\hat{6}$ has a further manifestation, one that has consequences beyond more local harmonic and linear considerations. As mentioned above, the sustained C of bars 9–12 marks not only the first major neighbour-note prolongation in the primary theme but also the abandonment of the chains of thirds and the first departure in surface thematic content. At subsequent appearances, precisely this point of departure *within* the theme becomes the structural point of departure *from* it. At the restatement of the subject, for instance, this moment (bars 27–31) coincides with the change in tonal direction that eventually concludes with the V/V harmony articulating and indeed underlying the whole of the transition. Similarly, it is a magical reharmonization of the neighbour (bars 153–6) that sets the development on its modulatory course following a literal restatement of the first eight bars of the opening theme. A repeat of this same reharmonization within the following ornamented presentation of the theme at the new transposition level (bars 165–8) secures yet another tonal shift and prepares the arrival of the passage of triple counterpoint that culminates in the first main climax of the section, on the neighbour-note cadence discussed above.[13] In this way, then,

[13] Not coincidentally, the reharmonized prolonged neighbour results in the brief tonicization of key areas a third apart: E minor to G minor to the B flat minor that begins the section of triple counterpoint.

the prolonged upper neighbour becomes the agent of structural change, and the move to it an event of increasing drama as the movement unfolds.

As might be expected in a late nineteenth-century symphony, this drama – and much else besides – reaches its high point in the coda. The prolongation of the upper neighbour in bars 402–5 following the canonic treatment of the first two phrases of the opening subject resembles the original treatment of this section of the theme. But the melodic prolongation itself begins an octave higher, so that its characteristic octave ascent in the second bar takes the music up to c'''', the highest note so far, and one not to be exceeded in the remainder of the movement. In the continuation – based on the final portion of the theme but departing from it – the C-B melodic progression is isolated from its original context, where it is the start of a local scalar descent, and turned into a sequentially treated motive (bars 406 ff; Example 11). This is the first time in the movement that the

Example 11. Bars 406–8

progression C-B is given such a direct surface statement, and it is a harbinger of the peroratory cadential gesture of bars 422 onwards (see below). A restatement of bars 406–9 two octaves higher leads to a cadential segment derived from bars 15–17 of the exposition. This segment is noteworthy for the pervasive subdominant emphasis of its first phrase, its recapturing of the highest C, and its harmonization of that note and the immediate resolution of b''' as IV-I, the first appearance of this harmonic succession as the movement now stands. As the music settles at bar 422 on the extended tonic $\frac{6}{4}$ prolongation – the cadential gesture referred to above – the C-B motive finally becomes the most prominent surface event (Example 12) and leads to the closing cadence. It is further worth noting that in the following expansion of bars 422–5, the C-B motive is no longer presented

Example 12. Bars 422–7

as an elaboration of an E minor triad but is reharmonized with C minor proceeding to G major (bars 426–9; Example 12). It does not take much effort to see the relationship between this subdominant progression, in which C and B function as the tonic and third degree of their respective triads, and the subdominant progressions in E minor in which those notes function as the third and fifth degrees (Example 13), nor to recognize the C minor-G major progression as a last reminder of the C-G harmonic subtext that grows out of the neighbour-note relationship at so many other points in the movement.

Example 13.

The entire passage considered in the last paragraph (bars 394–429) directly sets up the closing elements discussed above: the ascent to the final c'''' and the neighbour-note close. The coda of the movement thus presents a compacted synthesis of all that has gone before; and it is surely as much to this as to the forceful scoring, timpani strokes or even the traditionally solemn association of the plagal cadence that the close owes its enormous power. Yet the coda does more than synthesize: it effects a gradual transformation of the neighbour-note principle from an underlying structural premise to a prominent surface gesture. As such, this portion of the movement functions as a climax not only in the obvious surface sense – by means of dynamic intensification, thematic fragmentation and alteration, expansion of register, and so forth – but in that deeper way as well: by bringing to the fore something that had been functioning below the movement's surface. It works a dramatic reevaluation of the fundamental materials of the movement – of the music so far heard – and creates a sense of directedness, of attainment that reveals the entire movement as a series of implicit statements driving towards the final, explicit realization of its coda.

This very difference between the implicit and the explicit provides a key to at least one of the issues surrounding the rejected opening of the Fourth Symphony. With the four 'extra' bars presenting the C-B relationship directly on the surface right at the start, the end result is made manifest from the beginning. The movement does not gradually expose, make concrete and reinforce a series of compositional potentialities but rather suggests the main plot line at the outset and then elaborates in greater detail what has already been set forth in summary. Thus, at the end of the process in this version, what occurs is not the final revelation of something of which one has only slowly been made aware but a return to something that was known to be present from the start, whose full significance, however, can only now be understood, since it has been affected and shaped by what has happened in between.

The presence or absence of the introductory bars, then, makes a difference to the movement considerably out of proportion to the amount of music involved. Yet from the point of view of traditional analytic concerns, the movement remains essentially the same, whether those bars are present or not; viewed synoptically, at least, the underlying relationships and interconnections remain unchanged. Such concrete musical relationships – even of the complexity found in the first movement of Brahms's Fourth Symphony – are relatively easily recognized and, perhaps, can even be established according to fairly simple, comprehensible criteria. However, the choice among the many possible ways to expose these relationships – the dramatic choice, that is to say – is particularly subjective and unverifiable; for both composer and analyst, it is a choice that lies, as Edward T. Cone put it in the title of a well-known article, 'Beyond Analysis'.[14]

Thus it may be impossible with normal analytic means and assumptions to understand Brahms's indecision about this small but significant detail. Both versions of the movement are effective, as he clearly realized, and both satisfy the traditional criterion of the 'well constructed piece'. The choice between them appears to be almost an impulsive one, something that can be understood only as a matter of irreducible personal taste, of an individual sense of drama. The evidence of indecision, then, acts as a reminder that, first, the choice among options is often highly irrational – not even a composer, let alone an analyst, can say definitively that one is better than another – and, second, that even in the most carefully organized music and even at the strictest level of integration, no matter how 'inevitable' the apparently flawless surface of a completed composition appears, the work is still open, and further options remain. More specifically, that Brahms could vacillate in this fashion confirms the integrity of a structure that could stand up to two such different scenarios; and his irresolution also suggests that no matter how closely argued his music may be, for Brahms the element of improvisation is never really far away.

[14] *Perspectives of New Music*, 6 (1967) 33–51.

APPENDIX

Brahms and England

Handlist for the exhibition at the London Brahms Conference, Goldsmiths' College, 8–11 July 1983

Nigel Simeone

1 Johannes Brahms. Photograph (of the silverpoint drawing by Laurens).
Inscribed by Brahms: 'Sir George Grove. (40 Jahre später!) J. Br.'
Lent by the Royal College of Music

2 Brahms's visiting card.
Lent by Robert Pascall

3 Kate Loder (Lady Thompson). Photograph of the portrait by Alma-Tadema in the Royal Academy of Music.
Lent by the Royal College of Music

Ein deutsches Requiem

The first performance in this country was given at the home of Kate Loder (Lady Thompson) on 10 July 1871, with Cipriani Potter and Kate Loder playing the orchestral part in a reduction for piano four hands. The conductor was Julius Stockhausen. George Macfarren refers to this occasion in his paper 'Cipriani Potter: his life and work' (*Proceedings of the Musical Association* X, 41ff.):

> [Potter's] last appearance, I can scarcely say in public, but in a large assembly, was on the 10th of July in the year 1871, in which year he died. Lady Thompson then gave in her drawing rooms the first performance in England of the German Requiem of Brahms, a large number of ladies and gentlemen constituted the chorus, and the pianoforte part in the form of a duet (there being no possibility of a band in the space), was played by Lady Thompson and Mr. Potter. His enthusiasm on that occasion extended itself to everyone who was concerned in the performance. The occasion was memorable as introducing a composition of the rarest merit to a first hearing among us; Mr. Julius Stockhausen, who had carefully trained the singers, conducted the music, and the audience were aglow with interest in the work and its rendering. . .

4 *Ein deutsches Requiem*. First edition of the piano-vocal score. Leipzig & Winterthur: J. Rieter-Biedermann [1869]
Lent by Nigel Simeone

5 Cipriani Potter. Photograph of the lithograph by S. Bendixen in the Royal Academy of Music.
Lent by the Royal College of Music

6 *Ein deutsches Requiem*. Arrangement for piano four hands [by Brahms]. Leipzig: J. Rieter-Biedermann [plates of 1869]. Presumably a copy of this arrangement was used for the performance at Kate Loder's house.
Lent by Oliver Davies

7 *Ein deutsches Requiem*. Programme for the Philharmonic Society Concert, St James's Hall, 2 April 1873.
Lent by Nigel Simeone

8 *Ein deutsches Requiem*. First edition of the full score. Leipzig & Winterthur: J. Rieter-Biedermann [1868]
Lent by Nigel Simeone

9 George Alexander Macfarren. Carte-de-visite photograph by Fradelle & Marshall, London.
Lent by the Royal College of Music

10 William George Cusins. Carte-de-visite photograph by Fradelle & Marshall, London.
Lent by the Royal College of Music

11 Charles Santley. Carte-de-visite photograph by H.J. Whitlock, Birmingham.
Lent by the Royal College of Music

12 *Ein deutsches Requiem*. Programme details for the first performance in Manchester, 26 November 1874. The conductor was Hallé.
From: Thomas Batley, ed. *Sir Charles Hallé's Concerts in Manchester* (Manchester, 1896).
Lent by Nigel Simeone

13 Charles Hallé. Carte-de-visite photograph by Elliott & Fry, London.
Lent by the Royal College of Music

14 *Ein deutsches Requiem*. First edition with English text of the piano-vocal score. Leipzig & Winterthur: J. Rieter-Biedermann [1872]
Lent by Nigel Simeone

15 Sextet in B flat Op. 18. Programme for the Monday Popular Concert, 25 February 1867. The first performance in England. The performers include Joseph Joachim and Louis Ries.
Lent by the Royal College of Music

16 Johannes Brahms. Autograph note (unpublished) to Louis Ries, written on the verso of a visiting card.
Lent by Robert Pascall

17 Piano Quartet in A Op. 26. First edition of the score and parts. Bonn: N. Simrock [1863].
Lent by Nigel Simeone

18 Piano Quartet in A Op. 26. Programme for the Monday Popular Concert, 17 November 1873. The performers include Hans von Bülow as pianist, together with Ludwig Straus, Henri Zerbini and Alfredo Piatti.
Lent by the Royal College of Music

19 Quintet in F Op. 88. Programme for the Monday Popular Concert, 5 March 1883. The first performance in England.
Lent by the Royal College of Music

20 Quintet in F Op. 88. First edition of the score. Berlin: N. Simrock [1882].
Lent by Nigel Simeone

21 Clara Schumann. Carte-de-visite photograph by Fritz Luckhardt, Vienna.
Lent by the Royal College of Music

22 Clara Schumann. Album leaf in Clara Schumann's hand, comprising the opening bars of Brahms's cadenza to Mozart's Piano Concerto K. 466. Signed and dated 'London 20th of March 1867'.
Lent by Robert Pascall

23 Piano Trio in C minor Op. 101. Programme for the Monday Popular Concert, 19 March 1888, including the first performance in England of the Trio Op. 101. The pianist is Clara Schumann.
Lent by the Royal College of Music

24 Piano Trio in C minor Op. 101. First edition of the score. Berlin: N. Simrock [1887].
Inscribed by Brahms to Fanny Davies. A note in pencil at the top of the title page reads: 'Brahms played from this copy in Baden-Baden – with Joachim and Hausmann.

Clara Schumann turned over! An upright piano in a little sitting room at the Deutscher-Hof. Sept. 1890'.
Lent by the Royal College of Music

25 Piano Trio in C minor Op. 101. Programme for the Saturday Popular Concert, 6 April 1889, including the Trio Op. 101 played by Fanny Davies, Joseph Joachim and Alfredo Piatti.
Lent by the Royal College of Music

26 Fanny Davies. Carte-de-visite photograph by Elliott & Fry, London.
Lent by the Royal College of Music

27 Alfredo Piatti. Photographic postcard, London.
Lent by the Royal College of Music

28 Joseph Joachim. Cabinet photograph by Elliott & Fry, London. Mounted with a musical quotation in Joachim's hand, comprising the opening four bars of Brahms's Hungarian Dance No. 1. Signed and dated 'London 1884'.
Lent by the Royal College of Music

29 Ilona Eibenschütz. Cabinet photograph by Elliott & Fry, London.
A pupil of Clara Schumann, Ilona Eibenschütz made her debut in England at the Monday Popular Concerts in January 1891. In 1894 she gave the first performances anywhere of Op. 118 and Op. 119, both at the Monday Popular Concerts. After her marriage in 1902 she retired, settling in England. She died in 1967.
Lent by the Royal College of Music

30 Quintet in G Op. 111. First edition of the parts. Berlin: N. Simrock [1891].
Lent by Nigel Simeone

31 Quintet in G Op. 111. Programme for the Monday Popular Concert, 2 March 1891. The first performance in England.
Lent by the Royal College of Music

32 Clarinet Sonatas Op. 120. First edition of the score. Berlin: N. Simrock [1895].
Fanny Davies's copy, signed on the first page of each sonata by Fanny Davies and Richard Mühlfeld. Together they gave the first English performances in June 1895.
Lent by the Royal College of Music

33 Clarinet Sonatas Op. 120. Concert announcement for a recital at the Bechstein Hall, London on 4 December 1905, including both sonatas.
Lent by the Royal College of Music

34 Piano Concerto in D minor Op. 15. First edition, early issue, of the solo piano part. Leipzig & Winterthur: J. Rieter-Biedermann [plates of 1861; issue of c. 1864].
Lent by Nigel Simeone

35 Piano Concerto in D minor Op. 15. Autograph letter (unpublished) from Brahms to Theodor Leschetitzky, January 1874. With the original (part autograph) envelope. A fascinating letter concerning the performing material for the concerto, written over a year before the eventual publication of the full score. Brahms mentions a manuscript full score but says that Leschetitzky's conductor could use the solo piano part.
Lent by Robert Pascall

36 Theodor Leschetitzky. Cabinet photograph by Charles Scolik, Vienna.
Lent by the Royal College of Music

37 Piano Concerto in D minor Op. 15. Programme for the Philharmonic Society Concert, St James's Hall, 23 June 1873. An early English performance of Op. 15 by Alfred Jaell, a pupil of Moscheles and a noted interpreter of Chopin. This performance, like the one discussed by Brahms in his letter to Leschetitzky (No. 35) was given before the publication (in 1875) of the full score.
Lent by the Royal College of Music

38 Piano Concerto in B flat Op. 83. Etching of Brahms by Ludwig Michalek, with an autograph inscription from Brahms to Bechstein, including a musical quotation comprising the opening two bars of the concerto.
Lent by the Royal College of Music

39 Piano Concerto in B flat Op. 83. Programme for the concert at the Crystal Palace, 14 October 1882.
The first performance in England with Oscar Beringer as soloist, conducted by August Manns.
Lent by the Royal College of Music

40 Oscar Beringer. Photographic postcard, London.
Lent by the Royal College of Music

41 Johannes Brahms. Cabinet photograph by Brasch, Vienna. Stamped 1895.
Lent by the Royal College of Music

42 Announcement for the Berlin Philharmonic Orchestra concert, 10 January 1896.
On this occasion Brahms conducted both piano concertos, with Eugen d'Albert as soloist, and the Academic Festival Overture. This concert was the last time Stanford met Brahms (see Stanford, *Studies and Memories* (London, 1908), 114).
Lent by the Royal College of Music

43 Eugen d'Albert. Cabinet photograph by Gottheil & Sohn, Königsberg. Stamped 1896.
Lent by the Royal College of Music

44 Johannes Brahms. Print of Brahms conducting by W. von Beckerath, Hamburg.
Lent by the Royal College of Music

45 Symphony No. 1. Autograph letter (unpublished) from Brahms to Joachim, March 1877, concerning arrangements for the first English performance.
Lent by Robert Pascall

46 Charles Villiers Stanford. Carte-de-visite photograph by Elliott & Fry, London.
Lent by the Royal College of Music

47 Charles Villiers Stanford. *Songs of Old Ireland*. London: Boosey & Co. [1882].
Dedicated to Brahms.
Lent by the Royal College of Music

48 Symphony No. 1. Programme for the concert at Crystal Palace, 31 March 1877, conducted by August Manns. The second performance in England.
The programme note is by Grove.
Lent by the Royal College of Music

49 August Manns. Carte-de-visite photograph by The London Stereoscopic & Photographic Company.
Lent by the Royal College of Music

50 Crystal Palace. Two plans, one of the surrounding parkland, the other of the Palace itself, from a Crystal Palace programme of September 1899.
Lent by Nigel Simeone

51 Symphony No. 2. First edition of the full score. Berlin: N. Simrock [1878].
Lent by Nigel Simeone

52 Symphony No. 2. Programme for the Crystal Palace concert, 22 March 1879, including August Manns's second English performance of the symphony.
Lent by the Royal College of Music

53 Symphony No. 3 First edition, second issue, of the full score. Berlin: N. Simrock [1884].
Lent by Robert Pascall

54 Symphony No. 3. First edition, second issue, of the full score. Berlin: N. Simrock [1884].
Presentation copy from Brahms to Richard Barth, Brahms's autograph inscription dated 27 January 1885. With Barth's bookplate, showing an alp, with Brahms's 'alphorn' motif from Symphony No. 1.
Lent by Nigel Simeone

55 Symphony No. 3. Programme for the Richter Concert, St James's Hall, 26 May 1884. The second performance in England.
The programme note, by Charles Barry, mentions that this performance used material supplied by Simrock before publication. The English premiere was given at the Richter Concerts fourteen days earlier.
Lent by the Royal College of Music

56 Hans Richter. Portrait photograph by Barraud, London.
Lent by Nigel Simeone

57 Symphony No. 3. Programme for the Crystal Palace concert, 18 October 1884, conducted by August Manns, including the third performance in England.
Lent by the Royal College of Music

58 Symphony No. 4. First edition of the full score. Berlin: N. Simrock [1886].
Lent by Nigel Simeone

59 Symphony No. 4. Programme for the concert by the Meiningen Orchestra at St James's Hall, 21 November 1902, including Symphony No. 4 and the *St Antoni Variations*. The conductor was Fritz Steinbach, with Mühlfeld as principal clarinet. The analytical notes are by Tovey.
Lent by the Royal College of Music

60 Fritz Steinbach. Photographic postcard, Berlin.
Lent by Nigel Simeone

61 Adrian Boult. Autograph letter, to Nigel Simeone, 11 July 1978, referring to Joachim's orchestration of Schubert's Grand Duo, Brahms's Symphony No. 3, and Steinbach:

Dear Nigel – Thankyou for your letter – I don't think there is anything spectacular about Joachim's work – I believe Brahms made some suggestions to him about it. Isn't that in Tovey somewhere? It is interesting about the 3rd Symphony. I wonder if there is anything more to it than the inevitable flatness of a gramophone after you have heard the real thing. I heard Steinbach a good deal before the first war & his Brahms (& most other things too) was incredible somehow. One always felt that nothing else would do – & so you are getting some of it (I hope) at second hand!. . .

Lent by Nigel Simeone

62 'O Heiland reiss die Himmel auf' Op. 74 No. 2. Proof copy of the score, containing a number of corrections and alterations in Brahms's hand.
The autograph manuscript of this motet does not survive and this proof thus constitutes the primary source for one of Brahms's most important works for unaccompanied choir.
Lent by Robert Pascall

63 'O Heiland reiss die Himmel auf' Op. 74 No. 2. First edition of the score. Berlin: N. Simrock [1879].
Lent by Robert Pascall

64 'O Heiland reiss die Himmel auf' Op. 74 No. 2. First edition, later issue, of the parts. Berlin: N. Simrock [plates of 1879].
Lent by Robert Pascall

65 Georg Henschel. Carte-de-visite photograph by The London Stereoscopic & Photographic Company.
Lent by the Royal College of Music

66 Georg Henschel, *Personal Recollections of Johannes Brahms* (Boston: Richard G. Badger, 1907).
Lent by Oliver Davies

67 Georg Henschel. *Serbisches Liederspiel* Op. 32. Berlin: N. Simrock [1879].
Dedicated to Brahms
Lent by Nigel Simeone

68 Johannes Brahms. *Thematisches Verzeichniss der bisher im Druck erschienenen Werke von Johannes Brahms* (Berlin: N. Simrock, 1887).
Georg Henschel's copy, with all the works after Op. 101 listed in Henschel's hand on additional sheets.
Lent by Nigel Simeone

69 *Zigeunerlieder* Op. 103. Programme for the Monday Popular Concert, 26 November 1888. The first performance in England. The singers included Georg and Lilian Henschel; Fanny Davies was the pianist.
Lent by the Royal College of Music

70 Lilian Henschel. Carte-de-visite photograph by Elliott & Fry, London.
Lent by the Royal College of Music

71 *Lieder und Gesänge* Op. 57. First edition. Leipzig & Winterthur: J. Rieter-Biedermann [1871].
Lent by Nigel Simeone

72 *Lieder und Gesänge* Op. 57. Programme for the Monday Popular Concert, 17 January 1887, including two songs from Op. 57 sung by Lilian Henschel.
Lent by the Royal College of Music

73 Johannes Brahms. Announcement of Brahms's funeral. Vienna, April 1897.
Lent by the Royal College of Music

74 C. Hubert H. Parry. Carte-de-visite photograph by Elliott & Fry, London.
Lent by the Royal College of Music

75 C. Hubert H. Parry. *Elegy for Brahms*. Autograph full score. Though this work was composed in 1897 it was apparently never performed during Parry's lifetime. Stanford conducted the first performance at the Parry Memorial Concert in the Royal College of Music on 8 November 1918.
Lent by the Royal College of Music

76 Johannes Brahms. Medal by A. Scharff for the Gesellschaft der Musikfreunde, Vienna, to celebrate Brahms's sixtieth birthday on 7 May 1893.
Lent by Robert Pascall

ACKNOWLEDGEMENTS

Warmest thanks are due to the Royal College of Music, in particular Oliver Davies, and to Robert Pascall, for so generously lending material for this exhibition.

Index